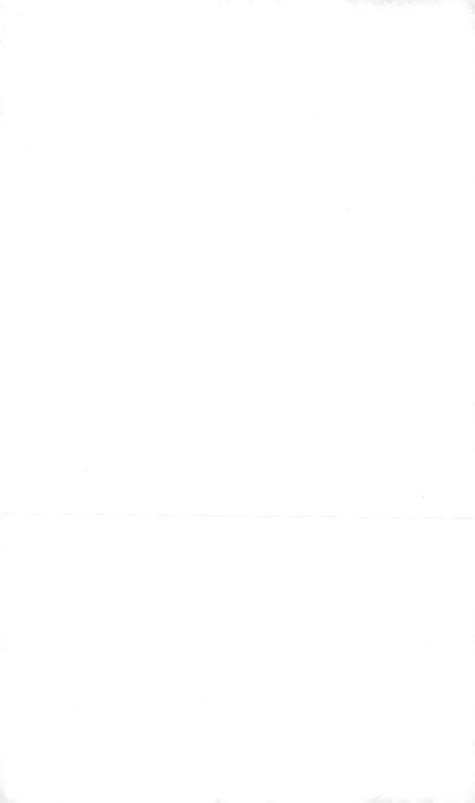

THE
VALUES
COMPASS

What 101 Countries Teach Us About
Purpose, Life, and Leadership

MANDEEP RAI

SIMON & SCHUSTER
New York London Toronto Sydney New Delhi

Simon & Schuster
1230 Avenue of the Americas
New York, NY 10020

Copyright © 2020 by Mandeep Rai

First Simon & Schuster hardcover edition January 2020

SIMON & SCHUSTER and colophon are registered
trademarks of Simon & Schuster, Inc.

For information about special discounts for bulk purchases,
please contact Simon & Schuster Special Sales at 1-866-506-1949
or business@simonandschuster.com.

The Simon & Schuster Speakers Bureau can bring authors to your
live event. For more information or to book an event contact the
Simon & Schuster Speakers Bureau at 1-866-248-3049
or visit our website at www.simonspeakers.com.

Interior design by Silverglass

All images courtesy of author, except for image of India by Raghu Rai,
and image of the Democratic Republic of the Congo by Angela Fisher
and Carol Beckwith.

Manufactured in the United States of America

10 9 8 7 6 5 4 3 2 1

Library of Congress Cataloging-in-Publication Data has been applied for.

ISBN 978-1-5011-8338-6
ISBN 978-1-5011-8340-9 (ebook)

For my beloved children ~ Naryan and Saiyan
May you, and all children, be rooted by your values and thus have
everlasting wind beneath your wings.

You are the source of all values and virtues
and it is with your grace that they are bestowed.

—Ang 4 of the Sri Guru Granth Sahib Ji,
by Guru Nanak Dev Ji

Your beliefs become your thoughts,
Your thoughts become your words,
Your words become your actions,
Your actions become your habits,
Your habits become your values,
Your values become your destiny.

—Mahatma Gandhi

Contents

Introduction 1

PART I: CHANGE VALUES

PART II: CONTINUITY VALUES

PART III: CONNECTION VALUES

PART IV: COMMUNAL VALUES

PART V: CORE VALUES

THE
VALUES
COMPASS

———

Introduction

Leading with Your Values

"Who will want to marry you if you go there?"

The moment the word "Oxford" passed my lips, my mother was immediately and implacably on the warpath. It was from there I had just returned, after an unsanctioned trip in my parents' car for an interview at the university.

Many parents might have expressed support or encouragement, or even pride. But not my mother. To her, a name like Oxford epitomized the British ruling class: the people who had changed her native India so much during the Raj, and were ultimately responsible for her ending up in a place where she was alienated, alone, and the frequent victim of violent racial abuse. She envisioned losing me, her best and only friend in our village, to a place where I would become exposed to drugs, and end up marrying an upper-class white boy called Sebastian.

Marriage. At eighteen, it felt like a cage to be avoided as long as possible: the end of freedom and happiness. Then as now, what I valued most was the power to set the course of my own life, not to be constrained by the expectations of others. For my mother, nothing was more important than that I be married off in the right time and to the right kind of boy: a Sikh, preferably from Punjab, with the appropriate creed, background, and parentage. Both of us feared most what the other desperately wanted. It was the first time in my life I really understood the importance of values. For her, family and heritage held sway. I was moved by the desire for freedom, exploration, and a thirst for knowledge. We both wanted the best for me, but we couldn't agree on what that was. Our starting points and basic assumptions had become irreconcilable. Our values were in conflict.

All of us will have moments like this in our life, where the choices, challenges, or opportunities facing us reveal something important about our character, desires, and personality. A decision about whether to prioritize professional aims or family needs; to pursue the best-paid job or the most meaningful; to do the things we want, or those that support our health and well-being. We face big, defining decisions, but also a constant drumbeat of choices about how to spend our time. Every day we are making decisions that set both the short- and long-term course of our lives. Whether we acknowledge it or not, these decisions are being steered by the principles we believe in and consider to be most important: values that are working away in our subconscious.

Many of us constantly question how to be our best selves, and live the most fulfilling version of our lives. Those conundrums are hard to answer without an appreciation of values. You need to understand your own values and those that are held dear by your core people, the company you work in and the community you live in. Values hold the key to so many of the things we aspire to. Quite simply, they are the foundation of our entire lives: the lasting and fundamental beliefs we hold and act against, however our circumstances change. Everything else—the decisions we make, the ambitions we nurture, the relationships we build—is simply a representation and amplification of our fundamental values. Our values are running our lives, yet not enough of us understand what they are, their power, and how we can use them. The more we know and understand them, the more clarity we have over what matters to us, and the more confidence we gain in making decisions toward that end. We need to know our values to better understand ourselves and what motivates us. And we need to appreciate the values of the people in our lives, to see the world through their eyes and help us to build sustainable and harmonious relationships.

Values represent the aggregation of our life experiences, personal aspirations, family inheritance, and cultural grounding. They determine the career, the partner, the lifestyle, and the goals that we all choose. And they set the limits on what we believe to be acceptable, fair, and just. We all have a fundamental personal code that we carry through life, and its language is values. A value is something that affects how we see the world, and also what we see. If you have been a victim of racism or social injustice, it is likely that equality and fairness will be important values to you, and that you are more likely to see injustice in the world than someone who has not. My own childhood experience in the Gloucestershire village of Churchdown, where my home was petrol-bombed, my nose broken so other children could see if I would bleed red or brown, and my parents would only leave the house with one of them in the trunk of the car (to avoid people seeing the house was unoccupied), has certainly left an indelible mark on me. We all have unconscious programming like this, based on our life circumstances and experiences. We need to be aware of this so that, rather than letting it guide our lives, we equip ourselves to choose powerfully. This is what an understanding of values helps us to achieve.

That moment with my mother was when I started to understand the importance of values as our personal bottom line. In the decades since, my understanding of how values define us as people, framing the direction we choose for our lives, has grown. And I have developed a clear understanding of *why* it is so important to both understand and reflect on your values. I believe there are five reasons:

1. They help us to understand ourselves, the beliefs that animate us as people, and the motivation that drives our personal aspirations.
2. They help us to understand other people, and the source of disputes that are often rooted in a clash of values, and can be resolved through better empathy for these contrasting perspectives.

3. They help explain our lives, allowing us to understand the values that were imprinted in us growing up, and how we choose to use or evolve those in the adult lives we have chosen.
4. They help us work out what we want in life, providing the compass to navigate from the things that motivate us to those we want to achieve.
5. They provide a tiebreaker, offering a mechanism to settle personal dilemmas and challenging life decisions—to see which option is most aligned with our values and will contribute to a more successful, fulfilling, and happy life.

Over the last twenty years, across a career that began in investment banking and shifted into venture capital, international development, and broadcast journalism, I have traveled to almost 150 countries. This journey has opened my eyes to how values define behavior, relationships, and culture all over the world. Reporting for Reuters and the BBC World Service, I have seen up close how values shape the life of a country and its people. Every time I visited a new country to report, I was struck by the same realization. Wherever you go, there is something apparent yet unspoken, a sort of cultural language that dictates so many aspects of everyday life. You notice it on the streets, in the cafés and shops, in business meetings, around kitchen and dining tables, and simply while working your way across the towns, villages, and cities. You see it from how a country responds to major events, to how individuals and local communities interact.

As I visited more countries, I was increasingly inspired by the values I saw, and how they were being used by individuals and communities to create change: to evolve into better versions of themselves. It was reporting from Ladakh, in the far north of India, that this perception settled. Almost two decades before the issue started animating governments across the world, Ladakh had banned single-use plastic bags. The lead came not from NGOs or local government, but a volunteer group, the Women's Alliance of Ladakh. Outraged by the litter problem that plastics were creating in the hands of both locals and tourists, the Women's Alliance succeeded in having them outlawed, while manufacturing and selling cloth bags that fund environmental protection and conservation in the local area. It was another twenty years before the Indian government committed to outlawing single-use plastics, way behind the pioneering efforts of the women of Ladakh.

Values are fundamental to us as people, and for organizations they provide the same cultural and moral foundation. When you engage with a company, as an employee, supplier, or customer, you feel the difference when there is a guiding purpose and a strongly held set of values. It makes you feel part of something bigger and more meaningful than a business transaction or an employment contract. Leaders of standout companies like Paul Polman, former CEO of Unilever; Ajay Banga, CEO of MasterCard; and Chip Bergh, CEO of Levi Strauss, told me that they use values to make decisions on everything from product development to hiring, remuneration, company culture, and sustainability. In other words, they have built entire business models around a specific set of strong and distinctive values. A company that understands its role and purpose, and is successful at attracting both loyal customers and employees, will invariably be one driven and guided by its values. That is why this is a book as relevant for those starting and leading companies, institutions such as schools, or even their own families, as it is for individuals.

We also live in a world of division, technology, and volatility—one that values are essential to navigating. Values provide an anchor in an environment where the news is being manipulated, politics has become confrontational, and traditional sources of faith have dwindled. Technology bombards us with information and sows personal doubt. As we all seek to make our way in a world where old certainties have been eroded, an understanding of our personal values becomes more important than it has ever been.

Values can spring from different places and parts of our lives. There are those that were instilled in us from a young age, taught and handed down to us, or acquired through experience. And there are those we aspire to, mold ourselves on, and wish to be the defining principles of our life. A value can be intrinsic or it can be adopted: the important thing is that it is entirely true to you as a person, and that you find practical ways to honor and express it.

HOW TO USE THIS BOOK

This book is predicated on the belief that there is no better model for values in action than the countries of the world. The value that defines each country stems from a wide variety of sources—from a nation's history, its geography, its religious topography, its traditions, its demographics. A nation's core value has been shaped in many cases over centuries or millennia, handed down from generation to generation, constantly evolving but never fundamentally altering.

As geopolitical, economic, religious, and environmental change has evolved around them, these values have largely remained the same. Indeed in many cases, it is values that have helped sustain nations through crisis and change. Governments, constitutions, colonizers, civil wars, and political movements may come and go. Borders shift, countries are wiped off the map one generation, restored the next, and then altered some more. But values remain, the irreducible core of national culture and identity. American entrepreneurship stems from a promise that has for centuries attracted immigrants to explore new geographical, scientific, and technological frontiers. Pakistani courage is the product of how its peoples have had to fight for their place in the world, ever since its founding in the bloodstained aftermath of Partition. Hungarian competitiveness arises from a history that has seen the country invaded and conquered on an almost unremitting basis since the thirteenth century. French protest is a tradition that connects the *gilets jaunes* of 2018 with the *sans-culottes* of 1789. Every nation's upward spiral, inconsistent and confusing though it may be, has evolved around—and in turn helped to shape—its defining value. Through sharing the stories of values from around the world, illustrating their power and the rich variety that exists, I hope to inspire you to start discovering and making the most of yours.

Of course, to elect a single value for 101 countries is not to suggest that the tapestry of people, communities, and cultures that make up a nation state is homogenous. Nor is it to claim any objective truth about what value should represent a country: the ones chosen here are the fruit of many conversations and passionate debates, and I expect you will disagree with some of the conclusions. The purpose is to illustrate the extent to which a value can inform the life and culture of a nation, and to understand how the same is true of our own lives. However diverse and heterogenous a nation, and however complex and multifaceted a life, it is both possible and valuable to distill down the singular factors that motivate and inspire it. The discipline of trying to understand these core drivers is as important as the conclusion itself.

The book takes you on a tour of 101 countries, explaining and exploring the values that make them tick. I have spent time in every country discussed here, and reported from most of them—in some cases a number of years ago, so I am aware my experiences will not always reflect the changes that have happened since. The experiences and observations included are based on the people I have met, stories I have covered, and the insight I have been offered by a combination of friends, experts, and total strangers.

I have grouped the values into five sections, which reflect the different areas of our lives in which values can help us to make decisions and find direction:

Change Values: These epitomize how nations and their people have shaped and responded to change.

Continuity Values: These have kept tradition and memory alive, often against great odds.

Connection Values: These shape our personal relationships, with friends, family, colleagues, neighbors, and strangers.

Communal Values: These are universally recognized in communities, companies, and countries, dictating behavior and social norms.

Core Values: These define our core personality and motivations in life.

I believe there is a lesson in every country and every value listed here: a perspective on how we can be better in many different ways. They are all important and instructive. But we have to choose. No one has 101 defining values. For each of us, some are always going to be more important than others. The purpose of this book is to help you work out which, and why.

As you read, I encourage you to think about the values that closely reflect your own. What stories inspire you? Which ones have the most relevance to your life and experiences? What values described here do you aspire to? Which relate to the things that make you happiest? What do you read and immediately recognize yourself in? Which values jump out at you? Which ones in your life have been violated or stepped on?

Note down each value that grabs you, the ones that feel most personal and relevant. Make a list, fold the corners of the page, or add highlights on your e-reader. Be discriminating—only choose those values that really feel like *you*. On average, this should leave you with a list of about fifteen to twenty. At the end of the book, I'll take you through the process of how to boil down this list to a final five, and how to make use of these values in your personal and professional life. Finally, don't be restricted by the exact wording of the values outlined here. Everything is open to your interpretation, and indeed I would encourage you to make it personal. If you want to interpret Kenyan togetherness as teamwork, Nigerian drive as making money, or Nicaraguan poetry as the sheer power of language, then go right ahead. Values are whatever you value.

When you're at the beginning of any process, the end is often a good place to start. At Harvard Business School, you do an exercise where you are asked to imagine what your eulogy will be. What will other people say about you after you're gone? I found this one of the most clarifying, eye-opening things I have ever done. Once you know the end, the kind of person you want to be and the life you want to live, everything starts to fall into place. The question then becomes how you get there. And the answer to that, is by letting your values show you the way: shaping your aims and guiding your decisions. So let's get started, and begin the journey of discovering yours.

Part I: Change Values

At some level, all of us are exercised by the question of how to create change. We want to change people's minds, change the course of our lives, change our communities and even society. At the same time as we plan and hope for change, we will also find it forced upon us—unexpected changes in our life circumstances that require us to change course. Whether big or small, change is something we are all searching for, and having to cope with.

Countries whose history has been defined by creating and responding to change—economic, political, religious, and demographic—are the ideal model for how it can be achieved in all its forms. They show that change is never just the product of one simple thing. Moderates, pragmatists, and compromise brokers have as much a part to play in the process of change as activists, idealists, and campaigners. Change is about building a groundswell, achieving something, and then forging something meaningful and lasting as a legacy. Together, these countries show what the full tool kit needed for achieving change looks like.

Pragmatism

Gengzhen, Xi'an, China.

I was wedged tightly into the back corner of the bus, which showed little sign of slowing as my destination hurtled toward us. Not knowing when it might next stop and realizing that I might soon be very lost indeed, I started to panic. In desperation I grabbed the arm of the woman sitting next to me and pointed out through the window, as unambiguous as I could be that I needed to get off the bus, now.

The response was immediate: she raised her fist and gave the ceiling of the bus such a thump that there was no chance the driver would not hear it. Taking me by the hand she carved a path through what seemed an immovable crowd of people, before snapping something to the driver, who immediately brought the vehicle to a halt—not at a bus stop, but on the hard shoulder of the freeway. Unperturbed and still grasping my hand in hers, my guardian angel hopped down the stairs, practically high-jumping over the tall roadside barriers in her business skirt to lead me across three lanes of fast-moving traffic. Depositing me at my intended stop, she gave a curt nod, turned heel, and marched back onto the freeway to make the return journey and flag down the next bus.

This was one of my many encounters with hardheaded Chinese pragmatism: a deeply practical approach to getting the job done that you can find across China's politics, business culture, religious tradition, education system, and economy, which is now the second largest in the world.

"It doesn't matter whether a cat is black or white, as long as it catches mice." That quote, or some version of the same thought, is one of the most famous sayings of former Chinese premier Deng Xiaoping, who as leader of the People's Republic from 1978 to 1987 was the primary architect behind the opening up of the Chinese economy, laying the foundations for the global powerhouse that it has since become. Deng's words, from one of the most prominent exemplars of Chinese pragmatism, capture a mind-set and approach that focus rigorously on the ends, without worrying too much about the means.

When it comes to politics, pragmatism means China does not generally let the concerns and protests of outsiders get in the way of doing what it believes is in its own best interest. Whether censoring large parts of the internet or tightening its control over nominally independent Hong Kong, the Chinese approach has been to carve its own path and pursue its own interest, however much others might disagree with or deplore its actions.

Deng's famous sayings follow in a long tradition of Chinese political, social, economic, and military thought that is steeped in pragmatism. Confucianism, rather than being a religion that directly instructs, is a system of thought that encourages people to think and behave ethically, and which leans more toward pragmatism than ideology. "I have no course for which I am predetermined, and no course against which I am predetermined," Confucius writes in one of the tracts attributed to him.

This approach informs many aspects of Chinese life today. Practices that might be deprecated from a moral or ethical standpoint in some countries are readily embraced here as an everyday reality of doing business and getting on. One survey found 35 percent of Chinese companies saying they paid bribes or made gifts as a regular occurrence, while cash payments to doctors in advance of a major medical procedure are also common, though this practice was officially banned in 2014.

The Chinese way is not to wring hands over the technicalities and the broader implications, but to take the clearest course of action to get a desired result and fast. Faced with a rapidly growing population in the late 1970s, Deng's government introduced a one-child policy, which remained in place until 2013, and has been blamed for the widespread infanticide of baby girls. More recently, current President Xi Jinping has circumvented the political constraints on his long-term plan for China's development by simply abolishing the two-term limit on premierships, potentially allowing him to rule indefinitely.

You might, very reasonably, be robustly opposed to some aspects of current Chinese government policy, but in broader Chinese culture there is something important to be learned—how pragmatism can help us all to steer a steady course in the face of change, when surrounded by forces that threaten to blow us off track.

Potential

**Chief Kibala of the Pende People,
Democratic Republic of the Congo.**

Of all the places in the world I have visited, none have elicited as strong a response as Congo. *Don't go!* I was repeatedly told. *It's the most lawless place, where no one can protect you or be responsible for what happens!*

I couldn't help feeling that perhaps they were right, when I crossed the border overland and was subjected to a bizarre sight: rich Congolese being transported on elevated metal platforms, their de facto thrones, in a scene that would not have been out of place in a medieval court.

At first glance, Congo does feel out of control. People wander around carrying guns, there is no serious law enforcement, and corruption is endemic. The civil war that lasted from 1994 to 2003—and in pockets for years afterward—claimed six million lives either in the fighting or the famine and disease that resulted. Conflict has continued on the eastern border with Rwanda, with dozens of armed militias estimated to still be active and millions of Congolese internally displaced. DRC's recent history is one of ruthless exploitation by rulers both foreign and domestic: from the rapacious imperialist Leopold II, who turned Congo into a de facto slave state funding the global rubber, copper, and ivory trade; to the kleptocracy of Mobutu Sese Seko, who enriched himself while leaving his country saddled with debt. Today, the finger is pointed at multinational corporations as the new exploiters of Congo's vast mineral wealth, estimated by some to be worth up to $24 trillion (yes, trillion).

Yet for all the complex and conflict-riddled reality, there is another Congolese story, one of potential. The DRC is the world's poorest country by per capita GDP, but its natural resources give it an opportunity to be one of the richest. Less than 20 percent of the Congolese population has access to electricity, but the country holds the potential to power the entire continent with a planned hydroelectric dam. The nation is currently one of the world's hungriest, and is reliant on imports for its food supply, yet the available agricultural land has the potential to feed not just the DRC but most of the continent. With proper road and rail infrastructure, Congo could connect much of Africa by virtue of its central location, but it currently has fewer kilometers of road than the U.K., a country barely a tenth of the size.

Slowly but steadily, changes are being made. Congo's investment promotion agency describes it as a "land of many potentials," but these go beyond the vast mineral wealth and untapped economic capacity. The economy, from a low base, has been growing, foreign investment is rising, and much needed infrastructure is getting the green light. Central to this is the Grand Inga Dam, which would be the biggest infrastructure project ever undertaken in sub-Saharan Africa, creating the world's largest hydroelectric plant.

And, most importantly, there is human potential. It can be seen in the work of Dr. Denis Mukwege, a gynecologist who has become the world's leading expert in treatment of rape and sexual violence survivors, and a prominent campaigner against rape as a weapon of war. His team has cared for over forty thousand women, providing medical, legal, and psychological support. Dr. Mukwege's work saw him awarded the Nobel Peace Prize in 2018, as well as earning him an attempt on his life by militiamen.

Congo is war-torn, hungry, and poor, but it is also joyful, striving, and full of hope. It is a nation of problems that could provide a continent with solutions.

Few countries have as traumatic a past, but perhaps none has a more promising future. The DRC is looking past its problems and toward its extraordinary potential. And who among us could not benefit in some way from attempting to do the same?

Problem Solving

These cars live a long life, Havana, Cuba.

Stepping off the plane and into Cuba is like stepping back in time. You see vintage 1950s cars gently rolling through the streets; colorful little food huts accepting ration books; and people walking around not clothed in the latest fashion labels, but with handmade clothing and patched-up glasses. This is the real Cuba: the Cuba of the peso economy, where life is governed not by the economic imperative, but deeper human needs: to be together, to create, to have time and space to think.

Yet Cuba is far from being some bucolic throwback, or a place left behind by technology or progress. In fact, the country is a medical innovator, leading the world in pioneering treatments for lung cancer and becoming the first to successfully prevent HIV transmission between mother and child. It is a beacon for literacy, with a globally renowned education system that attracts students from all over the world. And it is one of the most successful Olympic nations, with one in every seven athletes sent to the last three Games achieving a medal—a ratio bettered only by the United States, China, and Russia.

How are these things possible in a country where only 5 percent have access to the internet at home, in which the average monthly wage is equivalent to $25, and just 2 percent own a car? How can Cuba, one small Caribbean island, compete with geopolitical giants and even outdo them? The answer is *resolver*: the Cuban art of problem solving.

It is through the spirit of *resolver* that things that should be impossible, given the shortages and infrastructure problems Cuba faces, become possible. It is *resolver* that allows a nation with famously inconsistent internet access to be home to a thriving creative economy. *Resolver* means that a health care system facing frequent medicine shortages can deliver rock-bottom infant mortality rates and impressive life expectancy.

Through *resolver*, Cubans make the best of often trying circumstances. It means, thanks to patch job after patch job, extra miles will be eked out of an old car, one that might be written off anywhere else in the world. It means a doctor will do everything in his or her power: to beg, borrow, or even steal from their own supplies of medicine to keep a patient alive against the odds.

It was *resolver* that allowed Cubans to survive the desperately difficult decade after the fall of the Soviet Union, with the nation's global trade plummeting by over 80 percent and triggering a brutal recession that saw the Cuban economy shrink by over 10 percent in three successive years from 1991. These straitened economic conditions left Cubans having to adapt fast to harshly reduced circumstances, finding new solutions for situations where they no longer had money to spend. As Philip Peters of the Lexington Institute think tank wrote in 2002: "Students recall wearing shoes made of tire scraps and adhesive tape. Parents allowed children to play in the street all day because fuel shortages brought vehicular traffic to a near-standstill. Factories closed; workers were laid off. Farmers replaced their tractors with horses and oxen." In other words, Cubans adapted and survived. The wheels may have fallen off its economy, but Cuba found a way to keep going, some way and somehow.

Whether it is to fix a problem, earn enough to get by, or get hold of something that is in theory restricted, Cubans will find a way. Given the severe limitations on access to the internet (only just starting to be lifted at the time of writing), you might assume that you can forget about access to YouTube videos, sports highlights, and the latest films and TV. Except Cubans get around the problem: *paqueteros* (packagers) download a selection of the most popular content, upload it onto USB drives, and distribute it throughout Havana and across the country on a weekly basis (forming *el paquete semanal*, the weekly package). It is literally a human internet: transmitted by hand and on foot in place of a telecoms infrastructure.

What is the source of this unique ability to solve problems and make the best of things? After spending a month in Cuba, I became convinced that it was because people don't just live in the communist system; they believe in it. In a society where money doesn't do all the talking, there is more respect and a stronger sense of community. The skills of the gardener, doctor, artist, and tradesman are celebrated equally. It's an energizing, balanced, and progressive environment to live in. Because time is not synonymous with money, work is limited to healthier hours. There is a prevailing sense of freedom, one that gets creative juices flowing (as evidenced in the many innovations of *resolver*), and comes alive in the music, dancing, and art that fill every evening. I worked with a residential artist in the day, and was whizzed around to exquisite salsa in the evenings.

It is not for everyone, and it would be naive to ignore both the severe economic challenges Cuba now faces, and the many who continue to seek the dangerous escape routes to the United States in search of a better life. But it would be equally mistaken to underestimate the extent to which many still believe in the system, which helps explain the lengths to which people go to make things work.

In all our lives we will face situations where the solution seems elusive or impossible. Through *resolver*, Cuba shows us that barriers to success do not have to be absolute: the obvious path may be blocked off, but that doesn't mean there isn't another way, one less accessible but which still gets you to where you need to be. Not all may be inspired by its economic and political model, but anyone can learn from the Cuban capacity to always find a way. If you have that resolve, that inner knowledge that failure is not an option and setbacks won't stop you, you can achieve almost anything.

Equality

Nyhavn Canal, Copenhagen, Denmark.

Denmark is one of the only places in the world where I have never felt objectified, patronized, or threatened. You can walk down the street, speak up in the workplace, and let your hair down without having to worry. I believe this is rooted in a fundamental Danish value, that of equality.

In Denmark, equality means something more than fair treatment regardless of your sex, race, or religion. It is about something more fundamental—an idea that people should aspire to be more similar than they are different. Where in many countries equality is treated by governments and corporations as an obligatory action, in Denmark it is a deeply ingrained instinct.

Danish equality has its roots in the idea of *Janteloven* (The Law of Jante), a concept coined by the Danish novelist Aksel Sandemose in his 1933 satire, *A Fugitive Crosses His Tracks*. In it, Sandemose created the fictional town of Jante, satirizing the place where he had grown up. Its rules included "you're not to think you are anything special," "you're not to imagine yourself better than we are," "you're not to think you are more important than we are," and "you're not to think you are smarter than we are."

Although the initial creation of *Janteloven* was as a joke, over time it has taken on a more serious guise and become shorthand for the Danish obsession with equality: the principle that the collective trumps the individual, and the greatest faux pas is to boast about your abilities or achievements.

Although *Janteloven* was codified in the 1930s, the ideas that inspired it have much deeper roots. A British diplomat visiting Denmark in 1692 noted, "Scarcely have I known a nation whose national mentality is of such a monotonous uniformity as here."

While some have criticized the *Janteloven* mind-set for encouraging mediocrity, it ultimately created a remarkably equal society. According to the European Union, Denmark ranks near the top in the bloc for gender equality, while its income inequality is the lowest among the thirty-four countries in the OECD, the Organisation for Economic Co-operation and Development.

These impressive figures are underpinned by a social model that is designed to enshrine equality between men and women, rich and poor. Child care is affordable so that both parents can go to work without losing most of their salary. Maternity and paternity leave allowances are generous and can be split between the parents. High rates of income and inheritance tax balance out wealth inequality. And college is free to all, with Denmark's higher education ranking as the third best in the world.

The government mandates generous entitlements, and often companies go further. A Danish CEO told me that his company offers three months of fully paid leave to both parents, and encourages fathers to take six months off after their children are born. This, he said, is simply what people expect; similar policies exist at famous Danish companies including LEGO. Ensuring equality is seen not as a burden, but a facet of competitive advantage in the talent market. The same is true for employees: those who work excessively long hours are not praised, but instead seen as a person without balance or a well-rounded life.

Even those who reject the government and corporate status quo are focused on equality. In the commune of Christiania, founded in the 1970s on a series of abandoned military barracks, around one thousand citizens live in a semiautonomous state where decisions are made by consensus at community meetings. Entering the community, you pass a sign that reads "You are now exiting the EU." From my visit there, I remember not just the color and the distinctive culture of the commune, but also the abiding feeling that everyone is to be treated the same, and that we have value no matter our gender, race, or background.

Though its record on equality is prouder than most, Denmark is still no utopia. At 15 percent the gender pay gap is higher than in sixteen of the other EU countries. And, despite the generous maternity leave allowance, research shows women are still losing income over the long term as a result of having children. The perception that Denmark may have lost some of its momentum on gender equality has led to new developments. A feminist political party, F!, has started to gather support and a nationwide profile, campaigning for pay equality and a 50-50 split on parental leave.

Denmark not only epitomizes the value of equality, but also demonstrates the advantages it creates. As such an equal country by global standards, Denmark is also often ranked as the world's happiest. It's an important reminder of the real prize of equality, which is to remove the barriers that women and minorities face in the vast majority of countries, industries, and careers. So much effort is currently expended on trying to overcome structural inequality: time, ingenuity, and emotional energy that we will be able to use in so many other ways once those very necessary goals have been achieved. Denmark offers a glimpse of what that future looks like and what may eventually be achieved by removing (or at least lowering) these barriers. It shows that the real importance of equality is not as an end in itself but what it enables: for people to achieve, whoever and wherever they are.

Efficiency

Jüri Ratas, prime minister of Estonia.

Opening a bank account, filing a tax return, getting a doctor's appointment or medical prescription. For many of us, these are some of the most laborious and time-consuming processes we face, associated with days wasted and tempers lost. But in Estonia they laugh at our long queues, stubby pencils on strings, and rolling battles with telephone customer service representatives. For them, all those things are done online, at the click of a few buttons. Voting, banking, health care, even registering the birth of your child, is all readily accessible without delay. Red tape is untied, bureaucracy unwound, and frustrations dampened. It sounds too good to be true, right? Not in Estonia.

This is the reality of life in the world's most advanced digital society, one that has raced ahead of the world in embracing digitization as the key to effective government and an efficient life. Efficiency has been the driving mission of Estonia since the collapse of the USSR and its independence in 1991. At the time, the country was so technologically backward that it could take up to a decade to get a private landline telephone connection. Yet the moment in time allowed Estonia, under the leadership of a thirty-two-year-old prime minister, to skip a generation and invest in budding digital and internet technologies.

I interviewed current prime minister Jüri Ratas, who explained how swift the progress has been, as Estonia has evolved from a communist backwater into a digital economy that is both a hub for start-up activity and a haven for those who want to live their lives harnessing the efficiency of technology. On the business side, Estonia's digital revolution has birthed notable internet companies including Skype (one of the first in Europe to earn a billion-dollar valuation), TransferWise and Bolt (formerly Taxify), an Uber competitor. It is now home to more start-ups per capita than any European nation except Iceland and the Republic of Ireland, encouraging entrepreneurs from around the world with its e-residency program, which allows anyone to register to start a company in Estonia and access its beneficial tax, banking, and payment systems. Over fifty thousand people have already taken advantage.

In everyday life, digitization has removed much of the bureaucracy and many of the legacy systems that most other countries still wrestle with. You can file your tax return in minutes, with information that has been automatically populated over the course of the year, or you can check with your child's school how they are getting on with their homework. All these seamless interactions between the individual and the state are underpinned by advanced systems of data exchange, and the parity of digital signatures with physical ones, which has existed since 2000. At birth you are issued a unique digital identifier, beginning a life that will be lived more online than in any other country on earth. You start learning about computer science and programming in kindergarten.

Having leapt ahead of the rest of the world, it is now leading the way, pioneering technologies including delivery robots, and turning its attention to the national security challenges of the digital era:

how information and systems can be protected from hostile cyber-attacks.

The Estonian experience reveals the gap between the potential and reality of technology for many of us: in our lives, careers, and across society. While the digital tools exist to live and work more seamlessly than ever before, too often legacy systems and attitudes get in the way of ease and efficiency. Digital tools should be the salvation of modern life, saving time and money and sparing frustration. Estonia shows that a determined approach to digitization can deliver extraordinary dividends. And if a country of 1.3 million people can do it, why not every business? On a micro level, the Estonian approach to living digitally could let us all be a little happier, less stressed, and with more time to focus on the things that really matter.

Protest

The skyline of Paris, France.

There is nothing more French than going on strike. Even the Eiffel Tower, France's national icon and most important tourist attraction, doesn't get a free pass. Of course, the day I chose to visit, the upper levels were closed because of a strike over a new ticketing system opposed by staff. But although protest might be inconvenient, it is also a brilliant, beautiful, vital part of any functioning society—and France is justifiably proud of how it has, over the course of centuries, shown the world its enduring power.

Protest is fundamental to France, validating the national motto of *liberté, égalité, fraternité*. Protest is about *liberté*: achieving freedoms and indeed having the freedom in the first place to make your voice heard. It is about *égalité*: a fairer society, where the rights of women, workers, and all minorities are supported—a society of equals, with well-being at its heart. And it is about *fraternité*: solidarity and supporting each other.

This is a country built and shaped by protest. From the 1789 French Revolution to the student uprisings of 1968, the history of France has been set by labor strikes, uprisings, and the belief in popular power. Protest in all forms has instigated the fall of the monarchy, the separation of church and state, and the establishment of workers' and women's rights. And you see it in all its forms, wherever in France you go. Perhaps the most notable I have encountered was a group of farmers, naked but for their yellow vests, who had blockaded the motorway exit I wanted to use. Agree with this kind of approach or not, it cannot be ignored—and often it works.

Jacques Soppelsa, former head of the Sorbonne, explained the protest culture to me by saying that "French people are the sons of Voltaire," referencing the eighteenth-century philosopher and satirist who made widely influential arguments for civil liberties, religious freedom, and freedom of speech.

The nonconformist, radical, and suspicious-of-authority approach he staked out has become characteristic in French society, as those who seek to impose change upon it often find. Take Uber. The ride-hailing app has been subject to protests all over the world, but none more vigorous than in Paris. In response to its arrival, the national taxi union called strikes, causing road closures across the capital and disrupting traffic to both major airports. Tires were burned, Uber vehicles vandalized, and tear gas used on the streets by the police. All in a day's protest.

Other demonstrations have lasted months. Notably, the *gilet jaune* protests that began as an uprising against tax rises on gasoline, ran for more than thirty consecutive weekends from 2018 to 2019. Yet the violence and deaths that resulted from rioting on the streets and accidents at traffic blockades led some to condemn the protestors and the damage they had caused. Counter-protest movements, including the blue vests and red scarves, marched in the thousands against the violence—a reminder of the complexity and nuance of protest culture.

There are structural reasons that help explain why protest is so embedded in French society. These include the power of the trade unions, which while numerically relatively weak (with just 8 percent of French employees today unionized), have an institutionally strong role in how companies are managed. And there are cultural ones: the tradition of students and workers, parents and pensioners standing up for themselves and effecting change by taking to the streets. July 14, the most important date in the French calendar, commemorates the nation's most famous protest: the storming of the Bastille, political prison and symbol of royal power, near the beginning of the French Revolution.

Rights and freedoms—women's rights, employment rights, LGBTQ rights, and the freedom of personal, political, and religious expression—have had to be won and defended through history. Protest has been central to that. Protest is what leads to progress: it's also what allows anger at injustices to find an outlet, and not stay bottled up in dangerous ways. Everyone has a right for their voice to be heard. France shows the world what it looks like when that happens.

Hope

President Nana Akufo-Addo, Accra, Ghana.

To understand why Ghana is a nation defined by hope, you have to understand its president, Nana Akufo-Addo. His election in 2016 was not just a new beginning, but also the culmination of a near-two-decade campaign for the presidency. He first tried in 1998, losing in his party's primary. Ten years later, in 2008, he finally became the candidate, receiving the most votes in the first round, before losing the runoff by less than half of one percent. It was the closest election in Ghana's history. Four years later, another close election was lost again. Most politicians would give up after one failed bid at high office, let alone two. But Akufo-Addo did not. He never let his hope for success—for his country and himself—subside, and at his third attempt in 2016 was finally successful.

"Our best days lie ahead," he said at his inauguration. "Though our challenges are fearsome, so are our strengths. Ghanaians have ever been a restless, questing, hopeful people."

Since his election, Akufo-Addo has not let up on promoting his hope for Ghana to fulfill its potential as a nation. When I interviewed him, he spoke most passionately about his desire to help young people seize the future, "to create the conditions to allow them to see that yes, there's every reason to think out of the box, there's every reason to try new things, there's every reason to dream. Because there can be a result from your dreams, there can be a result from your creativity. That's the society that I'm hoping to try and build."

In many ways, the current president echoes Ghana's first, Kwame Nkrumah. The founding leader of modern Ghana, the first British colony in sub-Saharan Africa to gain independence, Nkrumah launched his presidency in 1957 with a powerful vision of hope. "I am depending upon the millions of the country, and the chiefs and people, to help me to reshape the destiny of this country," he said when the Gold Coast became Ghana.

Hope is integral in the culture—and it is not just preached from the political mountaintop. It is also something embraced by every Ghanaian, particularly in a song you hear all over Ghana: *Dabi dabi ebeye yie* (One day, one day it will be all right). More than a song lyric, this is almost a national motto: that the future will be better than the past.

Hope is not just something verbally expressed, but brought to life by visual symbols like traditional Ghanaian beads. In a practice that has been revived by bead artists like Kati Torda, Ghanaian women wear them around their waists, wrists, and necks, in strings that symbolize the hope for marriage, fertility, and good fortune.

It is also seen in the return of a once huge diaspora to Ghana. In the mid-1990s, an estimated 10 to 20 percent of the Ghanaian population lived abroad, but now many are coming back, a wave of "reverse migration" that is investing its talent and belief in helping the country to fulfill its vast potential.

Amy Frimpong, who worked in the U.S. for years before returning as executive director of the National Theatre of Ghana, told me that she often gets asked why she gave up a stable job that earned in a month what a job in Ghana would pay in a year. "I tell people it's because I want to give back," she said. "Whether you're here or outside, a lot of people have a love for the country; and when they come back, they're coming to assist, not to compete." I heard a very similar story from others I interviewed, ranging from musicians to lawyers. Korieh Duodu, a top media and anticorruption lawyer, decided to return to Ghana and qualify there to add to his UK practice, hoping that by spending time in both countries he could make a bigger impact on the world. Amy and Korieh, and many others like them I met across entertainment, education, and professional services, are all buying into the hope of what Ghana could still become: "an independent nation that will be respected by every nation in the world," as Nkrumah defined it in 1957.

In doing so, Ghanaians offer an example to the rest of the world. Because what life, what career, what organization does not depend on hope to succeed? Nothing good ever came without the essential optimism of hope: that tomorrow will be better, that obstacles can be overcome, and that the impossible can be achieved. Hope is what gives us life and keeps us going. And Ghana shows us what it really means to live with hope in your heart.

Justice

Night vigil, Procesión del Señor Sepultado, Guatemala.

For thirty-six years of its recent history, Guatemala was dominated by civil war. And since the signing of a peace treaty in 1996, it has been defined by a decades-long battle to win justice for its victims. As a result, Guatemala has established itself as a pioneer for how justice can be sought and—however imperfectly—achieved in the aftermath of horrific crimes.

The duration of the fight for justice may eventually outlast the war itself, one that saw over 200,000 people killed, more than half a million displaced from their homes, and hundreds of villages razed to the ground, with most of the dead being indigenous Ixil Mayans. The atrocities committed by the military against the Ixil have subsequently been acknowledged as genocide.

The battle for justice in Guatemala is rooted in the principle that the atrocities that happened must never be allowed to be repeated.

Nunca Más, never again, as a report capturing the memory of survivors was titled. It is a process that has collectively activated the legal system, religious leadership, human rights organizations, and community activists to record the memories and experience of victims—a total of 6,500 personal testimonies were recorded and the history of over 55,000 victims documented in a project led by the country's Catholic Church—and seek restitution.

Another game changer was the Historical Clarification Commission, which was established as part of the 1996 peace treaty. It recommended that the state should investigate and hold responsible those who had committed crimes during the conflict, not offer them amnesty. Still, the results have been slow-going. Former dictator Efraín Ríos Montt was initially found guilty of being the author of genocide and crimes against humanity, and sentenced to eighty years in jail: the first head of state to be found guilty of genocide by a court in their own country. But only days later the ruling was struck down and he died in 2018 in the midst of an ongoing retrial. Military intelligence chief José Rodríguez Sánchez, whose trial went on for over a year and heard testimony from over one hundred eyewitnesses, was found to bear no criminal responsibility for the genocide the court confirmed that the military had perpetrated against Guatemala's indigenous population. Even as the Ixil finally won official recognition of what their community had suffered at the hands of the state and army, they had to watch a high-ranking member of the military escape responsibility for it.

Justice dominates the political landscape in Guatemala, and it is also prevalent in wider culture and communities. For a month I lived at a school overlooking Lago de Atitlán, working on my Spanish and talking to locals who would often speak of justice and their hopes for it. The still waters of the lake, many told me, reminded them of the depth, patience, and calm that have powered the long and still unfinished search for justice. Others lament that the search for justice has been undermined by institutional corruption and widespread criminality, including high levels of violent and organized crime.

Now the pursuit continues, in search of state reparations for the families of victims, restitution of land, and more comprehensive education for all Guatemalans about the Ixil community, its culture and customs. If justice cannot be found one way, it will be found by another. Guatemalans know that a solution cannot be delivered by solely the legal stroke of a pen, through the collection of memories, or support given to survivors. It is about all these things, brought together to create change, and deliver something meaningful from the memory of atrocity. True justice must help to shape the future as much as it seeks to excavate and address the crimes of the past. A justice that only looks backward is worth little compared to one that actively faces forward, toward a better and changed world.

Adaptability

Luxembourg Stock Exchange, Luxembourg City, Luxembourg.

Normally when you go into a shop to buy something, you know what language you will be speaking. But not in Luxembourg. Here you often find yourself playing a game, where the customer or shopkeeper waits for the other to pick one of several available languages, and set the tone of the conversation. This is all a testament to the adaptability that is core to Luxembourg, a place of multiple languages, numerous nationalities, and intermingling cultures.

Adaptability is taught to Luxembourgers from a young age. The education system progressively ensures every child is taught Luxembourgish (a real language, though one that exists more to be spoken than written), German, French, and English. Though French is most prevalent, it's typical that someone will slip into whatever suits the situation. In a diverse and multilingual society, Luxembourgers are used to adapting to what is in front of them, a product of their nation's long history of being handed back and forth between neighboring powers, and a contemporary population that is majority immigrant, containing over 170 nationalities. Depending on the area you are in, or the restaurant you walk into, you can feel as if you are moving from Germany to France and then Belgium, all within a few meters.

Just as Luxembourg had adapted to a combination of Burgundian, Habsburgian, Dutch, Napoleonic, and German rule over the centuries, so too has its economy adapted to encourage significant foreign investment. The favorable tax environment has made the European Union's smallest member state one of its main financial centers, home to 141 banks from twenty-six countries. And because the Grand Duchy is reliant on maintaining a thriving financial sector based on foreign investment, rather than on natural resources or homegrown industry, it has to be adaptable in making regular upgrades to its legal, tax, and regulatory framework to maintain competitiveness in a global market. That ability to keep adapting and attracting investment from across the globe has made Luxembourg one of the world's wealthiest countries per capita, and the EU's richest on the same basis.

This model in turn made the country pro-immigration; 80 percent of population growth between 2011 and 2016 arose through foreigners settling, with especially high numbers from other EU countries, notably France, Italy, and Portugal. Almost half of the entire population is from overseas, with another 350,000 traveling in every day to work. But adaptability is a two-way street, and those who come to live and work in Luxembourg for any length of time are also given an opportunity to more closely acquaint themselves with the local culture and language. This is facilitated through official "welcome and integration" contracts, which are voluntarily offered to those who are staying in the Grand Duchy for more than two years, and provide free language training, lessons in Luxembourgish culture, and the opportunity to vote in some local elections. Foreign workers in Luxembourg are also entitled to take two hundred hours of leave over the course of their career to learn the native language.

A melting pot that wants to retain its distinctive national culture and language, Luxembourg shows that being adaptable does not prevent you from holding on to the things that are most important to you. The national motto, "We will stay what we are," represents a strain of resilient national identity that has survived multiple instances of foreign invasion and rule. To adapt does not mean to change everything, and to meet the needs of others does not demand that you surrender your own principles and identity. Today, there is a growing movement to popularize Luxembourgish in education, government, and popular culture, while the question of whether it should supplant German and French as the official language was debated in Parliament following a petition. Instead, adaptability is about responding to change in a way that reflects values and principles. Getting ready for the future does not mean we have to forget about what defined us in the past. It is about evolving, growing, and learning—and knowing who we are and having the strength to be open to change.

Compromise

Door within the Saadian Tombs, Marrakesh, Morocco.

King Hassan II of Morocco once likened his country to a tree whose roots were in Africa but whose branches extended across to Europe, a visual that harkens back to a history shaped by an eclectic combination of African, Arab, and European influence, and a nation now accustomed to political, religious, and social compromise.

Since the nineteenth century, Morocco has been both the source and subject of frequent compromise. In 1905, it was at the center of a tussle between the European imperial powers for supremacy, which concluded in 1912 with the partition of Morocco into French and Spanish protectorates, an arrangement that would last until independence in 1956. Since then, Morocco has agreed to five separate constitutions, the most recent in 2011 in the aftermath of protests that took place during the Arab Spring, but which stopped short of overturning the Moroccan ruling status quo of constitutional monarchy, as occurred in neighboring countries from Libya to Egypt and Tunisia.

Many have credited the survival of the monarchy with its willingness to embrace compromise. Most immediately this was witnessed in the form of concessions King Mohammed VI made to respond to the protests in 2011, including transferring the right to choose a prime minister from the monarch to the people, and formally recognizing the elected leader as the head of government. The changes also strengthened the powers of Parliament, including making it easier to investigate officials for corruption, and stepped up the commitment to human, women's, and religious rights. In the spirit of compromise, all major Moroccan political parties endorsed the new constitution, and it was passed in a referendum with overwhelming support. The reforms may not have delivered everything the protesters sought, but endorsement was still given to a series of measures that were seen as the beginning of a workable compromise.

The choice to find the middle ground was not a radical one; in fact, it was only the latest in a long history of compromise. During the reign of current king Mohammed VI, which began in 1999, a decision was made to offer reparations to former political prisoners, and a Reconciliation Commission was created to investigate human rights violations from his father's reign. Live television hearings were held, and the families of almost ten thousand victims were compensated. All were attempts to move on from the reign of his father, Hassan II, notable for the violent suppression of protest and imprisonment of political opponents. The king has also overseen updates of the Moroccan Family Code, giving women equal rights in a range of areas from marriage to family and the control of property after divorce.

Beyond politics, you can see compromise in everything, from how Moroccans—a diverse mix of people descended from groups including the Amazighs (Berbers), Spanish Christians and Jews, and sub-Saharan Africans—coexist and recognize each other's cultural and religious customs to how they barter when shopping. The country has actively prized its religious diversity, even as the non-Muslim population has shrunk, and with the Jewish community now a small fraction of the 250,000 it was when the state of Israel was founded. Regardless, synagogues and Jewish cemeteries have been maintained and restored, an annual festival is held celebrating shared Muslim and Jewish musical culture, and Morocco is the only Arab country to be home to a Jewish museum. Even the architecture reflects compromise among competing visions, with Arab, African, and European influences all visible, a beautiful mélange of color and creativity, one that harnesses a range of cultures to make bold statements and create a distinctive atmosphere.

There is another part of daily life where compromise is always on display; the place for which the country is perhaps most famous: the souks of Marrakesh. The experience of visiting the mazelike markets is known for being overwhelming (and for the inevitability of getting lost), but amid the noise and the color, the spirit of compromise remains. The bargaining that is part of any purchase in the souk is not intended to allow either side to "win" the best possible price, but rather to achieve an agreement that everyone can live with.

The art of effective compromise recognizes that we cannot get everything we want, and that there must always be give-and-take in any kind of negotiation or debate. The Moroccan example shows that change is not always swift, but that it can be achieved with evolution rather than revolution. The incremental, compromise-laden path to change may not be the most popular or fashionable, but in many circumstances it will prove to be the most effective. It is about how you create outcomes where everyone can benefit, and realistic, fair, and rational decisions get made. So if you want to make progress, get ready to do as the Moroccans do, and to compromise.

Drive

Miss Nigeria, won by Mildred Peace Ehiguese, Lagos, Nigeria.

Perhaps the most revealing question to ask anyone, anywhere in the world, is whether they expect the next year will be better than the last. It's a request that gets to the heart of the kind of lives people live, the hopes they hold and the dreams they nurture. When I posed it to market traders in Lagos, the response was immediate. "Oh yes, definitely. I know I will do better this year." It is this inner drive that unites and galvanizes the entire nation. This is not a place where you encounter laziness or complacency. Nigerians are driven to keep earning, achieving, and climbing.

This kind of drive is necessary in a country where neither the state nor infrastructure can be relied upon. If you're lucky, the electricity will work for a couple of hours a day; there will often be gasoline shortages; broadband is patchy and expensive. When you pass a cash machine, you feel the urge to empty it—unsure when you might next get the chance—but find withdrawals are strictly limited. There is no safety net to fall back on. In Nigeria, the individual is their own ruler, their own government, their own support network—like the media entrepreneur and filmmaker Jason Njoku, who until recently had to fly to London with hard drives of his films to upload them, because the local internet connection was so slow. In a country with as many as 370 distinct ethnic groups, the sense of difference is as strong as any feeling of collective community. Both the culture and the realities push people toward self-reliance: either find the drive within yourself, or fall far behind the crowd.

This message—that you can do it—stares back at you from wherever you look. Lagos may well be the world capital of personal development, from the torrent of motivational books sold by street vendors to the prosperity gospel of the dominant Pentecostal Church. In churches that can seat thousands, with names like "Winners Chapel," millionaire pastors preach sermons that sound more like get-rich-quick schemes than a study of doctrine. When it comes to work, the real job for many is not formal employment but the side hustle—buying and selling goods on the side, driving cabs, repairing phones. All around, there are role models who provide the template for the profits of drive and self-reliance. From business leaders, such as Aliko Dangote—who turned a $5,000 loan into a multibillion-dollar industrials business—to Elvis Chidera, a teenager who taught himself to code on an old Nokia 2690 and went on to land a job at a West Coast start-up, the stories of success are everywhere.

As a whole, Nollywood—Nigeria's booming film industry, responsible for over 2 percent of GDP and the second largest in the world by volume—represents the fast and furious, lean and scrappy approach that defines much of Nigerian culture. Its first hit, 1992's *Living in Bondage*, was an effective home video that sold over a million copies on VHS, mainly through street vendors. Today, a Nollywood film will be produced in seven to ten days, with a typical budget of around $10,000, compared to the year-long, multimillion-dollar production cycle of Hollywood. As Omotola Ekeinde, a famous Nigerian actor, told me, the reason Nollywood thrives is that everything is citizen-based: like much of Nigeria, it succeeds in the absence of government intervention, through the drive of the people supporting it.

Spending time in Lagos is an eye-opener. We talk about hardscrabble, bootstrapped entrepreneurship in Western economies, but that is nothing compared to the hustle and drive that the average Nigerian needs to get ahead. Drive fuels motivation and it can also create danger, a sense that nothing is off-limits. In some rural areas, friends would not let me travel without an armed guard equipped with an AK-47.

While you might not rely on drive to make up for electricity that doesn't work, or internet that keeps falling off, we all rely on drive to keep ourselves motivated, challenged, and inspired. You don't get what you want unless you are driven to succeed in your own way. That doesn't mean you have to go around high-fiving and hanging inspirational posters on your office wall. But it does require an inner fire to keep burning, and for you to keep stoking it. The next time you encounter some kind of problem or roadblock in your work or personal life, stop and think: is it really some external force holding you back, or is it actually you and your attitude toward it?

Diplomacy

Nobel Peace Prize Museum, Oslo, Norway.

Norway is a country that seems to have it all—extreme wealth in a society that focuses on redistribution; the tradition of monarchy alongside progressive governments; officially one of the world's happiest countries and probably one of the most beautiful. It stands for many good and just things, but perhaps the most notable among them is the pursuit of peace through the Norwegian talent for diplomacy.

When countries at war are looking for a mediator to help bring conflict to an end, they invariably turn to Norway for help. Over the last three decades, the country has established itself as the world's most prominent peace broker whose diplomatic activity in conflict situations is arguably unmatched, seeking to achieve peace in conflict zones as diverse as Colombia, Guatemala, Sri Lanka, Bhutan, Afghanistan, Myanmar, Mali, and South Sudan.

How did Norwegian diplomacy come to play such a central role in conflict resolution on this scale? In 1993, the Oslo Accords, an agreement between Israel and the Palestine Liberation Organization, created a so far unfulfilled framework for Middle East peace. Although the Accords were signed at the White House, with then President Bill Clinton overseeing a famous handshake between PLO chairman Yasir Arafat and Israeli prime minister Yitzhak Rabin, most of the legwork had been done in Norway, and in secret, coordinated by a Norwegian trade union think tank, Fafo, which hosted the negotiations under the guise of a research project on living conditions in the West Bank. Norway provided a peripheral, deniable back channel for talks that both sides initially approached with high levels of skepticism, and fear about being denounced by those on their own sides.

Since then, Norway has become the mediator of choice for many conflict zones. In complex negotiations with multilateral implications, a relatively small and independent nation, one without vested interests in the outcome, can be a more honest broker than a larger power whose greater influence and bargaining power also comes with perceived conflicts of interest. It helped to secure an agreement that brought an end to the Guatemalan civil war in 1996, and to achieve a cease-fire between the Colombian government and FARC rebels in 2012, after over half a century of conflict. When the U.N. was looking for a new special envoy to Syria in 2018, described as "one of the most thankless tasks in diplomacy," it turned to a Norwegian: Geir Pedersen, a diplomat whose experience stretched back to the Oslo negotiations. Since 2014, NATO has also been led by a Norwegian, the former prime minister Jens Stoltenberg.

If independence is one cornerstone of Norway's diplomatic success, another is its wealth. It ranks among the ten richest countries in the world per capita, with resources that have regularly been donated in the service of international development and diplomatic ends. Norway is one of only three countries that commit more than 1 percent of national income to overseas development. As the Syrian civil war turned millions of its citizens into refugees, Norway committed aid amounting to $240 per head of population, compared to $32 from Germany, $24 from the U.K., and $16 from the U.S.

Norway's diplomatic reputation has also been enhanced by the global reputation of the Nobel Peace Prize, awarded each year in Oslo. Admired around the world, the Peace Prize is the only one of five Nobel awards to be held outside of Sweden. Alfred Nobel stated no reason for choosing it to be associated in Norway, which at the time of his death was in a political union with his native Sweden, though the Nobel Committee has suggested it was linked to the Norwegian Parliament's work on peace resolutions in the 1890s. Many have sought to replicate the impact and influence of the Peace Prize, but none have so far come close. Norway's intrinsic relationship with diplomacy makes its status as the natural home for the world's peace prize unimpeachable. It has an integrity in matters of peace and diplomacy that perhaps no other country can equal.

Norway shows that, when it comes to managing complex situations and attempting to reconcile the seemingly irreconcilable, you don't have to be the biggest or most powerful voice in the room to effect change. Whatever your diplomatic ends, so much can be achieved by being independent, humble, and simply willing to engage where others are not.

Courage

Ashik Ali (Bhai Lal), descendant of Bhai Mardana, the musician who accompanied Guru Nanak Dev Ji, Lahore, Pakistan.

Pakistan, the land of my maternal grandparents, was the one place in the world where I almost failed to gain entry. Visa after visa was rejected until a contact in local government finally facilitated a permit. Then, tracing the journey my grandmother Mohinder Kaur had taken seventy years earlier during Partition, I was able to cross the Wagha border (with India) on foot and find my way to what I knew had been their village: Chak 94 Shankar near Shahkot. I even tracked down a man of 102 who had known them. He showed me their family home, the fields where their school had been, and the cattle sheds where the local Gurdwara (Sikh place of worship) had once stood.

This was no warm nostalgia trip. Sikhs have become a minority in what for many is ancestral homeland, including the birthplace of Guru Nanak, founder of the Sikh way of life. There are now just thirteen Gurdwaras in Pakistan, where there were once more than six hundred.

The remnants of a once thriving population, now numbering just tens of thousands, have faced repression and imprisonment without trial, with Sikhs having to close their businesses and withdraw their children from school. One of the last Gurdwaras in Lahore, which is invoked whenever any Sikh worships, as part of the final prayer (*ardas*) that laments the massacres that took place there five hundred years ago, is currently being sold off as a shopping center.

The Sikh experience is not an isolated one. In Pakistan, a country that still bears the deep scars of the deadly religious fighting that marked its birth amid Partition, all minorities face violence and repression. In parallel, ordinary Pakistanis of all faiths struggle to earn, educate their children, and simply survive in an environment marred by corruption, an absence of reliable state services, and terrorist attacks.

Yet in the face of such challenges, Pakistanis do not bend. They show the courage that is a defining national characteristic, one manifested in everything from protest and campaigning work to the establishment of citizen-led services to fill the gaps the government has left. And it is precisely through this courage that progress has been won and new rights granted.

A case in point is the Pashtun, a minority group of Afghani origin, who for the first seven decades of Pakistan's existence were denied the full rights of citizenship and remained subject to colonial-era law. The Pashtun were finally granted equal rights in November 2018, months after a groundbreaking series of protests that brought together tens of thousands under the banner of the Pashtun Tahafuz Movement. These protests represented a significant act of courage, in the face of years of harsh treatment from the military, the detention of numerous Pashtun leaders, and a media blackout.

The Pashtun had the courage not just to stand up for their rights, but also to stand against Pakistan's all-powerful military, one with a long record of crushing protest movements. They did just that, deliberately setting their movement on a collision course with the primary symbol of state power. And they won.

Minorities beyond the ethnic and religious have also battled courageously against the prevailing social tide. Pakistan's transgender community, which faces a culture of often murderous violence, has also fought for and won political progress, with a landmark bill passing Parliament that allows people to choose their gender and have it recognized on official documents, as well as measures to combat discrimination in schools. Pakistani elections now regularly feature trans candidates such as Nayyab Ali, who was ostracized by her family at thirteen, faced sexual assault, and was attacked with acid by a former boyfriend.

Courage is also a defining feature of the Pakistanis who believe in the power of volunteer-led services in areas from education to health. Among the most celebrated was the late Abdul Sattar Edhi, known as "Father Teresa," whose experience showed that work of this kind in Pakistan is fraught with risk and requires significant bravery. The social entrepreneur, who ran a nationwide network of hospitals and a volunteer-staffed, 1,200-strong ambulance force, was targeted by Islamists who robbed his hospitals and attacked his volunteers and ambulances. Undeterred, Edhi continued to run what is Pakistan's largest health care charity from a Karachi back alley until his death at the age of eighty-eight.

As Pakistan reminds us, courage is about the willingness to put your beliefs before your personal interests. It also means that, when you see a problem, you don't ignore it or sit back and hope someone else does something. You get involved. Syeda Anfas Ali Shah Zaidi sold her business to set up the Footpath School, a network of schools for street children that hosts classes in Karachi's public underpasses, bringing education to a handful of the 60 percent of Pakistani school-age children who are not in the system. It has persisted in the face of government opposition, educating hundreds of children a day. Sisters Asma Jahangir and Hina Jilani established the country's first woman-run law firm in 1980, and later one of its pioneering human rights organizations. Malala Yousafzai was shot for standing up for her right to be educated. The late Benazir Bhutto, the first woman leader of a Muslim-majority nation, was assassinated for standing up for her political beliefs.

Pakistan is full of stories of courage like theirs, of people who, against the odds, are helping to build a better and fairer country. In an often hostile environment for change, many Pakistanis put themselves in danger's path to push for progress. They show that it is not enough simply to want change and justice; it takes the courage to demand and achieve them in the face of all kinds of opposition.

Education

Nadine Hassassian, of Beit Jala,
Central West Bank, Palestine.

When it came time for the $1 million Global Teacher Prize to be awarded in 2016, the accolade didn't go to a representative of Finland's world-renowned school system, to a teacher from Singapore's table-topping academies, or one from Silicon Valley's tech-lite elementary schools. Instead, the winner was a woman who had grown up in a Palestinian refugee camp, and whose classroom provides a refuge for pupils who often face a dangerous and unstable world outside it.

Hanan Al Hroub was selected out of eight thousand candidates, winning recognition for her unique approach to working with children traumatized by their experience of living in violence in the West Bank. At her school near Ramallah, her approach revolves around games and play with six- to ten-year-olds, with teaching methods ranging from class singing to using balloons to help solve math problems. The methods were first developed after her family was shot at in their car by Israeli soldiers at a checkpoint, and she was left struggling to help her children cope with the traumatic aftermath. "Children are deeply affected by their environment," she has said. "I want to provide a safe environment for learning. I cannot influence the wider environment but I can influence the child. This is my philosophy."

Ever since, Hroub has become the global face of Palestinian education, the symbol of an important tradition that is essential to the Palestinian way of life. As a people displaced and dispersed, facing an unstable present and an uncertain future, Palestinians know there is only one way to ensure that their history, culture, traditions, and identity make it to the next generation: through education. This has been true since the establishment of the State of Israel on historic Palestinian land, during which an estimated 750,000 Palestinians fled or were expelled—losing almost everything, but never the ability to educate their children and give them the best chance in life. Education is valued as one of the ways to survive and fight back, a key to the future as well as one to unlock the past, and make sense of the present.

Talk to an educated Palestinian and they will often tell you about the significant sacrifices they, and their families, made to get hold of a degree: being sent abroad by parents who know they may never get to see them again; living with their whole family in cramped conditions and working night jobs just to be near a university; taking almost a decade over a degree that should only last a few years, because of the disruptions and challenges they have faced along the way. At home, makeshift classrooms pop up almost immediately to replace those lost when schools are bombed. (An estimated 180 of Gaza's 690 schools were damaged by Israeli bombing during the summer of 2014, adversely impacting the education of almost half a million children. Education infrastructure is also heavily reliant on foreign aid, and as such subject to changes in the political landscape.)

Yet despite the shortages and the challenges, Palestinians are by many measures among the world's most educated people. Gaza and the West Bank have one of the highest literacy rates in the Arab world, at 96.9 percent, while illiteracy in adults over the age of fifteen fell from 13.9 percent in 1997 to just 3.7 percent by 2013. Moreover, the enrollment rate of students in higher education increased by 940 percent between 1993 and 2011, and Gaza is also home to more PhDs per capita than almost anywhere in the world.

That has made education one of the most important Palestinian exports: so many people I encountered across the Middle East had been taught by Palestinians, who are called upon across the Middle East and indeed the world as teachers of unique renown. Hearing a Palestinian teacher at work is something special: you experience a combination of pure passion and extraordinary knowledge. I have never been more impressed by a speaker than when I heard my friend Nadine Hassassian speaking at the London School of Economics, with more conviction and clarity at the age of twenty-one than most world leaders can muster.

Yet despite the quality and prevalence of education, for many Palestinians the reality after graduating is often a bleak one. Almost 38 percent of male graduates, and 72 percent of women, were unemployed in 2017. In Gaza especially, mostly closed borders on both the Egyptian and Israeli sides severely limit the employment opportunities for young and highly educated Palestinians.

In many ways that grim reality reinforces the importance of education. Palestinians may be denied many of the essential rights that we take for granted in other parts of the world, but nothing can take away their ability to gain for themselves and their children the best possible education. The right to learning—the sharing of information, tradition, and expertise—is one that remains sacred and prized. Whatever else may be taken away, education is always something to hold on to.

Exploration

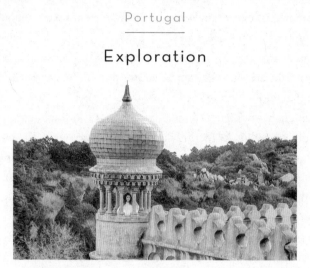

Yellow Tower of Pena Palace in the Sintra Mountains, Portugal.

Europe's westernmost country, looking out to sea, Portugal has been defined for centuries by its appetite for exploration. This began in the fifteenth century, when Portugal rapidly established itself as the Western world's foremost maritime explorer. In Europe's Age of Discovery, the nation was at the forefront, pioneering new technologies and reaching hitherto unexplored places. Its navigators were the first to navigate the Cape of Good Hope, to reach India by sea, and later the first Europeans to discover Brazil and Japan. In 1519 a Portuguese explorer, Ferdinand Magellan, led the first voyage to circumnavigate the globe. His is one of several Portuguese names synonymous with the discovery of the New World, including Vasco da Gama and—according to some theories—Christopher Columbus.

So how did a small strip of land in the corner of Europe become the world's leading sea power, and the driving force in opening up major new commercial arteries? What led them to disprove the prevailing theory that the Atlantic and Indian Oceans were landlocked, and eventually helped establish trade routes around the coast of Africa, and to South Asia?

The motivations of Portuguese exploration were multiple—from the commercial to the religious—but its foundations were undoubtedly the country's unique geography. "The Portuguese people . . . naturally faced outward, away from the classic centers of European civilization, westward toward the unfathomed ocean, and southward toward a continent that for the Europeans was also unfathomed," the historian Daniel Boorstin has written. Distant by land from the unexplored world but coastally primed, its borderlines led it to invest heavily in the potential of maritime exploration. Henry the Navigator, third son of King John I, was a central figure in bringing together the different talents and ideas that would eventually secure Portugal's supremacy. In the village of Sagres he established a "school" that brought together the leading lights in geography, navigation, and mapmaking. Its most important product was the caravel: a new, lighter design of ship with triangular sails, built to be more compact and better able to take advantage of the wind, widely regarded as a pioneering innovation.

With the handover of Macau in 1999, Portugal withdrew from the last of its former colonies, but the spirit of exploration has not gone away. From Angola to Mozambique and Brazil, a new generation of job seekers has returned to former colonies in search of opportunities and to escape southern Europe's economic stagnation. Only two other countries—Ireland and New Zealand—have a higher proportion of the native-born population living abroad than Portugal's 14 percent. Around a million Portuguese are estimated to live in France, twice the number who have made their home in the capital, Lisbon. In the U.K.'s National Health Service, one of the world's largest employers, Portugal is the sixth most represented nationality among the 203 who make up its workforce. Today, Portuguese remains the sixth most spoken language in the world, while large pockets of Christianity in places such as Goa (in India) are another legacy of its once vast imperial reach.

Driven by a combination of geography, ambition, and necessity,

Portugal has been Europe's most dedicated explorer for centuries: a navigator of things new and a creator of world firsts. As its history shows, only by exploration can we make discoveries and achieve progress. Exploration is as fundamental to every individual life, career, and business, as it is to a nation. We must all expand the horizons of our knowledge and experiences. Only by becoming explorers in our personal and professional lives can we keep our ambitions sharp and our minds fresh. It is how we avoid limitations and grow, learn, and improve in everything we do. Nothing or no one has ever succeeded without having the will and the courage to explore. Portugal points the way to a more adventurous and fulfilling way of being.

Influence

Urquhart Castle, overlooking Loch Ness in the Highlands of Scotland.

"We look to Scotland for all our ideas of civilization," the French philosopher Voltaire once argued. Since he said that in the eighteenth century, the world has indeed been influenced by numerous Scottish ideas and inventions. Pick up the telephone, turn on the TV, or drive down a tarmac road and you are experiencing the full extent of Scottish influence on the modern world.

From philosophy to innovation to modern economics, it was Scots who set the stage, and as such influenced their development. Whether Adam Smith's free market teachings, James Watt's steam engine, or Kirkpatrick Macmillan's bicycle, Scots have pioneered so many things that we today take for granted, and would never think could all have come from a single, small slice of an island nation. It's not just inventions, but whole institutions and nations, that have Scottish fingerprints on them. Scottish influence is everywhere, reflected in the many countries with large populations who can trace Scottish ancestry.

Compared to Scotland's own population of 5.45 million, there are diaspora populations of over 6 million in the United States, 4.7 million in Canada, 1.7 million in Australia, 100,000 in Argentina, and 80,000 in Chile, who can claim Scottish ancestry. Aided by the prominent role of Scots in expanding and administering the British Empire, and the wide reach of Scottish Presbyterian missionaries, enclaves of Scottish culture and influence were created during the eighteenth and nineteenth centuries that continue in various forms today. It was a Scot, William Paterson, who founded the Bank of England, then only the second central bank in the world. Scots and Scottish ideas were also fundamental to the creation and development of the United States. There are multiple Scottish signatures on the Declaration of Independence, while the framers of the U.S. Constitution, notably Thomas Jefferson, were students of Scottish Enlightenment philosophy.

Scottish influence on the world is not just the product of its distinctive history. It's also something we can still see around us. The UK's Open University, which has played a significant role in democratizing access to higher education, was founded by a Scottish politician, Jennie Lee. The biggest arts festival in the world happens annually in Edinburgh. Or look to Hollywood, and the number of Scottish actors who have become big screen stars: from Sean Connery in the 1960s and 1970s to Ewan McGregor and Gerard Butler today. Think of some of the world's finest restaurants, stocked with Scottish salmon and single malt whisky: the two biggest food and drink exports from not just Scotland, but the U.K. as a whole. Even the president of the United States, probably the most influential figure in the world, lives and works in the White House, a residence that was partly designed and built by Scottish stonemasons.

When in 2014 a referendum was held to decide whether Scotland should remain within the U.K. or become a fully independent nation, a passionate debate opened up about what the future should look like. Some saw independence as a throwing off of shackles, and a catalyst for unleashing Scotland's full potential. Others warned not to underestimate how well Scotland had done under the existing Union, benefiting from economic ties with England in particular, and the influence it had historically been able to wield. "We've run the English very efficiently for 300 years," the Scottish author William Dalrymple wrote at the time. "I see no good reason to stop now." With the future for Scotland still uncertain, and independence by no means off the table, we can be sure that Scottish influence will continue to be felt, both near and far.

And for anyone wondering how to make their impact—whether that is in their career, growing a company into a new market, or trying to launch a product—Scotland offers an example that size doesn't equate to power. It is the power of ideas that really travels and influences change; you can start by being small, peripheral, and unknown, but that doesn't stop you from changing the world.

Order

Haji Lane, Kampong Glam, Singapore.

A few days into my time in Singapore, I found myself craving some chaos; grit in an otherwise perfectly ordered oyster. And if that seems like a strange reaction, bear in mind this is the country where it's against the law to chew gum, to cross the road at a nondesignated point, or to forget to flush a public toilet. Order, rules, and regulations are everywhere you look, covering all aspects of daily life.

In every sense, Singapore is a nation governed by an overwhelming sense of order. It is often described as a fine country, because you can be fined for almost anything, from eating a certain kind of food (the durian fruit) on public transportation to flying a kite too near passing traffic. Even the laws that aren't on the statute book are commonly understood: during the rush hour you will never dawdle even for a second on the city's public transport system; once the elevator doors are closed all conversation ceases; and if you are invited for dinner, whatever you bring must not be food (implying, as that does, that the host will not be able to fully provide). Not for nothing has the island nation been variously described as "the most meticulously planned city in the world," and "the country run like a corporation." Both are testament to the ordered vision of its founding father and longtime ruler, Lee Kuan Yew. He took what was essentially a swamp and led its evolution into one of the world's most advanced economies. In the last decade, Singapore has also been ranked as the healthiest country in the world (though it has more recently struggled in this area), the best place to do business, and the place where the fewest people report struggling to afford food or shelter. It is regularly one of the highest performers in global education rankings, which it topped in 2016. As a small city-state that was started from scratch and without many natural resources, Singapore is the ultimate example of what can be achieved through a singular vision, brought to life by carefully planned order.

In a water-scarce country, effective policy has ensured that Singapore is now regarded as one of the world leaders in water conservation and management, having maximized its efforts to collect all available rainwater, create the infrastructure to recycle and reclaim water on a large scale, and undertake major projects to clean previously polluted rivers.

This fundamentally ordered approach in managing the limitations and constraints of the city-state has also extended to housing policy. Approximately 80 percent of Singaporeans live in government-provided social housing, around which amenities from schools to shops are built to create self-contained communities. There are quotas to ensure an ethnic mix, and avoid the development of monoracial communities.

Bans, quotas, and regulation may not be everyone's idea of fun. But Singapore shows how wielding the rule book can be an important part of achieving the outcomes you seek. And what goes for public policy in Singapore can equally apply to all of us in how we seek to achieve our ambitions at work and our goals in life. Though we might chafe against rules and procedure, order has an important role to play in even the most creative of pursuits. What's left to chance generally won't happen. But as Singapore shows, what is carefully planned in an orderly way will probably succeed. We quite rightly celebrate creativity, rule-breaking, and disruption in today's business world. But they are worth nothing if not based on a core of order. Without that, nothing gets done.

Impact

Award-winning straw dome, an earthen home, Senec, Slovakia.

When the Slovak government was looking for a symbol to promote the country to tourists and foreign investors, it chose the butterfly. Like the insect that flaps its wings and eventually causes a storm on the other side of the world, it wanted to capture Slovakia's capacity, as a "small big country," for making an outsize impact.

Right at the heart of Europe, and crowded on all sides by much larger neighbors, Slovakia prides itself on the ability to punch above its weight. It not only wants to make a difference in the world, but also prides itself on the ability to do just that. Slovakia, and Slovakians, are obsessed with the question of how they can make an impact and be a force for positive change.

"Good idea, Slovakia" is what the national promotional slogan has evolved into. And there can be no doubting that Slovakia is a place from which some of the world's most innovative companies and commercial ideas are evolving. It is home to the most advanced flying car start-up, AeroMobil, which has created a vehicle that could potentially cover distances equating to a middle-distance flight. Another pioneering business model is the Ecocapsule, a miniature dwelling that entirely powers itself through a combination of solar and wind energy. These are not just ideas for their own sake, but exist to address some of the biggest questions the world faces: What will transport look like in a more populous world? How can we reduce the reliance on energy sources that are slowly making the planet uninhabitable?

The Slovakian desire to leave an impact is rooted in self-sufficiency, and the desire to take control over your own destiny. AeroMobil's founder, Stefan Klein, has spoken of how he first dreamed of building a flying car as a child, living in communist Czechoslovakia and dreaming of flying across the Iron Curtain to Austria. There is something about the Slovak environment—at the heart of Europe, surrounded by exquisite nature—that makes you want to connect and contribute to the world around you: making a difference for yourself, your neighbors, and even the rest of the world.

Slovaks know that you can only make that impact by having the strength to carve your own path. Elena Mallickova is now a senior diplomat, which sounds unexceptional enough, until you learn that she faced rejection after rejection, from the university who told her that a woman couldn't study International Relations, to the Foreign Ministry that told her there would never be a job for her. She built another career as a broadcaster and foreign editor, and two decades later was able to realize her lifelong ambition. Now she uses her position to support and spotlight Slovakians who are making a difference around the world, helping to create the Goodwill Envoy award, given annually to a handful of Slovakian leaders who have made an international impact in industry, science, the arts, and acting.

The desire to make an impact is reflected in Slovakia's choice of leaders. In 2014 it elected a political novice and independent candidate, Andrej Kiska, as its president. Kiska was best known as an entrepreneur who created one of Slovakia's largest charitable bodies, Good Angel, which supports families of sick children with their medical bills. Since 2006, it has distributed over 34 million euros, and while he remained president, Kiska donated his monthly salary to the cause. In 2019, Zuzana Čaputová became Slovakia's first woman president.

Whether through philanthropy at home, or blazing a trail abroad, Slovakians are focused on the impact they can make on the people and world around them. Most feel an obligation, one passed down through the generations, to make a difference and leave a mark.

It's a question we would all do well to ask ourselves. Are we using our talents, our resources, and our time to the maximum possible benefit? What more could we be doing to help people and contribute to solving the problems that our communities face? There is more that all of us can do, in however small a way, if we see the world through the Slovakian lens of how to make an impact.

Forgiveness

Desmond Tutu, archbishop emeritus of
Cape Town, awarded the Nobel Peace Prize for his work with the
Truth and Reconciliation Commission, South Africa.

"If there are dreams about a beautiful South Africa, there are also roads that lead to their goal," Nelson Mandela once said. "Two of these roads could be named goodness and forgiveness."

If there is one global figure in recent history who above all others can be associated with forgiveness, it is Mandela. The Government of National Unity he headed from 1994, and the institutions it created to deliver justice for the horrors committed under apartheid, have become the model for how countries can deal with the aftermath of internal conflict, violence, and sectarianism.

"Forgiveness is the centrepiece of his government, institutionalised in the truth commission," wrote *The Economist* in 1997, referring to the Truth and Reconciliation Commission that was established to lay bare the crimes of the previous four decades, acting in the words of its chairman, Desmond Tutu, as "an incubation chamber for national healing, reconciliation, and forgiveness." The commission, whose proceedings were broadcast to the nation, heard the testimony of over twenty thousand victims and more than seven thousand perpetrators. It was empowered to grant both reparations and amnesty, and widely praised as providing a victim-led process for the crimes of apartheid to be addressed without violence or retribution. "Good apartheid victims wept, they did not rage," the South African author Sisonke Msimang has written. "They cried out but they dared not swear. The ugly side of grief—vengeance and the nihilism of loss—have had no place in the vocabulary of the new South Africa. We are a nation founded on the benign principles of tolerance and forgiveness, not on the craggy rocks of fury." It was within that framework that South Africans were used to speaking about the past.

Now, almost a quarter of a century has passed, and many doubt that legacy, and its effectiveness. Archbishop Tutu himself has been deeply critical of the failure to follow through on the findings and recommendations of the commission he chaired. "The tardy and limited payments of reparations to victims of humans rights violations eroded the very dignity that the commission sought to build," he wrote in 2014. "The fact that the government did not prosecute those who failed to apply for amnesty undermined those who did. The proposal of a once-off wealth tax as a vehicle for those who had benefited from the past to contribute to the future was stillborn."

In a country that remains officially the world's most unequal nation, where children are drowning in outdoor pit latrines (as of 2018, still used by over 4,500 schools nationwide), and only 10 percent of white-owned land has been redistributed to black South Africans since the end of apartheid, unrest is now growing on issues from race relations to student fees, land reform and the quality of the school system. You have only to visit a township, and contrast it to the houses of white neighborhoods—with their high walls, guard dogs, and servants—to see the extent to which race remains a dividing line in modern South Africa. These challenges are bringing a new perspective to the process of forgiveness, as those who have grown up in a post-apartheid nation reach for a more profound moment of social and economic transformation: to achieve structural as well as surface-level change. The time may have passed for Mandela-era forgiveness, but that does not mean the process is over or the book is closed.

"In South Africa we've had something of a truncated process of forgiveness," Mpho Tutu, daughter of Archbishop Tutu and coauthor with him of a book on the subject, has said. "Economically the realities of South Africa have barely changed and there are some people who are quite satisfied with the idea that, 'Well you forgave us, now let's just march on into the sunset together without anything having to change.' That's not a full forgiveness process, full forgiveness is when the relationship after is different from the relationship before and that has not happened yet."

Ubuntu can be defined as humanity toward others. In some parts of South Africa, there is a practice whereby when someone has made a mistake, they are taken to the center of the village and surrounded by their tribe for two full days, who speak about all the good this person has done. Believing that the core of each of us and therefore humanity is good, a mistake is seen as a cry for help. The community unites in this ritual to encourage the person to reconnect with their true nature. The thought is that unity and affirmation have greater power to change behavior than shame and punishment.

If the early years of post-apartheid South Africa showed the power of forgiveness, recent times have demonstrated its limitations, as well as its complexities. It demonstrates that forgiveness can be a messy, long-term process, one that defies simple definition and strict terms. South Africa reminds us that forgiveness can only really be achieved when the root of wrongdoing has been not just apologized for, but meaningfully altered, guaranteeing that the future cannot mirror the past.

Dynamism

Zen yet still energetic dance at the Golgulsa Temple, Gyeongsangbuk-do, South Korea.

ali-pali. Hurry up! You could use this one phrase to sum up the culture of South Korea, a country where nothing and nobody is static. Dynamism rules the day: a need to be ahead of the curve that is fueled by the fear of being left behind.

Stop. Breathe. Take a minute to understand what this looks like. Consider that the average Korean takes 56 steps in a minute, compared to 35 in Japan, 29 in the U.K., and 25 in the U.S. The country has the world's fastest internet speeds, and is pioneering the shift to 10 Gbps connectivity. According to one dating company, the average time from a first date to marriage is just over ten months. Even relaxation is done in a hurry, with South Korea home to a growing number of "nap cafés," where you can pay by the hour for a bed to rest during your lunch hour, or any other precious moment of downtime. The name of the trend? *Fast healing*. People almost never stop working, and they hardly get any sleep, by international standards, as a result. According to the OECD, South Korean workers complete an average of 2,069 hours of work per year. That compares to averages of 1,713 in Japan, 1,669 in Australia, and 1,363 in Germany. It can be no surprise that, when the OECD surveyed sleeping habits among eighteen countries in 2014, South Korea came bottom of the pile: its average of 469 minutes' shut-eye a night compared to 530 in France, 518 in the U.S., and 514 in Spain, the three most sleep-rich countries.

Dynamism means that you never settle for what you have, and you are always looking past today to what the future can and should hold for you. It is rooted in a sense of unease—that your life might not be progressing as it should, or that others around you are proving more successful. It's why Koreans are always looking for what their next job should be, and planning far ahead in their family lives. It's not uncommon to hear couples in their twenties discussing how they will afford their third child. The same attitude explains the famous Korean affection for the latest fashion or new technology. South Korea is home to tech giants including Samsung and LG, and Seoul is often seen as one of the world's most technological cities. While fast fashion in the West might mean a turnaround of a concept in a few weeks, in South Korea it might be done the same day. It's this dynamism that is also fueling the global phenomenon of K-pop, attracting a fandom of young people all over the world.

A dynamic environment is also a practical one, where design is minimalistic and honed for efficiency; this attention to detail is something you quickly come to appreciate. It's also one that requires you to take breaks from the otherwise hectic pace of life, as my brother and I did on a retreat to a Buddhist monastery.

For a country that was, in the aftermath of the repressive Japanese occupation (ending in 1945) and the Korean War of the early 1950s, one of the world's poorest, it had been a remarkable transformation. At the beginning of the 1960s, South Korea's trade output amounted to just $33 million annually. Life expectancy was fifty-five and only 9 percent of the population enrolled in higher education. By 2015, trade had topped $96 billion, life expectancy had risen by twenty-seven years, and the university population had grown to over 70 percent of the total.

Would such an extraordinary acceleration have been possible without a culture that has dynamism at its core? As South Korean president Park Chung-hee said in a speech in Germany in 1964, to a group of Korean miners who had come to Europe to make a better living for their families: "Although we are undergoing this trying time, we are not supposed to pass poverty on to our descendants. We must do our part to end poverty in Korea so that the next generation doesn't experience what we are going through now."

A country without any real natural resources to speak of, South Korea has become a forward-looking, high-performing, and globally leading nation not least because of the determination and dynamism of its people. Dynamism has ensured that South Korea has gone from being one of the world's poorest countries to among its richest.

If we are to achieve our own ambitions, we all need some of that dynamic internal motor. Being dynamic means never accepting the status quo, never settling for what you have, and always trying to find ways to improve yourself. Dynamism is the polar opposite of complacency, the enemy of drift and stasis. It is a shared trait among the most successful people and companies—full of energy, but also the keen desire to make progress and stay ahead. With dynamism in your life, you never stop thinking ahead or asking what comes next. You don't stop, because there is always more to do, and further to go.

Moderation

The open doors of Al-Zaytuna Mosque, Medina, Tunis, Tunisia.

The spark that lit the Arab Spring came not from Egypt, Syria, Libya, or Lebanon, but a country less associated with revolution—Tunisia—and it began not with a mass protest but a single street vendor named Mohamed Bouazizi. Refusing to pay a bribe to local government agents, he was beaten and his produce and weighing scales confiscated. When he went to retrieve his property and was turned away, he got some gasoline, returned to the municipal building, and set himself alight. A few weeks later he died of his wounds in the hospital, but not before his suicide inspired protests that would unseat Tunisia's president of twenty-three years, and set off a chain reaction across the Arab world.

Tunisia may have ignited the Arab Spring, but its response in the aftermath set it apart from its regional neighbors as a nation that has moderation in its political, religious, and social fabric. Of all the countries where the status quo was overturned in 2011, Tunisia alone has succeeded in engineering a democratic government that has kept dictatorship and religious extremism at bay. Two sets of elections, the first since the 1950s and judged free and fair by international observers, have since taken place. A new constitution was adopted in 2014 that ensures equal representation for women on all electoral lists. And, since 2011, Tunisia has been ruled by a series of coalition governments that have united secular and Islamist parties. From fractious beginnings, a moderate approach has ensured relative political stability.

The moderation that sets Tunisia apart is rooted in its relatively relaxed attitude to religion. It is an Islamic country that does not always feel like one. I remember being surprised to see people openly sitting on their terraces drinking, with no concern about being seen in public with alcohol. I was even allowed to visit the mosques in the Medina of Tunis, which are closed to non-Muslims.

Where most Arab countries have a strong religious and military involvement in politics, post-revolutionary Tunisia has worked hard to minimize both influences. The Islamist Ennahda Party is avowedly moderate, and in 2016 formally separated its political and religious activities, even in the face of opposition from some supporters. Ennahda has worked hard to distance itself from suspicions that it wants to enforce an Islamic agenda in a country where there is widespread expectation that the state should be secular.

Still, the evolution of democracy in Tunisia has not been without its difficulties, from internal disputes within political movements to accusations that the different parties have become too similar and fail to represent the people. For many, the political consensus that emerged has actually been *too* moderate, afraid to enact the bold reforms needed to turn around an economy struggling with low growth and high inflation and to curb a public sector that has become unaffordable. But these are problems and disagreements happening within an essentially democratic framework, a stark counterpoint to the dictatorship, theocracy, and martial law that exist on Tunisia's doorstep.

These moderate leanings are not a novelty of the post–Arab Spring era, but something with a long history in Tunisia. Women's equality has long outpaced that of other countries elsewhere in the region, stretching back to reforms made in the aftermath of independence in 1956, including equal divorce rights. In recent years, landmark laws have been passed to protect women against violence (which over half of Tunisian women have experienced) and to create equal rights in inheritance.

These (relatively speaking) progressive policies have been guaranteed by the prominent role women play in Tunisian politics. As of the May 2018 elections, 47 percent of local government representatives are women, and Tunis has elected Souad Abderrahim, who does not wear the veil, as its first female mayor. None of this is by accident: it is the product of decades of campaigning, by activists like Ahlem Belhadj whose work extends back decades. The role played by women in public life is one of the foundations on which Tunisia's moderate culture and society rests.

Such moderation extends into every facet of life. It is a country where the sweets are not too sweet, the colors not too colorful, and the architecture far from showy.

This temperance in many things has delivered perhaps a rare example of political stability in the region and a progressive stance on social issues. Tunisia shows the benefits of moderation for individuals, organizations, and indeed countries as a whole. By moderating our views and beliefs, we create more room to understand those of others, and to allow everyone to be heard. Moderating our ambitions might sound counterintuitive, but it can help us to be less self-obsessed and see the bigger picture. In a megaphone world, moderation doesn't feel like the obvious course to follow. But, as Tunisia shows, it isn't always the one who shouts loudest that goes furthest.

Freedom

You know your value when it is violated. Petro Poroshenko
served as the fifth president of Ukraine.

A revolution can be a strange thing to witness from within. It is not just about people marching on the streets and massing in huge numbers, but also about the quiet intensity you see on people's faces—in how they talk and plan, even when the streets are empty, the weather conditions are harsh, and the gatherings are only small.

As Ukraine's revolution got under way in the winter of 2014, I was in Chernivtsi, some five hundred kilometers from the center of events in Kiev. At first glance you would not have known a revolution was beginning. The place felt deserted, the weather was so bad you could hardly get into the city via the main roads, and there was a sense that everything was in lockdown. The cars that were on the road had chains over the tires to crush their way through the ice.

Yet among the bitter cold and the frozen snow, a quiet fire was burning in the people I met. In cramped cafés, people intently followed the latest events on TV, congregated in small groups to discuss what was happening, who was going to Kiev, and what they could do next. It was a strange feeling of living something momentous in real time, even when it was happening hundreds of miles away. I did not witness rousing speeches or mass rallies, but instead small pockets of people who had come together in the singular cause of freedom. "We don't want to be told what to do," one told me. "We don't want a Russian president acting through a shadow, or a Polish president or an American president. Just leave us alone. If no one interfered in Ukraine, we'd be fine."

There are few people more accustomed to fighting for their freedom than Ukrainians. "We've been fighting for our freedom for centuries, it's in our genes and that's what drives us forward. We believe in ourselves, we want to be free, we want to be strong, we want to be proud of ourselves. Look at Ukrainians and how much they've sacrificed for freedom even in the last hundred years," then-Minister of Finance Oleksandr Danylyuk told me. But despite this commitment to freedom, Ukranians are not free by most measures. According to the Heritage Foundation's freedom index, Ukraine is the least free European nation once factors ranging from business and employment freedom to government integrity, property rights, and judicial effectiveness have been taken into account. Out of 180 countries ranked, 149 are deemed to enjoy greater overall freedom than Ukraine.

Perhaps it is this lack of freedom that explains why Ukrainians fight so hard in pursuit of it. Rabbi Yaakov Dov Bleich, chief rabbi of Ukraine since 1990, told me, "it's a unique thing that the Ukrainian people have. It may be because they were persecuted for so many years and they were subjugated and they didn't have the independence that some of us take for granted, that they yearn for freedom, they appreciate that freedom."

The revolution of 2014 may have succeeded in bringing down Viktor Yanukovych's government, but it has not yet brought the true independence that the people want above all else. "We are still not free, as our president is weak and now stuck, having made the promises he did to get into power," my friend Elmira told me. "For us, freedom is not to do what we want when we want, but to have the freedom to practice our own way of living. We want free and fair elected authorities and for our nation not to be robbed."

It is this absence of true liberty that makes freedom so central to the identity of Ukraine: a search for something that, through its history, has so often been denied. Freedom is something so fundamental to our lives that we often only appreciate it when it is taken from us. By the same token, the search and the fight for freedom, from oppression of any kind, is one of the most galvanizing forces that exists. That is what has turned freedom from Ukraine's value into its national mission.

Vision

Sheikh Zayed Grand Mosque, Abu Dhabi, United Arab Emirates.

In 2007, I turned down several job opportunities and chose to move to Abu Dhabi. Despite the fact that I had just got married, and my husband, Gavin, was still living and working in London, it was an easy decision: the power and distinctiveness of the UAE's vision, for itself and my role in it, put everything else in the shade. As this episode of my life unfolded, I found that the vision that had drawn me to Abu Dhabi in the first place was something shared by almost all of the people I encountered: everyone was working on their own big plan, a microcosm of a nation that runs on building and creating visions of the future.

The government's vision was clear: to tell the story of what the UAE and Islam stood for, in a world where the religion had seen its reputation tarnished in many parts of the global media. I was the second employee at twofour54 (the media zone named after the emirate's coordinates) and went on to create Ibtkar, the first media venture capital fund for MENA—Middle East, North Africa. As a Sikh, I was drawn to their vision of standing up for people being misunderstood and discriminated against.

Such vision has been the cornerstone of a young country that only came into existence in 1971. What was then mostly desert has now become one of the world's most prosperous and forward-looking economies. The region's rich natural resources help to explain its prosperity, but its infrastructure, innovation, and the rich range of services on offer to citizens speak to something more than natural advantages. The UAE has been built not just on the vast quantities of oil it sits above, but perhaps more fundamentally on its most precious resource: the vision of its rulers and people.

The nation's founder, Sheikh Zayed, was heavily influenced in creating his vision for the UAE by the time he had spent in Europe. He made it his mission to bring the quality of schools and hospitals he had seen to the new nation. He later said, "I was dreaming about our land catching up with the modern world." That meant that at the moment the UAE was founded, a clear vision was already in place. He has said, "All the picture was prepared. It was not a matter of fresh thinking, but of simply putting into effect the thought of years and years."

It took vision to create the UAE in the first place, uniting seven separate emirates under one national banner, creating a new identity and collective mission where none previously existed. The vision of Sheikh Zayed, who was the UAE's president for its first thirty-two years, has since been advanced by his successors. This is a country that continues to be built on plans for how to grow, harness new technologies, and give its people the best possible life.

Whichever direction you look in the UAE you see vision: in the skyscrapers and the major developments—the Burj Khalifa (comfortably the world's tallest building) to the Dubai archipelago that physically represents a world map through the design of its islands, or the Palm Jumeirah, an island designed in the shape of a tree. You see it in the UAE's social fabric, with an education system that funds its citizens to study anywhere in the world they choose, and a government in which there are dedicated ministries for happiness, tolerance, and artificial intelligence, and a third of the ministers are women. And you can see the hope for a better and more sustainable future, one symbolized by the creation of Masdar, which will be the world's first city powered exclusively by renewable energy sources.

Above all, the mind-set that nothing is impossible predominates. This is a country with the wealth, the focus, and the committed citizenry to make things happen, and fast. The vision that has seen cities of the future rise out of the desert continues to fire progress toward what is coming next. Vision is what has driven the world's great inventions, its most important companies, and its most significant social movements. It is also what drives us all, whatever we may be doing in our lives. Founding a business, building a career, starting a family. All these things take vision: without one, it's hard to see where all this work is actually taking you. We all need vision in our lives—once we know what we want the end to look like, it becomes so much easier to get started.

Entrepreneurship

CEOs from left to right: Marc Benioff (Salesforce), Karl Mehta (EdCast), Chip Bergh (Levi Strauss), John Milligan (Gilead), Ajay Banga (MasterCard), Mandeep Rai (Creative Visions Global).

We all know America as the nation that was founded in revolution and that has prided itself on never taking a backward step since. The biggest and the most powerful; the dominant power economically, culturally, and militarily. But what makes America America? What among the familiar ideas of ambition, progress, patriotism, and success is the value that truly distinguishes this vast, sprawling country of countries?

In the view of Professor Nitin Nohria, dean of Harvard Business School, the U.S.'s secret ingredient is about something more than the quest for success. In his view, it is the American attitude to change and ability to pivot that is its defining characteristic.

"Some might say that America values economic success above all else, that it is ruthless in its quest for money, but at closer examination it may be an economic powerhouse because of its unquenchable appetite for experimentation, for change, for innovation and for opportunity," he said. In other words, it is entrepreneurship—the pursuit of the new, in search of personal success and collective progress. A desire to build things, pioneer ideas, and achieve what has never been previously possible.

In the United States, there are no regrets over businesses that failed or ideas that didn't pan out. It's always on to the next thing, the new opportunity, something bigger, better, and smarter. As Nohria puts it: "What ultimately makes America different is its ability to be unsentimental about change." This idea, that there is more to gain from change than there is to lose, has been embedded since the American Revolution, and the break from British rule. It is fundamental to the American psyche and reflected across its political, corporate, and cultural worlds.

Fundamental to this entrepreneurial culture is the American belief that there are more lessons to be taken from failure than from success— you're a learner, not a loser. A string of ventures that went south doesn't make you a dud, but someone with the guts to have had a go, and who now has valuable experience to go again. In business, at least, Americans are better than most at recognizing and admitting what was missing or mistaken before, and making sure they get it right next time.

This mind-set means America is culturally conditioned to pursue change and shift gear when circumstances require it. Among entrepreneurs the idea of the pivot has become increasingly commonplace as companies adapt to a fast-changing technological landscape. We hear all the time about disruption, but this is increasingly a world where companies have to disrupt themselves, developing products that will displace their existing ones, and ripping up the old business model in order to make space for a new one.

It is this attitude that makes America the capital of risk taking, the "home of the brave" as its anthem tells us. According to the World Economic Forum, the U.S. is second only to Switzerland as the world's most innovative economy. In what is still a relatively young country, where young companies thrive, the no-regrets attitude means boldness is in the blood. Don't sit around wondering what you might have to lose; instead focus on the opportunity to win, and decide what you need to change to do so.

For some the American system is too Darwinian, whether in its approach to health care, or the concentration of wealth that means some of the world's greatest prosperity lives alongside unaccountable poverty. Yet despite its undoubted challenges, there is still a lure to America, whether you are a business, an artist, or a professional looking to make it big. The American Dream might have taken on some tarnish in recent years, but a large part of the ideal, and the attraction, still remains. After decades of the American Century, the U.S. is still facing forward, ready for its next move. It's still a fundamentally entrepreneurial country, where anyone can make it.

And if we want to be successful in our lives, we all need the ability to be entrepreneurial. Whether it's changing course to seize a career opening or to respond to a personal or professional crisis, our lives will throw challenges and opportunities our way. Our success will depend on how effectively we can thrive in these changing circumstances. That is especially true as the world speeds up, careers become less reliable, and new skills are constantly needed. Increasingly, our capacity to succeed will be tied to our entrepreneurial capabilities: the ability to adapt and thrive amid new and unexpected circumstances. We all need to get as comfortable with change as America has frequently been.

Part II: Continuity Values

The natural complement to change, and an idea of equal importance, is continuity. We are defined by so much more than the span of our own lives. As individuals, families, communities, and countries, our inheritances shape us in so many ways. It is the continuity of tradition, language, culture, belief, and community that makes us who we are. These continuities provide our roots, grounding us in a world of constant change, imbuing us with the wisdom of our elders, and connecting the past with the present.

And there is no better way to understand the nature—and importance—of continuity than to study the countries where identity and memory have been kept alive for centuries, despite war, oppression, occupation, and ethnic cleansing. As these stories show, the battle for continuity against all odds is one of the unifying expressions of the human spirit.

Survival

Haghpat Monastery, founded in the tenth century, Lori Province, Armenia.

To understand Armenia, a country whose population is dwarfed by a global diaspora almost three times the size, you need to look beyond its borders. As such, the most striking encounter I had with an Armenian was in Turkey, meeting a grandmother who had been taken from her homeland at the age of ten and never returned. She had been given a Muslim name, later married a Kurd, and raised her family as Muslim Turks.

Yet when I visited her with her Armenian grand-niece, it all came flooding back: the language, the memories, her Armenian name. Right down to the small details of her house, decorated Armenian-style with small side tables and embroidered cloths, you could see that this woman had never really stopped being Armenian, even though she had lived the vast majority of her life in a different country, under a different name, raising her family in a different culture.

A country that is today under thirty thousand square kilometers and populated by just over three million people was once an empire that stretched from the Caspian Sea to the Mediterranean, across much of modern-day Turkey, Syria, and Iraq. The Armenian civilization is also one of the world's oldest, thought to have existed in one form or other for up to 2,600 years. That is the essence of Armenian survival: the ability to withstand so many efforts to destroy the nation, its culture, landmarks, and collective identity, but to not let oneself or one's nation be destroyed. Their instinct to endure is unparalleled—and rooted in a national longing for the places that have been taken from them.

Mount Ararat, one of the most potent national symbols of Armenia, now lies within Turkey's borders. But, far from being forgotten, it is commemorated across Armenian society. Children, restaurants, and one of the nation's most prominent soccer teams are named after it. Every house has a framed picture of it. In the face of loss, Armenians resolve not only to survive, but also to preserve collectively memory and identity even more staunchly.

Most of all, Armenians long for the terrible crime that was perpetrated against their people to be recognized. Between 1915 and 1918, up to 1.5 million Armenians were slaughtered by the Ottoman Empire, which Turkey still refuses to recognize as genocide. The mass murder of its people, the loss of its historic lands and sites, and the dispersal of its nation means Armenia cannot escape the need to look back, remember, acknowledge, and commemorate. Over a century later, the battle for recognition remains current and poignant. Only twenty-eight countries formally recognize the killings as genocide, with the United States, the United Kingdom, and Australia among those who do not. The refusal of some nations to formally acknowledge the genocide, in some cases out of a desire to avoid diplomatic tensions with Turkey, is an ongoing source of pain to Armenians, especially those who live in the countries in question, as part of one of the world's largest ethnic diasporas. That battle for recognition is one that continues to have deadly consequences. In 2007

Hrant Dink, an Armenian-Turkish journalist who edited a newspaper for Turkey's Christian Armenian population, writing frequently about the genocide, was assassinated in the street in Istanbul.

Yet this history of loss does not make Armenia a nation defined by victimhood. "We really hold on to one another and our identity so that it stays strong—the culture, food, language, and songs," my friend Arpine says. Armenian, classified as a distinctive Indo-European language with numerous unique characteristics, is an important part of that.

Perhaps no one has captured the Armenian spirit of survival better or more memorably than William Saroyan, the Armenian American novelist, whose words need no accompaniment:

> *Destroy Armenia. See if you can do it. Send them from their*
> *homes into the desert. Let them have neither bread nor water.*
> *Burn their houses and their churches. See if they will not live*
> *again. See if they will not laugh again. See if the race will not live*
> *again when two of them meet in a beer parlor, twenty years after,*
> *and laugh, and speak in their tongue. Go ahead, see if you can*
> *do anything about it. See if you can stop them from mocking the*
> *big ideas of the world, you sons of bitches, a couple of Armenians*
> *talking in the world, go ahead and try to destroy them.*

Austria

Tradition

Philharmonic Ball in Wiener Musikverein, Vienna, Austria.

Barely visibly or consciously pregnant (for I had only just found out myself) I felt giddy for more reasons than one as I was whirled around a Viennese ballroom floor by a gentleman with a distinct resemblance to Jane Austen's Mr. Darcy. This was a Viennese winter ball—an event that is at once elegant, antiquated, and magical—from the grand setting to the finely attired orchestra and dance moves that have been honed and handed down through generations.

Attend one of these events and you are not just signing up for an evening of formal dance. You are entering into a tradition stretching back over two centuries, wearing the dress and performing the dances exactly as they might have been done by the great-great-grandparents of the Viennese in the room. If it looks like something from a period drama that's because it is; but in Austria, the tradition lives on, more popular than ever.

For the first three months of the year, winter ball season dominates

Vienna, with around 450 events being held, mostly organized by the guilds of traditional Austrian industries from coffeehouses to confectioners. Everywhere you look people are buying their costumes, dancers are practicing, and the sound of orchestras rehearsing Beethoven and Mozart follows you down the capital's original cobbled streets. It is like stepping back in time into a very privileged slice of Austrian high society.

Austrian balls, which began in 1814 during the Congress of Vienna that negotiated an end to the Napoleonic Wars, are a tradition that contains many more. At the annual Vienna Opera Ball, debutantes are formally introduced as the curtain-raiser, echoing a tradition that has long since petered out in other aristocratic societies—in the U.K., which hardly disdains its traditions and history, the queen last received society debutantes in 1958. At the heart of every Viennese Ball is the waltz, the oldest ballroom dance, and a tradition that Austrians begin learning as children.

Just as you can dance tradition in Austria, you can also eat and drink it. A slice of culture that predates even the winter balls is the *Kaffeehaus*. Many European countries are known for their coffee culture, but Austria's attachment is unique even among this competition. Since the first one opened in 1683—supposedly using coffee beans left behind by a retreating Turkish army—Vienna's coffeehouses have been the places where artists and writers, politicians and intellectuals have come to work, gossip, plot, and observe. The coffeehouses have hosted luminaries from Freud to Trotsky, and been credited as the birthplace of everything from great literature and music to pioneering soccer tactics. At Café Frauenhuber, you can take your morning coffee where Viennese have been doing the same since 1824, and where patrons were once entertained by Mozart and Beethoven. It is inspiring to sample the wares of Café Korb, opened by none other than Austro-Hungarian Emperor Franz-Josef in 1904, and known as the haunt of Nobel Prize winners. Whether you are seeking cake, conversation, or creative inspiration, there is a coffeehouse for you in Vienna, as has been the case for well over three hundred years.

Tradition does not just exist in Austria; it is also treasured in its modern context. When surveyed in 2016, 90 percent of Austrians said that it is vital to protect and keep their traditions alive. This affection for longer customs may spring from an ambiguous relationship with more recent history, especially the complex legacy of the Second World War and Austria's role in Nazi war crimes and genocide. (For decades, the prevailing narrative was of Austria as a victim of Nazism, not a contributor. Unlike Germany, it did not acknowledge its role in the Holocaust until the 1990s, or open its first official memorial until the year 2000.) As of 2018, attempts are still ongoing to secure reparations for the $1.5 billion of property estimated to have been stolen from Austrian Jews. It has often been easier to harken back to the traditions of the Austro-Hungarian era than to grapple with more challenging recent history.

The source of Austria's love for tradition may be complex, but its importance is nevertheless clear to see. Traditions—whether religious, communal, or familial—are a cornerstone of identity, helping us understand who we are as people. They offer continuity between past, present, and future, connecting us with those who came before and providing something to pass on as a legacy. Tradition reminds us of where we are from, points to what remains sacred over the ages, and therefore to what really matters. In a changing world, traditions provide a precious dose of continuity, grounding, and fundamental values.

Stability

Statue of Lenin in Independence Square, Minsk, Belarus.

Belarus has some of the appearance of a modern European nation, but still largely operates, in the words of one journalist, "like a mini-USSR preserved in amber." Since 1994, the country has been led by the same president, Alexander Lukashenko, who has been called Europe's last dictator. It can sometimes feel like a place of smoke-and-mirrors. There are large open boulevards with no one walking on them. Huge Soviet-era hotels with no one staying in them. A democracy that isn't in practice democratic. An economy that is growing but in real terms stagnating.

Yet while some might consider this as a lack of progress, for many Belarusians it simply represents the welcome stability that has delivered a steady economy and slowly rising living standards for most of the post-Soviet era. The revolution that roiled neighboring Ukraine in 2014 might have been a major threat to Lukashenko, but research found that 60 percent of Belarusians preferred to have its political and economic center of gravity remain Russia, which is responsible for over 40 percent of its export trade. Under Lukashenko, Belarus has sought to play East and West off against each other: benefiting from Russian support while working to limit economic sanctions from the U.S. and EU.

Stability is core to modern Belarus, and something it has preached on the international stage, arguing in favor of strong nation-states and government in its own model. "We are absolutely convinced that only a strong state can ensure the safety and well-being of its population," Belarus foreign minister Vladimir Makei has said at the U.N. General Assembly. "If we are truly interested in . . . global stability, we must not weaken the states, but help them to grow stronger."

For the most part, Belarus is a country where people live in neutral, toeing the line and accepting the limitations of their political and economic freedom in return for a relatively safe and peaceful existence. Protest is tightly regulated and in some cases prohibited outright, including on March 25, the anniversary of 1918's Freedom Day, which commemorates the establishment of the short-lived Belarusian People's Republic.

This stability and widespread popular neutrality are maintained through a highly centralized system that vests overwhelming power in the hands of the state. The vast majority of Belarusians work for the government or state-owned enterprises, under contracts that have to be signed on an annual basis. The state even briefly introduced a tax on the unemployed, one declaring them "social parasites," which was swiftly withdrawn amid a rare bout of protest. Many people work side hustles to top up their state salary, but levels of entrepreneurship are low and in keeping with the national ethos of playing it safe and not taking unnecessary risks. Politically, parliamentary elections are held to elect representatives who have little influence over the direction of the government, while the presidential elections are not regarded as free and fair.

With a supportive elite, and a dependent workforce, the Lukashenko regime has to date succeeded in projecting itself internally as the guardian of stability: a price worth paying for political and economic safety. In a world obsessed with change, Belarus stands apart for its refusal to go along with the tide. Nations are primarily a product of evolution from within their historical and geographical context. In this case, while Belarus's political model may be off-putting to Western eyes, its focus on the maintenance of stability over the pursuit of progress offers a worthwhile counterpoint. Change is often sought but not always beneficial. In all our lives, we also need to think about what is better maintained and kept the same. Sometimes, a little stability is exactly what we need.

Rootedness

**El Tío, the Lord of the Underworld,
Cerro Rico Mine, Potosí, Bolivia.**

Go underground in Bolivia, and you have to pass the devil to get there—literally. Step into one of the country's tin, copper, or silver mines and you will encounter the Bolivian equivalent of a scarecrow: a sandbag dressed as the devil, at whose feet workers will leave gifts of food, drink, and money in exchange for good luck. Go down into the mines themselves and you can see why. Soon the light has long gone, oxygen is getting scarce, and it's becoming hard to breathe. It's a harsh, claustrophobic environment where you would gladly welcome divine intervention to survive on a daily basis.

A visit to a Bolivian mine is salutary, helping to explain a national culture that is steeped in spirit, and as rooted in its past and indigenous culture as Bolivia's economy is in rich mineral resources.

Bolivia is a country where history is everywhere and roots matter.

The present, and hopes for the future, are informed in so many ways by the past, symbols and remnants of the famous civilizations that have occupied a country of mountains, desert, and rainforests. It is a country where the earth is like a rainbow—red soil, green lagoons, multicolored geysers—and where the indigenous people—the largest concentration in the world, making up 62 percent of the general population—hold sway, creating blockades and halting transport if oil and gas exploration threatens to destroy their precious land.

Indigenous pride has grown since the election of Evo Morales, himself an enthusiastic wearer of traditional dress, as Bolivia's first native president in 2006. Morales has since passed antidiscrimination laws to protect Bolivia's indigenous peoples against prejudice that had become widespread. In an even more powerful statement, he led an effort to retitle the nation as the "Plurinational State of Bolivia," through a new constitution adopted in 2009 that recognizes the rights and languages of thirty-seven different native groups. Native Aymara and Quechua women visibly display their heritage with the distinctive, *chola* fashion: wide, layered dresses and shawls in bright colors, topped off with a ubiquitous bowler hat (an addition from the early twentieth century, when a consignment of hats ordered for European railway workers were found to be too small, and given away to local women).

Indigenous culture is displayed not just in Bolivian dress, but increasingly in its architecture. In recent years, a fashion has sprung up for buildings that are as colorful as indigenous clothing, and replete with Aymaran symbology from representations of Inca temples to details that echo important parts of the natural world: water, wind, and mountains. These *cholets* predominate in El Alto, one of the country's largest cities, adjacent to La Paz. "It might look like Vegas, but it's all grown out of our pre-Columbian roots," said the leading creators of *cholets*, Freddy Mamani. His patrons reflect the unusual fact that Bolivians are not shying away from their roots as they grow wealthier, but actively embracing them and bringing new life to ancient symbols and ideas.

Customs rooted in Aymaran tradition predominate throughout the

Bolivian calendar. During the month-long Alasitas festival that begins in January, people will purchase miniatures that represent their hopes for the next year (tools if they want to buy a house, a crib if they are trying to have a baby, monetary bills for prosperity), which are then blessed by priests. In February there is the Carnaval de Oruro, a celebration of indigenous heritage featuring tens of thousands of musicians and folk dancers. While each May, Tinku takes place: a festival of ritualized street fighting between villages, with the symbolic intention of spilling enough blood to appease Pachamama (Mother Earth), a goddess central to indigenous culture, and fertilize a strong harvest. Another cornerstone of indigenous culture is the celebration of the solstices. These include the greeting of the sun on June 21, winter solstice in the Southern Hemisphere and New Year in Bolivia. Hands are raised to welcome the first beams of sun, acknowledging the importance of Tata Inti (Father Sun), while a llama, Bolivia's national animal, is sacrificed in honor of Pachamama. This reflects a year-round custom where, in advance of major construction projects, a llama sacrifice (often of an unborn fetus) will be made before a priest blesses the ground.

We should all have such an appreciation of our roots, whether as an individual or as part of a family, community, or organization. We cannot truly understand ourselves as people without knowing something about our ancestry, and listening to the wisdom of elders today who provide the link to our past; where we come from, and the places and experiences that have shaped our culture and the history of our family. The same is true for institutions. How many times do you hear about a business that lost its way because it forgot what it had been built to do? Finding the next step, whether in life or business, is as much about knowing where you started as about where you want to end up.

Peace

The waterfalls and pools of Costa Rica.

Costa Ricans will not generally greet you with hello and goodbye. Instead, the standard salutation is *pura vida*: a phrase that literally translates to "pure life," but which actually stands as a much deeper symbol of life in Central America's happiest country and, in every sense of the word, its most peaceful.

Pura vida, which carries the meaning of everything from living well to being positive and a sense of happiness and contentment, is as much a statement of intent as a greeting. To someone who has never visited, that might sound a bit cloying. After all, do people really want to live surrounded by others saying how happy they are, and how happy we should all be?

To step foot in Costa Rica is to understand that *pura vida* is simply a fact of life. It is a place that feels like a paradise: from the beaches to forests, volcanoes and butterfly farms. It's the Caribbean coast meets the Central American rainforest, where you can zip line between the treetops one day, climb the peak of volcanoes the next, descend into bat caves, and have a forest bath—in such lush surroundings, you become naturally open to all the scents, sights, and sounds of the earth. The people, the environment, and the culture are so peaceable that it just wouldn't occur to those present to feel anything other than deliriously happy. You are lulled by the surroundings into exactly the state of contentment that *pura vida* symbolizes. There's truly nowhere else like it.

This sense that the normal rules don't apply is reflected in some of the country's policies. For instance, it has no standing army, having abolished it in 1948, to invest the defense budget in health care, education, and social security. For many nations, not least one in a conflict-riven region, this might appear (or actually be) an act of desperate naïveté. But in Costa Rica, it has worked, helping to create thriving education and health services, while making it the most peaceful nation in Central America, according to the Global Peace Index.

Abandoning its army is not the only way that Costa Rica has sought to further the cause of peace. In 1980, President Rodrigo Carazo donated land that would become the base for the United Nations University for Peace. In 2001, along with the U.K., Costa Rica co-proposed a resolution for the establishment of an International Day of Peace, now marked annually on September 21. And in 1997, the country passed a law mandating the teaching of conflict resolution in all of its schools.

And while many of the planet's natural ecosystems are under an onslaught of human and climate pressures, Costa Rica has also decided to declare peace on its rainforests, once ubiquitous but increasingly threatened. Once 75 percent forest-covered in the 1940s, the country had just a 26 percent canopy by 1983. Reforestation work to reverse that trend has now brought the figure back over 50 percent, with a government target of hitting 70 percent by 2021. That has helped ensure Costa Rica remains one of the most biodiverse nations on the planet, home to over 500,000 different species, including some that are unique to it. Costa Rica's record is equally impressive on clean energy, having supplied over 98 percent of its electricity needs through renewable sources in 2016: principally wind, hydro-electric, and geothermal power.

Costa Rica has proved itself as a nation where peaceable, sustainable solutions can deliver meaningful change and an impressive quality of life for people. According to several indices, it ranks as the happiest place on the planet. It is a nation not without its challenges, especially when it comes to poverty and income inequality. But as a whole, Costa Rica shows that peace does not have to be an idealistic vision; it can also be a practical, long-lasting reality.

Nature

Land iguana, endemic to the Galápagos Islands, Ecuador.

A pure, raw, dense, and beyond delicious bar of chocolate is being passed around, from one member of a group to the next. Each person is taking a piece, and around half, maybe 60 percent, of it has been consumed. Then it changes hands again, and the remainder is promptly buried into the soil. "The rest is for you, Pachamama," the group leader declares.

This deep and moving respect for nature is intrinsic to life, politics, and the economy in Ecuador. It's even written into the constitution, which includes the statement that the people "hereby decide to build a new form of public coexistence, in diversity and in harmony with nature, to achieve the good way of living." That may not sound like the most radical statement in the world, but its mere existence represents a significant departure from the socioeconomic model prevalent in most parts of the world. It signifies something radical: the idea of a country that honors nature (Pachamama, Mother Earth) before everything else.

This is *buen vivir*—literally the good way of living—focused not on the individual but rather on the individual's place both in society and most importantly the natural environment. From the Ecuadorian perspective, the good life is not about people prospering through their own endeavors, but by interacting respectfully with each other and the world around them. Economic development is not seen as a good unless it is done in respect of the needs of communities as a whole and the environment. As a philosophy, it is nothing less than a direct rebuke of free market capitalism as it is practiced in large parts of the world.

Ecuador's reverence for nature is not just a good intention, but one with legal and constitutional force. The 2008 constitution was the world's first to bestow specific rights on nature: "the right to exist, persist, maintain and regenerate its vital cycles, structure, functions and processes in evolution," and gives the state power to act in ways that protect nature and restrict activities that could damage species or ecosystems.

Nowhere are these beliefs more evident than on the Galápagos, the natural wonder of a country obsessed with nature. Here, hammerhead sharks speed by, iguanas prowl, blue-footed boobies waddle, albatrosses feed, flamingos dance, and cacti rule. There is no better place to experience the wonder of nature in its full, multispecies, multicolor wonder. On these islands, the vast majority of animals and birds you encounter can be found nowhere else on the planet. Anywhere else in the world, they would have become an overdeveloped tourist theme park, but despite its high volume of yearly visitors, the Galápagos remain an environment still ruled by its most important inhabitants: the birds, plants, and animals. There is very little development, because Ecuador isn't willing to alter the natural environment on the basis it might make a few people richer. It is already serving a more important purpose, to house some of the world's most unique and biodiverse populations, to oxygenate the air and nourish the waters. Even Ecuadorians must originate from the Galápagos to live or build homes there.

Ecuador's commitment to nature and *buen vivir* has faced some struggles as it competes with national economic needs. The Yasuní nature reserve in the country's northeast vividly represents this conflict: home to around a third of the world's amphibian and reptile species, it also sits above almost 850 million barrels of oil. From 2007 to 2013, the Ecuadorian government ran a pioneering plan to try and raise the money that could have enabled them to leave the oil untouched and avoid an unaffordable loss of income. But the donations did not materialize, and extraction of some of the oil has now begun. This has been done reluctantly, with alternatives still being sought.

Ecuador and *buen vivir* point the way toward a new socioeconomic model that prioritizes the habitat, and not just its inhabitants. When the rights of nature hold sway as much as the demands of profit, a new approach to development becomes possible, one that wider climate concerns will likely help to accelerate.

But Ecuador's honoring of nature is not just about a new form of environmentalism, it is—as the name of the concept suggests—about a better way to live. It is designed to preserve great quality of life for everyone, creating an environment in which there is the room to breathe, to enjoy earthly pleasures, and to nurture our physical and mental well-being. All my Ecuadorian friends who had moved abroad to study or work have now gone back because the quality of life is simply better. They can work to live rather than vice versa, in an environment that sees being outdoors and in nature as more important than slaving away in service of "prosperity."

Numerous studies show how spending time outside and in nature is good for our health and state of mind. We are better and happier when we get out from behind the screen and outside into the world. Ecuador reminds us that honoring nature isn't just good for the environment, but good for us as people. When Pachamama is revered, respected, and replenished, we receive the same benefits, many times over.

Recognition

Chair for the toastmaster, Tbilisi, Georgia.

"... and now, we must mention ... Georgia!"

By this point in the evening, you have been through many toasts already. But there is always room for one more, because in Georgia, one toast is never enough. Sit down for a *supra* (feast) with family and friends, and you encounter a tradition that is as much about recognizing the people around the table as eating the food placed upon it.

You have entered the realm of the *tamada* (toastmaster). If the meal has a special significance, then someone will be hired for the occasion. More often, it will be a senior member of the family or group. At a *supra* I attended, a gathering of family and friends in a spacious restaurant on the outskirts of Tbilisi, the uncle took on the role of *tamada*.

Before anything is served, and glasses are filled for the first of what would be many toasts, the *tamada* makes a point of greeting and introducing everyone around the table, individually, whether they are close family members or guests. The first toast is then given by the host to the *tamada*.

And then the toasting begins in earnest, as much if not more of an event than the meal itself. The first, in honor of the gathering and why it has been brought together. The second, to thank the family who is hosting, recognizing their generosity. The third, a toast to parents, husbands and wives, and partners. The fourth, a toast to ancestors, descendants, and those who are no longer with us; a bridge between past, present, and future. The fifth is for Georgia itself. The sixth for shared memories, even things that seemed bittersweet at the time, but can now be fondly remembered. And the seventh and most important, a toast to each individual present, celebrating them for who they are and for their unique achievements.

Everyone around the table is then given the opportunity to respond to the *tamada*, and offer their own toast in turn. As you can imagine, by this stage toasting has become competitive, with everyone trying to upstage each other, and offer ever more creative and fulsome tributes. This is toasting as you have never seen it before or elsewhere; and if you want to leave before it is over, then get ready to negotiate with the *tamada*, who will implore you to stay for just one more toast: for the ancestors, for the children, for Georgia!

A small but strategically significant country, nestled between Asia and Europe, and fought over throughout its history by neighboring superpowers, Georgians love to recognize their colorful history, and what makes them unique. Once the toasts at a *supra* have finally been exhausted, the folklore singing begins. Just as there is a toast for everything and everyone, there is a Georgian folk song for anything you could think of: healing, work, marriage, travel, and dance; songs in honor of God, Georgia, peace, love, long life, and friendship, following a tradition that is thought by some to be as much as three thousand years old. Georgia's language is as ancient and distinctive as its music, with a unique thirty-three-letter alphabet that has been recognized as a cultural artifact by UNESCO. Georgian: ქართული ენა

Surrounded by much bigger powers than itself, Georgians revel in their ability to make their mark. A country of only four million people can feel, thanks to its influence, like one three or four times the size. In Russia, you will find Georgians aplenty on TV, as leading doctors, artists, musicians, and authors. What stands out most powerfully is how people are positively determined to focus on each other's strengths, accomplishments, and capabilities. It is about recognizing the best in people, and gaining a perspective that can also help you see the best in yourself: exactly the sort of ethos that you need to build empowered, successful teams. It is a healthy outlook on life that you need, whether you are trying to be a good parent, teacher, or business leader. It is about self-esteem, respect for others, and ultimately dwelling less on what you can't do and focusing on what you can do and do well.

Introspection

The bear is the unofficial ambassador for Berlin,
promoting peace, understanding, and tolerance, at the
Brandenburg Gate, Berlin, Germany.

When walking down the streets of a German town or city, take a moment to look down. There's a good chance that you will encounter a *stolperstein* (stumbling stone): a brass plaque where a cobblestone used to be, with a name, date of birth, and date and place of death. You might not realize it while rushing to your next destination, but you have just stepped on part of the world's largest memorial to the Holocaust, one of sixty thousand plaques that the Berlin artist Gunter Demnig has cemented across Europe in a project to commemorate those murdered by the Nazis.

The *stolpersteine* are not universally popular, and in Munich there is a local authority ban on them. But, part of the national fabric as they have become, they represent something fundamental about modern

Germany: the importance of introspection in coming to terms with the Nazi past and forging a new national identity in the traumatic aftermath of the war. The German word is *Vergangenheitsbewältigung*, which loosely translates as "overcoming the past," and is very much focused on engaging with difficult issues rather than seeking to avoid them. Germany's urge is not to excuse or turn away from what happened, but to expose it, question it, and ask what can be learned.

When you are constantly stepping on history, there is no escaping it. And Germany makes a virtue of looking back to absorb the horror and draw the lessons of the past. When I first visited the country and asked some German friends what we should see, the first places they took me to were the Holocaust memorials and museums. Visiting them, I was struck not just by the memory and horror that they evoke, but also by the thought of how many other people my friends had taken on this tour, and how many times they had themselves confronted this wound in the national memory.

Introspection applies not just to the Nazi past, but also to what followed, and the legacies of the police state that was East Germany for over four decades until 1989. The surveillance files of the Stasi secret police have become a central source for Germans who want to know how they and their families were spied on, with extensive efforts made by the government and historians to restore the records, which in many cases means piecing together torn or shredded papers that run into the millions. It is the only way people can come to terms not just with the reality of past events, but also with the questions that arise from them. Why did people collaborate with the Nazi slaughter and Stasi surveillance? Did they really have any choice? Could it have been different, and what can be done to stop it from ever happening again? Germany chooses to grapple with the difficult, in some ways impossible, dilemmas of the past, where other countries are too ready to wipe the record.

The emergence of a right-wing nationalist party, the AfD, has put the question of remembering Germany's past back onto the frontline political agenda. In part, it represents a strain of opinion that demands

Germany stop apologizing for its history. But even within a party that is beyond the pale for many Germans, such a view sparks controversy. One senior figure, Björn Höcke, was condemned by the AfD leadership for a speech that condemned Berlin's Holocaust memorial as a "monument of shame in the middle of our national capital." Protesters retaliated by installing a minor replica of the memorial outside Höcke's house.

For Germany, the introspection over the past and how it should be remembered continues. That bravery in facing up to difficult history offers an important lesson, because there is nothing to be gained through trying to forget what happened. What is swept under the carpet never remains there forever. It is always better to reflect, confront, and be able to speak about the past, rather than acting like it never happened at all. That is how we remember, and use the lessons of history to shape a better future.

Storytelling

Bookstore in Limerick, Republic of Ireland.

Many countries have monuments and relics that people visit to seek support or inspiration. But only Ireland has a stone that hundreds of thousands of people a year bend backward and kiss in order to gain "the gift of the gab": the Irish silver tongue that is something between eloquence, flattery, embellishment, and mythmaking.

Mystery surrounds the origins of the Blarney Stone, now located in the southwestern province of Cork, with its provenance variously attributed to figures as diverse as the biblical prophet Jeremiah and the fourteenth-century Scottish king Robert the Bruce. But there is nothing mysterious about what it has come to represent: the cornerstone of a national culture of storytelling for which Ireland and its populous diaspora is famous around the world—from the man in the pub to world-famous writers like James Joyce, Samuel Beckett, and now Sally Rooney.

With an Irish narrator, a story is never just a story. It is a living, changing thing: a tale destined to become taller with each telling, a format whose details change according to the context, the audience, and the person telling it. The truth is one thing, but far more important is the ability to stretch, twist, and uplift it into the creation of a memorable story, one that gets better every time it is wheeled out. In the narrative sense, blarney is never outright falsehood, but rather the truth of an event adapted and enhanced so many times that it has traveled some distance from the original. This is born not from a desire to mislead, but rather to entertain, and to embellish further with each new narration.

Storytelling is how the Irish talk their way through both the pain and pride of their past: a proud history that stretches back millennia, tinged with national traumas including the Great Famine of the mid-nineteenth century and the Troubles of the twentieth. Stories commemorate the past, keeping it alive and passing living memory from one generation to the next. And they help balm the still raw wounds of events that have left an indelible imprint on families, communities, and society as a whole.

Through storytelling, the tragicomedy at the heart of the Irish experience finds expression, creating humor out of bleakness. As Frank McCourt wrote in his memoir, *Angela's Ashes*: "Worse than the ordinary miserable childhood is the miserable Irish childhood, and worse yet is the miserable Irish Catholic childhood . . . nothing can compare with the Irish version: the poverty; the shiftless loquacious alcoholic father; the pious defeated mother moaning by the fire; pompous priests; bullying schoolmasters; the English and the terrible things they did to us for 800 long years."

Stories are an important window onto Ireland's recent past, but also link back to more ancient traditions and culture. Seanchaí (traditional storytellers, literally "the bearers of old lore") still keep alive an oral tradition that has transmitted history, law, and customs down the generations for over a millennium. Large tracts of Celtic folklore and history were transmitted not through being written down, but by these oral poets who passed the stories on to their successors. Stories are also part of how Ireland has knitted together the many different nationalities and cultures that have arrived on the island down the centuries.

Anyone who has ever heard an Irish friend or relative gather a group around them to tell a story knows the power of this tradition and its importance. Storytelling is about so much more than transient entertainment and amusing anecdotes. It is about connecting people and turning shared history (whether from last week or the last century) into something that bonds families, friends, and communities together. Stories unite us, engage the senses, and create something to believe in. Every individual, every organization, and every nation has its own story: in fact when you distill it down, often our story is all we have, the core foundation of our place in the world. We should all learn how to curate and tell ours, even half as well as the Irish do.

Care

**Attention to detail over years (70–80 AD) created
the Colosseum, in Rome, Italy.**

After the Colosseum and the Leaning Tower of Pisa, the overprotective mother is probably one of Italy's most famous national symbols. It's not just a cliché that Italian *mammas* care more about their children (especially their sons) than is either normal or perhaps healthy. A survey once showed that a third of Italian men see their mother every day. And Italian adults are more likely to live with their parents past the age of thirty than almost anywhere else.

Care is an Italian value that has taken over almost every aspect of life: from how you dress, to what and when you eat, to the car you drive. Though Italy can sometimes seem like a chaotic place from the outside, it is a deliberate one: it matters how you look and are seen, how you come across to people, and that you adhere to the many small but important conventions that govern everyday life.

It starts when you get up in the morning. For Italians, throwing on the nearest available T-shirt is not an option. You think carefully about the combination of colors, fabrics, and accessories. That belt with those shoes? That color? It's not for nothing that Italians are world-renowned for their fashion sense. Working hard on how you look is not confined to dressing for work or going out. You could be nipping to the corner shop or taking the trash out, and even then you'd still throw on a simple dress and some lipstick; it's the least you can do.

The same holds true for another cornerstone of Italian culture: food and drink. For a nation that takes justifiable pride in its food culture, there is no sipping coffee from cardboard cups or forking takeaways out of polystyrene trays. Time, and care, are taken over feeding and watering oneself. In the morning, Italians don't grab their coffee as part of the commuting rush. They take it at the bar of the café and drink standing up, from a ceramic vessel, enjoying the ritual as it is meant to be, taking the time it takes, maximizing the quality of the experience. And of course it's not just when or where you eat, but what you eat, that Italians care about. Italians care about what goes on their plate and would never serve up either ingredients that are out of season or dishes that are not traditional to the local area. Indeed they care so much that the arguments about exactly how to make the best tomato sauce, or the method for perfect carbonara, can be both extensive and heated. Staying with a friend, I once witnessed what appeared to be a significant marital dispute between her parents. So much so, that I thought divorce might be in the cards. But the next morning, she shrugged it off. They had been arguing about tomatoes.

In Italy there's even a correct way of going to the beach, to relax. You wear a little scarf to protect your throat on the journey there. Upon arrival, your shoes are exchanged for flip-flops. Under the sun lounger, there's a hook to hang your bag on. No throwing it lazily onto the ground. Everything designed to minimize sand in awkward places. There's a reason for all these things.

Italians care about things that many of us haven't even considered, or don't find the time to give proper thought to. In making sure to do things the "right way," stressing the small details, and insisting that time and care are taken to do it properly (whatever "it" is), they show the legions of us who rush thoughtlessly through our routines every day the benefit of caring that little bit more about what we do and why. And if you take care of the little things, and do things the way experience tells us they're meant to be done, it goes a long way to avoiding bigger pitfalls in life. That's why it always pays to do as the Romans do, and take a little care.

Endurance

Annapurna Circuit, peaking at Thorung La pass, Nepal.

As home to eight of the ten highest mountains in the world, Nepal's terrain makes endurance an unmissable fact of life—so much so that research has shown the Sherpa people, native to Nepal's mountainous regions, have biologically adapted to the harsh environment. A recent study suggested genetic differences between Sherpas and "lowlanders," with the former having more efficient mitochondria (cell structures that produce energy through respiration) and a greater capacity to generate phosphocreatine, an emergency energy source for the body when the oxygen supply is low. When you see them in action, it starts to become clear why this matters so much.

On my first visit to Nepal, my dear friend Mehdi and I had made it our mission to conquer the Annapurna Circuit, a roughly one-hundred-mile trek that is one of the most famous routes in the region, peaking at just higher than Everest base camp. We were young, reasonably fit, and youthfully naive. All that bravado vanished on the coldest night I have ever slept through, when it was so freezing that we had to sleep under seven mattresses piled on top of each other, because no amount of blankets could come close to keeping out the cold (think the princess and the pea, but in reverse!).

While we had started the adventure wearing shorts, with the sun on our backs, by the end blizzards were raging and the way forward had become almost unpassable. A week later, on the day we finally reached striking distance of the Cho Oyu summit, we set out at 4 a.m. At the start, the weather wasn't completely against us; but as dawn broke around six, the storms started, and the snow set it. Conditions became so bad we could hardly see ahead through all the hats, goggles, and scarves covering our faces.

As others were returning from the summit and coming back past us, they were telling us not to go on. A big storm was due at midday, and we agreed that if we had not made it by this point, we would have no option but to give up on our goal of reaching the summit. It was the last thing we wanted to hear, having come so far and gotten so close, but it was eventually the advice we were forced to take, tantalizingly close to the end when the storm closed in.

From that experience I learned to respect not just the immense endurance shown by Sherpas, to live and work in these conditions all the time, but also for their acceptance that there must be a reasonable limit to it all, the point where you admit it would be not brave but dangerous to try and go further. Sometimes endurance means that you must accept that the road ahead is impassable, and so you fall back and live to fight another day.

The Sherpas are far from alone in showing the distinctively Nepalese powers of endurance. The Gurkhas, Nepal's soldier tribe, are another prominent example. The British found this to their cost during the Anglo-Nepalese War of 1814–16, during which the forces of the East India Company were routinely bested by Nepalese warriors. Indeed, the Gurkhas made such an impression that the British Army sought to recruit them as part of the resulting peace treaty: an arrangement that has continued for over two centuries.

Today's Gurkhas are not just respected for their extraordinary endurance as soldiers (Johnny Fenn, a former British Gurkha officer, has written that they will routinely complete an annual one-hundred-mile training exercise in 8.5 hours compared to 12 or 13 for their British counterparts), they also face a significant test of endurance to join the elite force in the first place. Young Nepalese aspiring to join the Gurkhas face a daunting recruitment process: only two hundred are chosen annually from a pool of over twenty thousand. To win selection they face challenges including the "doko race," an uphill 5 kilometer run that must be completed with 25 kilograms of rocks in a wicker basket attached to your head.

It is not just Nepal's fighting and mountaineering elites that show this kind of endurance. Consider Biresh Dahal, a Nepalese cyclist who for fourteen years, across seventy-two countries, has been riding a bicycle backward to promote peace. Or Min Bahadur Sherchan, who in 2008 became the oldest person to successfuly scale Mount Everest, and died nine years later trying to reclaim his title, at the age of eighty-five.

Every Nepalese has to show endurance to survive in one of the world's poorest countries, with 15 percent of the population living on less than $2 a day. Nepal also frequently endures major natural disasters, such as the earthquake of 2015, which killed approximately nine thousand people, made hundreds of thousands homeless, and affected an estimated eight million, a third of the entire population. The damage was so great that it is estimated to have cost up to 50 percent of the country's annual £20 billion GDP.

Yet in the face of these daunting challenges, from the economic to the environmental, Nepal endures. It shows, in our instant gratification era, the value of being in it for the long haul. And by doing so it demonstrates the importance of endurance in all our lives: to discover our limits, push ourselves beyond them, and learn to taste the sweetest successes of all—those we have to struggle to achieve.

Poetry

Inspiring mountains of Nicaragua.

Some countries have artists, architects, or athletes as the symbols and bearers of their national culture. Some are defined by geography, political ideas, or religious culture. Nicaragua alone is a land that lives, breathes, and expresses its identity through poetry.

Here there are more poets per capita than anywhere else in the world. The most famous and revered Nicaraguan, Rubén Darío, was a poet. The president, Daniel Ortega, was a poet in his youth and so is Vice President Rosario Murillo (the two are married). Every year, the world of poetry descends on Nicaragua's cultural capital, Granada, for the International Poetry Festival, one that brings together verse writers from over fifty countries.

In some countries poets narrate the national story, but in Nicaragua they actively help to shape it. Fundamental to the constant upheaval that has defined the country's political history, Nicaraguan poetry has been a weapon of revolution, a catalyst for social change, and a marker of national identity. Poetry has been a means to protest injustice, a record of people's hardship, and a vessel for aspirations and dreams.

Recent Nicaraguan history has been defined by the Sandinista revolution, which overthrew the Somoza dictatorship in 1979, before being embroiled in a bloody war with the American-backed contras that ran throughout the 1980s. The Sandinistas, defeated in 1990, returned to government in 2006, and have latterly faced large-scale protests from Nicaraguans who accuse them of displaying the same authoritarianism and corruption that they fought against during the revolution.

Poets have been at the heart of these political battles. One of the original Sandinista leaders, Sergio Ramírez Mercado, was a poet who claimed to be a reluctant political leader. "I'm a politician out of necessity," he told the *New York Times* in 1987, when he had become vice president. "I'd rather just be a writer." Mercado was not the only poet to rank high in the Sandinista hierarchy. Ernesto Cardenal, a Catholic priest who became famous for his writings against the Somoza dictatorship, served for years as the Sandinistas' minister of culture, though he later denounced the party for having betrayed the revolution. Other poets were martyrs of the revolution, including Leonel Rugama, killed at the age of twenty, and famous for his last retort to the National Guard soldiers who surrounded him and demanded his surrender: *Qué se rinda tu madre* (let your mother surrender).

Poets were fundamental to the Sandinista revolution, and as it faltered in the eyes of many, poets were among its most prominent critics. Another renowned poet, Pablo Antonio Cuadra, led protests that the Sandinistas were subverting Nicaragua's proud poetic and artistic culture for their own political ends, and undermining freedom of expression. He wrote in 1984 that the Sandinista policy toward the arts amounted to "Stalinization."

In a country that has rarely been far from a revolution for most of the last century, poets have been in the vanguard of Nicaraguan protest and popular dissent. Few dispute that this is in large part due to the influence of Rubén Darío, Nicaragua's preeminent writer and undisputed national hero. Darío is credited not just with molding his country's intellectual and literary culture, but transforming the Spanish language in the twentieth century. His name adorns roads, schools, squares, and museums throughout the country. In his native León, Nicaragua's second city, there are today over one hundred professional poets among a population of just 200,000.

Poetry has put Nicaragua on the map as well as helping the nation to navigate through repeated political and social turbulence. The national history is a testament to the power of the written word and the role it plays in all our lives. Poetry helps us to process what is going on around us and make sense of events we cannot always control. It is evocative, empowering, and above all galvanizing: giving people a voice, an outlet, and representation. Poets convey suffering, they capture experience, and they translate hope—everything, in other words, that makes us human.

Relaxation

No words required, Paraguay.

Every country you visit leaves its own mark on you. Spending time in a different culture can change the way you think—challenging your preconceptions, offering new experiences, and providing a new perspective. Paraguay's impact was to help me fully appreciate something that I had been told some years earlier, but never properly understood.

It was far from South America, in a room at London Business School, that a career advisor had once made a suggestion. "Do you know what you need to do? You need to sit and do nothing." At the time, I received the advice impatiently and it took years for its full significance to seep through. My visit to Paraguay, spiritual home of relaxation, was the catalyst.

Nestled between two giant neighbors, Brazil and Argentina, Paraguay has been described as an "island surrounded by land on all sides." It doesn't take long to see why. It is the opposite of the raucous, bustling way of life you find in the towns and cities of Mexico or Brazil. Paraguay's capital, Asunción, is renowned for its relaxed vibe. People don't treat the city like a racetrack, rushing as fast as they can from A to B, but will stop and smile and spend time talking to people—including those they have never met before. "It seems that the favorite local pastime may in fact simply be standing along the roadside waving to friends who appear to cruise the streets," one travel writer reflected.

It's the same in people's social lives. Forget dinners that are arranged weeks in advance only to be canceled the day before. In Paraguay, people take an altogether more relaxed approach. They will just call you up and invite you for a drink there-and-then and, rather than being indignant about being given no notice, you will just say yes. You'll then spend the afternoon doing nothing other than enjoying a *tereré* (cold maté tea), and sitting around. I have never visited a place where people are more comfortable with doing nothing: sitting and talking, watching the world go by, and simply enjoying the company of others. It takes relaxed to a whole new level—and it's wonderful. The ability to live in the moment is even reflected in the fact that there is no word in Guaraní, an indigenous language, for "tomorrow," only *koera* (literally: if dawn breaks). For Paraguayans, what matters is not what might happen in the future, but what is immediately in front of you.

This laid-back culture starts in school, where you will attend the same institution from when your education begins until the age of seventeen. There is no moving around, having to adjust to a new environment and leave behind all your friends. Instead you are given a stable foundation upon which to build long and lasting relationships, with the people you have grown up with from a young age, and whom you'll relate to most pleasurably for the rest of your life.

The same is true of family life, which revolves around a weekly get-together that happens on Sunday without fail. The whole family—sometimes over a hundred people, with siblings, cousins, aunts, uncles, and in-laws—will gather at the home of the elder member—generally a grandparent—and share the afternoon together over a barbecue. In some parts of the world, you would only get this many family members together in one place for a wedding, but in Paraguay it happens every week. It's not some stressful big occasion, but simply another part of a relaxed routine.

This easygoing attitude to life also extends to some operations of the state. Paraguay does not defend access to citizenship as some countries do, but is relaxed about who wants to become Paraguayan and where they come from. It is one of the easiest places in the world to become a citizen and obtain a second passport, which can be done in three years and without living exclusively or permanently in the country.

It is worth noting that Paraguay can experience this type of relaxation because—at least as a nation—it can afford to. Rich in natural resources, it has no pressure over water or energy supply, with its Itaipu Dam providing almost ten times the amount of renewable power the nation needs. Hydroelectric power accounts for 99 percent of the nation's electricity, of which Paraguay is the world's fourth largest exporter. That is not to say every Paraguayan has benefited from recent economic growth: almost 30 percent still live in poverty, especially prevalent among the large rural population. Relaxation, as a whole, is also at odds with much of its recent history, which has been anything but low-key. The Triple Alliance War, which pitted Paraguay against Brazil, Uruguay, and Argentina, was the deadliest in South American history. When it ended in 1870, 60 percent of the entire Paraguayan population was dead, including 90 percent of working-age men. The country also experienced widespread repression under the thirty-five-year military dictatorship of Alfredo Stroessner, during which an estimated four hundred people were murdered and over nineteen thousand tortured.

Although they live in one of just twenty-two countries where voting is mandatory, and despite a burgeoning protest culture against endemic political corruption, for many Paraguayans the political system is one they have little power to change. Stroessner's Colorado Party has provided all but one of the nation's presidents since his fall in 1989. Instead they focus on what is near to hand, most importantly the family and friends unit, which is the center of most people's lives.

Still, there is something remarkable about spending time in a place that puts no premium on it. One where there is no sense of people glancing at their watch and working out where they need to be next. With technology having made work a constant, the increasing struggle to switch off and relax has become a regular complaint. It makes countries like Paraguay, where relaxation is in the water, an essential counterbalance. Smartphones fill our heads with an endless, but often meaningless, torrent of information and communication. The ability to step back from that, and to meaningfully relax, allows us to appreciate the things—and above all the people—that nourish the soul. Relaxation might feel like "doing nothing" but, as my career advisor was trying to tell me, it is actually the foundation of what it means to be alive.

Irrepressibility

St. Mary's Basilica, Kraków, Poland.

Poland is the proud nation that, for 123 years of modern history, officially did not exist. From partition in 1795 to the end of the First World War in 1918, the name Poland was not to be found on any map of Europe, its land carved up and governed in three parts by the Prussian, Russian, and Austrian Empires.

Yet Polish identity, culture, and language (which was officially banned in most of the three regions) were kept alive, and since the fall of communism they have thrived afresh as an independent state. The irrepressible spirit that defines Poland is not just an intrinsic national characteristic, but also one that was fundamental to the preservation of the nation. And it's something that continues to live in the national culture. "I can't keep calm, I'm Polish" reads a poster I saw often in the country.

Poland's struggle for nationhood, and the spirit it has shown to maintain its culture and identity, are enshrined in the very first line of its national anthem: "Poland has not yet died, so long as we still live." The message could not be clearer. While we survive, wherever in the world, under whatever jurisdiction, so does Poland. That is the story of the nation in a stanza.

Defiance flourished during the Second World War. Poland's Armia Krajowa (Home Army) was the biggest resistance movement in Nazi-occupied Europe, one that saw both significant success in sabotage operations, and losses among its own fighters that ran into the tens of thousands. Poland's capital was the scene of some of the war's most compelling acts of defiance, from the last stand fought by the Jews of the Warsaw Ghetto in 1943 to the ultimately failed uprising the following summer led by the Armia Krajowa, the Polish resistance.

Later, Poland's irrepressible nature played a central role in the downfall of the Soviet Union. The founding of the Solidarity movement—the first independent trade union in a Soviet nation—is regarded as one of the key stepping-stones that led to the collapse of the Berlin Wall nine years later. The circumstances of its creation, in August 1980, were symbolic of Polish defiance. The movement's leader, Lech Walesa, evaded arrest by the secret police and scaled the wall of Gdansk's Lenin Shipyard to lead seventeen thousand workers on strike. Factories across the country would shortly join in a strike that after two months led to concessions including the granting of genuine trade union rights. Walesa's career after his initial rise to prominence became a symbol of the national spirit. He was arrested and imprisoned in 1982, won the Nobel Peace Prize the following year, and in 1990 was elected as the newly independent Poland's first president.

Walesa and the Solidarity movement were not the only Polish catalysts for the fall of communism. Another prominent player was Pope John Paul II, formerly the archbishop of Kraków. His 1979 visit to his homeland provided a rallying point for Polish opposition to Soviet rule, just as the Catholic Church had helped to keep alive the flame of national identity and culture during the years of partition.

Polish history shows us that keeping alive things that matter is not a passive act. Preservation will often mean resistance against those who want to destroy something or appropriate it for their own purposes. Polish irrepressibility is about never taking no for an answer, not letting failure be an option, and continuing to fight even when you fear the worst. Protecting the things you hold dear, maintaining tradition, and ensuring a legacy require irrepressible belief in the ideas you are fighting for.

Precision

**Such robots are said to be the future,
Davos, Switzerland.**

Switzerland is synonymous with high-quality timepieces, but you need to see how the Swiss actually use their watches to fully appreciate the importance of precision in the national culture. Standing on the platform at a railway station, if a train is even twenty or thirty seconds later than expected, you will see a forest of watches raised to eye level in frustration. Where in other countries eyes would roll, in Switzerland it is more likely that heads will, such is the importance of punctuality. This extends across everything: business meetings, social occasions, public events. A minute late is too late. Swiss culture demands that it happens on time, all the time.

Effective timekeeping is just one facet of the national obsession with precision in all things. If you own part of a community garden, it will be inspected on a regular basis to ensure that everything is being properly maintained, the hedges are at the right height, and so forth.

If your patch doesn't come up to scratch, then you will be issued with instructions by the "hedge police" about what to do differently.

The train companies, not satisfied with making service run in a punctual manner, also insist that conductors (incentivized by another Swiss staple—chocolate) ensure the train doors always stop in exactly the same place on a platform—so commuters know where they should be standing, to ease congestion. And the search for precision does not stop at their human employees. To keep the grass adjacent to train tracks from overgrowing, they have drafted in a particular breed of Swiss sheep to deal with the areas lawn mowers cannot easily reach. In the Swiss pursuit of precision, no embankment is seen as too inaccessible. Flying into Switzerland, it is impossible to miss the incredibly neatly ordered symmetry of fields all carefully curated and with clearly defined boundaries.

Precision has also been a defining feature of some of Switzerland's most successful sons and daughters. Consider Albert Einstein, and his ultimately unfulfilled desire to develop a unifying theory of everything that could explain the entire functioning of the natural world; or the tennis superstar Roger Federer, widely seen as the epitome of elegance and precision in sport. Federer came up against many opponents who could run faster and further, and hit the ball harder. But none had the Swiss player's uncanny ability to make the ball go exactly where he wanted it to. It was the relentless precision of Federer's game that made him stand out as probably the greatest male tennis player of all time.

Davos, something else for which Switzerland is world-famous, is another testament to the Swiss art of precision. Where else in the world could a sleepy skiing village be turned into a destination where the corporate and political elite can be meticulously hosted each year? The infrastructure and security required to pull this off in the snow is extraordinary, and only Swiss precision makes it possible year after year.

To some, precision might feel like an obsession with detail that can be taken too far. But Switzerland, which has generally been good at shielding itself from economic shocks as well as geopolitical ones, and enjoys a prosperous economy for a resource-poor nation, demonstrates what can be achieved by focusing on precision in all things. Getting the details right matters because it builds trust, fosters a culture in which people can take pride, and ultimately helps deliver results: a well-maintained country, a political and educational system that works, and a nation that has through its policy of neutrality exempted itself from the major conflicts involving its near neighbors, and the damage they have wrought.

Being precise about the small things better equips you to take on the more important ones. It's about creating good habits, and where these exist, success will generally follow.

Heritage

Experiences with the Memory Project, in Eastern Uganda.

"You should not go there alone, it will be too much for your heart."
For hours a tune had been playing, as we sat talking under the shade of two banyan trees. The women I had been interviewing, as part of the Memory Project to record the stories of Ugandan women with HIV-AIDS, agreed to take me to its source.

We walked together until we reached the gate of a house. A teenage boy sat on the porch with a *rabab* (lute)-style string instrument. He carried on playing while the women told me his story. An orphan, he had watched his whole family die around him. In fact, he had watched his father—loudly denying that his wife, and therefore he, could have contracted AIDS—cut his wrists and those of his family to share their blood and prove they were not infected. His mother had become ill and died, then so did his sister, two brothers, and father. Now he waited for his fate, playing this same tune at five funerals and continuing to play it until his own came.

The boy was one of two million orphans in Uganda, 43 percent of whom had seen their parents die as a result of the global pandemic, not only losing family and everything that they provided and represented, but also having to face down the stigma around AIDS and its causes. Children with little or no living memory of their parents were being denied this essential inheritance: a knowledge of where they had come from, the land, livestock, and artifacts they were entitled to, and the people they could turn to for help.

The loss of a parent at a young age is traumatic for so many reasons. But in Uganda, an additional layer is the loss of family history and heritage that is so fundamental to the national culture. Here they say that a child is known before they are born: defined by their place, their family, their language, and their tribe. Children with little or no living memory of their parents were being denied this essential inheritance.

The Memory Project was designed to address this problem, providing an accurate written account from one generation to the next, helping children to understand who their parents really were, and crucially to have a full appreciation of their culture and heritage. Working with both parents and children, the initiative created Memory Books that recorded the family tree, assets, and history, designed to answer the questions any child might ask of a parent at the point when they no longer could. It was about supporting families to prepare for the trauma of parental death and its aftermath. And it was about equipping children with the identity to succeed in a country where heritage is all-important.

A Ugandan will always want to know where you come from, what tribe you are a part of, and who your family is. From that, they can tell who you are. To lack this information in Uganda is like trying to travel abroad without a passport.

You have probably heard the phrase that it doesn't matter where you've come from, but where you are going. Ugandans passionately be-lieve in the opposite. Everything about you as a person, starting from your very name, says something about the place and people you have emerged from. In some western Ugandan tribes, you go not just by the name your parents give you, but also by your Empaako name: one of eleven or twelve "pet names" given to every member of the community, which becomes a lifelong signifier of your heritage and allegiance. As part of the naming ceremony, a tree is planted to symbolize the new life's connection with the land and tribe.

Uganda may be distinctive in its emphasis on heritage, but the importance of knowing who and where we come from is universal. We can't understand ourselves without knowing something about what our parents, grandparents, and ancestors did and how they were as people. For all of us, discovering the truth about ourselves is a lifelong process, and one that will always remain incomplete without a full appreciation of everything we have inherited. Aided by internet archives, the interest in family history has boomed in recent years. Genealogy is said to be the second most popular American hobby after gardening. We now have more tools than ever to discover our history and find clues about our ancestry. Heritage has never felt more important, nor more accessible. The closer we get to our roots, the taller we are able to stand.

Etiquette

Non bread being baked in Tashkent, Uzbekistan.

As one of the world's oldest civilizations with a history stretching back over 2,300 years, it should come as no surprise that Uzbekistan places a premium on etiquette. From everyday interactions to sharing hospitality and raising children, most aspects of Uzbek life follow a behavior that is carefully coordinated, long rehearsed, and deeply cherished.

One example is in the traditions surrounding *non*, Uzbekistan's national bread. A golden, tandoor-baked flatbread, it is only ever to be torn by hand and never cut with a knife. It is placed under the heads of newborn babies, and between the legs of toddlers learning to walk. An Uzbek child leaving home, whether to go abroad to study or for military service, will be asked by their parents to take a bite from a loaf of *non*. The remainder will be kept waiting for their safe return. My Uzbek friend's family practiced a similar ritual when her brother went off to the army:

half a loaf went with him, the other half stayed with his parents; a family separated, waiting to be joined back together.

Etiquette of this kind is not maintained simply for its own sake. It is also about being grateful for what you have and seeing beyond the obvious—not just a loaf of bread, but who has baked it (each producer has their own stamp), where it has come from, and what it represents. Etiquette is a way of honoring tradition, family, culture, and your elders. As an Ubzek proverb reads: "Respect for *non* is respect for country." And that means upholding all the etiquette that surrounds what might otherwise seem a humble flatbread.

This embrace of etiquette extends to how food is shared and hospitality offered. A meal is not something to be quickly or carelessly prepared and consumed. It is an event, one with defined stages, and which proceeds according to long-established convention.

It begins with tea, brewed with cardamom and cinnamon, served as soon as guests arrive. A tray is then brought down from the top shelf, with four compartments: nuts, raisins, dried apricots, and sweets. Warmed by the tea, your appetite is opened by these sweet bites. As more people arrive, the entire room stands to greet them.

With everyone present, and the appetizers having done their job, the meal proper is ready to begin. A *dastarkhan* (cloth) is carefully rolled out on the floor for everyone to sit upon. Great care is taken in the seating arrangement; no knees, let alone feet, are allowed to touch the cloth. Feet are tucked away and not to be facing anyone. The communal eating area is kept as pure and clean as possible. Instinctively, people are deeply considerate toward each other, the host, and the space.

Bread is served, broken by the host and offered to each guest in turn. And then each course is brought out individually, to be eaten piping hot. Dishes are passed around, people serving the person next to them first, before themselves. Food will be taken from the part of the plate closest to you, leaving others intact for the next person. Once everyone has been served, a short prayer is offered before the fast is broken.

As a guest, it struck me how carefully people were managing their behavior in this shared environment. The idea of bad table manners simply does not exist; from a young age, Uzbeks are trained to be polite and to observe etiquette, whether by observation or gentle reprimand.

And of course there is etiquette well beyond the dinner table, covering everything from greetings (which will differ depending on how well you know the person, whether they are a man or a woman, or an elder), to how hospitality is offered, and even the way in which two people ride a horse together (with the senior individual at the front). Here the rituals of etiquette say something important about the relationships at hand, and how respect is appropriately conveyed. They are a series of rituals that are actively embraced and enjoyed rather than considered obligations. Etiquette here is a defining feature, not an inherited layer on social and professional interaction.

Etiquette is something most of us think about at least some of the time—eager not to offend either people whose hospitality we are receiving, or business contacts in a culture different from our own. But beyond checking the boxes and seeking to avoid offense, do we actually stop to think about why we are doing those things, what these traditions represent, and how etiquette truly matters? It is worth doing so, because the more we scrutinize these apparently small things, the more we can appreciate their essential role in facilitating communication, conveying respect, and enabling integration. Good etiquette is about so much more than good manners. It is fundamentally about having strong relationships with people: understanding how they see the world and showing both empathy and respect for that. So next time you find yourself having to shake hands or eat dinner a certain way, don't just follow the instructions you are given—also stop to think about what they mean, and what they ultimately represent.

Resilience

A child at an orphanage on the outskirts of Ho Chi Minh City, Vietnam.

For the real story of Vietnam, don't visit the mountains, the caves, the paddy fields, the temples, or the war memorials. Instead, go to one of its numerous government and church-run orphanages. There you will see, as I did, that the legacies of a war that officially ended over four decades ago are still very much alive—and still being born. Children sit or lie in cots, many suffering from birth defects—missing limbs, swollen heads, or unformed spines—the course of their lives irrevocably set by an event that happened a lifetime before. There are almost as many of these orphanages as there are schools, hidden away by a government that would rather tourists looked elsewhere. Visit a place like this and you will understand that Vietnam, a country that saw one of the most brutal wars of the later twentieth century, and which some of the world's biggest economic and military powers have sought without success to bend to their will, is a nation that knows the true meaning of resilience.

It is hard to emphasize enough quite how bitter and far-reaching the legacy of "the war against the Americans to save the nation" was. Across North and South, there were estimated to be over three million Vietnamese deaths, civilian and military. (And bear in mind that before the Americans there were the French, and after the Vietnamese had defeated them both, they did the same to China.)

The suffering did not end with the war in 1975. Over the course of the conflict, the pesticide Agent Orange was sprayed over approximately 4.5 million acres of Vietnamese land. While the purpose was to defoliate the forests and to devastate the Vietcong's supplies, the impact has been devastating both in human and environmental terms. According to one estimate, over four million people are still living with the aftereffects, almost fifty years after the U.S. stopped using Agent Orange in 1971. Contamination of crops and the water supply has been linked with high incidences of some cancers, including childhood leukemia, and disabilities at birth which continue in second- and third-generation victims, many of whom live in orphanages. Land mines left over from the war have caused an estimated forty thousand deaths in the decades since. A country less resilient might have been broken by both the extraordinary loss of life and damage incurred during the war, and by the legacy that continues to affect people today.

Yet in many ways, Vietnam's recovery from the war has been extraordinary, and a testament to the resilience of both the nation and its people. In the immediate aftermath of the war, an estimated 70 percent of the population lived in poverty, a figure that has now dipped below 10 percent. While the market economy was long in coming (in the 1990s a family's ration of meat was just 200 grams for an entire month), in the last two decades Vietnam has become a full member of the World Trade Organization, liberalizing its economy and starting to see significant benefits. In 2017, Vietnam cemented its place as one of Asia's fastest-growing economies, with GDP growth of 6.7 percent, while foreign direct investment topped $17.5 billion. The consultancy

PricewaterhouseCoopers has estimated that by 2050 Vietnam will be one of the twenty largest economies in the world. And it's a progressive one: an estimated 25 percent of CEOs and board directors at Vietnamese companies are women, and Vietnam is ranked second across Asia for women in senior management positions. It also has a proud record on education, investing heavily and performing strongly on the global Pisa rankings. The resilience that carried the Vietnamese through a decade of punishing war—one that is literally imprinted into the country in the form of the hundreds of kilometers of underground tunnels that provided the infrastructure for guerrilla warfare—has passed down through the generations.

Vietnamese resilience has been evident not just within its borders, but also across a thriving diaspora. In the two decades after the Vietnam War, around 800,000 people fled the country to escape government repression and the economic depression. The boat people faced hazards from rickety vessels to perilous weather conditions and piracy. Estimates on how many died at sea range widely, but the United Nations has put the number at between 200,000 and 400,000. All of those who undertook the journey, and the many who have since left, helped create a thriving, four-million-strong diaspora that stretches from France to Australia, Japan, Canada, and Poland. Once they had settled overseas, they worked several jobs, in difficult conditions, keeping their heads down and doing what was necessary to survive and ultimately achieve the goal of returning home. As it is said, *"The best is to come back to your home village and to bathe in your own pond."*

That resilience remains much needed, especially in the face of the natural disasters that are a routine occurrence in Vietnam. The World Bank has called Vietnam "one of the most hazard-prone areas" in East Asia and the Pacific, estimating that 70 percent of the Vietnamese population is exposed to the risk of typhoons, flooding, drought, landslides, and earthquakes. Where most countries name their hurricanes or typhoons, Vietnam just numbers them: there are too many to record in any other way (although most of the earthquakes are relatively minor).

But the Vietnamese will not be beaten by their perilous climate any more than they have been by outsize military threats or the prospect of economic ruin. As my friend Thuy explained to me: "When times were tougher, my mother who was a professor would conduct extra classes, and raise chickens. The entire family would roast peanuts and grow vegetables to sell. My father learned Portuguese in order to go to Angola for a few years and earn extra money for the family."

Whatever the conditions, the Vietnamese usually find a way to pull through. More than that, they make the best of difficult circumstances. The harder the conditions get, the more intense their resilience and capacity to adapt becomes. And when you consider that most of us can easily turn a delayed train, a late delivery, or some other everyday inconvenience into an international incident, we could all do well to follow the Vietnamese example of how to respond when adversity strikes.

Part III: Connection Values

Connection is the most fundamental of human needs, something that we all long for throughout our lives. But in our attempts to connect we can often stumble: arguments and frustration are as much a part of relationships as love and support.

Fortunately, there are values from around the world that can give us a new perspective on our relationships and insight into how to build stronger ones. Some aspects of human connection may be universal, but there are many variations and differences that would never occur to you until you see them in action. The following are the countries that can teach you how to be a better friend, partner, colleague, and neighbor.

Honor

Near the River Drin, which runs across Albania.

I have to be honest, my entire life I have been confusing Europe's Roma for Albanians. It was not until I actually entered Albania that I learned who the Albanians were and what they stood for: honor in all things.

This European nation has a predominately Muslim population, a legacy of centuries of Ottoman rule, and due to its communist past it was isolated from the rest of the world until 1991, when the Soviet republic dissolved and the Republic of Albania was established. Scarfs meant many faces were concealed, and there was no language in common due to the division between standard Albanian and various dialects, so people's behavior told the story instead.

More than two thirds of Albania is mountainous, making it ideal to explore on foot. In northern Albania one discovers the fairy-tale landscapes of the Accursed Mountains. Southern Albanian walking routes run along the crystal waters of the Ionian Sea, up high ridges and panoramic peaks, through pine forests, olive and citrus groves.

However, if you prefer the past to the future, then strike further inland—here you enter a whole new world—a different world—from days long gone by, a world where ancient mountain codes of behavior still prevail. You'll feel as though you have entered a pre-mechanized time warp—where farmers work the land in much the same way as their ancestors did, the women continue to grow most of their food, and a donkey is still the favored mode of transport.

Driving into the most isolated parts of the country, it wasn't until my husband and I emerged from the safety of our vehicle that we experienced this nation. Suddenly people are taking you as their responsibility, you have an adopted family, coffee is being provided and cards produced for a game. You don't want to be a burden or take their time, but it is their honor to look after you. Because for Albanians, *Besa e shqptarit si purteka e arit, etj*: one's word—*besa*—is worth more than gold.

In a land where they have had many cultural influences, Greek, Roman, Byzantine, Venetian, and Norman, it is a real cultural melting pot, archaeological gold mine, and trekker's paradise. Yet the fiercely independent Albanian people are defined by their geography, with mountainous frontiers on all sides. What is there apart from your word? *Besa*, a word that first gained prominence in the Kanun of Lekë Dukagjini—an assembly of customary codes and traditions documented by the fifteenth century. And in the Kanun, the *besa* is described as the highest authority. "One's word, promise, honor and all the responsibilities it entails" lies so close to the heart of Albanians that is it often referred to as "Albanianism."

The "man of *besa*" connotes a man of honor, someone to whom you can trust your life and family. During one of the darkest chapters for the nation, when millions of Jews, gays, communists, and racial minorities were rounded up across Europe, many Albanians put up a fight to save complete strangers. While the Holocaust saw 90 percent of Poland's Jews killed, and 77 percent of those in Greece, it is estimated that Albania emerged from the Second World War with a population of Jews eleven times greater than at the beginning. According to Yad Vashem, the Israeli museum that holds the world's largest repository of documents and information related to the Holocaust, there is not a single known case of a Jew being turned over to Nazi authorities in Albania during its occupation. So Albania was recognized as "Righteous Among the Nations" at the United States Holocaust Memorial Museum in Washington, D.C., on February 2, 1995.

Honor may feel like a slightly archaic concept, but it is actually one of the most important things we have. If we don't honor our word, our responsibilities, our families, then we have lost something essential to our sense of self. Honor is not about some medieval notion of chivalry, so much as the fundamental principle that underpins trust and respect between people. It is about being true to our word, a principle that time and time again underpins trust and respect between people. Your *besa* says everything about you as a person. It is the last thing we should ever allow ourselves to give up.

Mateship

Mates on a ship, in the Whitsunday Islands, Queensland, Australia.

"G'day mate" is the universal Australianism. It's a phrase that is so much more than a greeting, one that you would be as likely to offer to an absolute stranger in a shop as your closest friend.

The word "mate," used so indiscriminately, is also one of the most significant in Australian culture. Anyone can be a mate, but only Aussies understand the true meaning and value of mateship, an idea and a cultural touchstone that is more meaningful to them than the universal concept of friendship.

Mateship symbolizes everything that it means to be Australian: open-minded and welcoming to strangers, fiercely loyal to your friends, generous to those in need, and committed to the collective. It is about pulling together, and pulling down those tall poppies that are growing too far away from the common good.

I experienced the power of mateship after one of the worst accidents I have suffered on all my travels. Studying for a semester at the

University of Melbourne, I joined a trip to Wilsons Prom, Australia's southernmost tip, and on our class trip there I made the fateful decision to venture out early and alone, eager to glimpse the sun rising over the beach. As I clambered onto some rocks to get the first peek, a wave suddenly crashed over the rocks, sending me flying and falling face-first. My nose and glasses were broken, I couldn't see, and I could taste blood in my mouth. My arm, which I'd thrown in front of me to cushion my fall, broke. I blacked out.

I still don't know who found me there or how long it was, but, someone did and I was soon reunited with my mates—Andy, Carolyn, Federico, Gael, Megan, Melicia, Nima, Tomer, and Pooja. The only problem was that we were hundreds of kilometers away from the nearest large town. Our trek had to continue, and so did I. It should have been a difficult, horrible experience, but my mates rallied around me in a way I have rarely seen: carrying my stuff and continually lifting my spirits. For the next three days of hiking, people never stopped checking on me and making me laugh (and laughing with me as I spent the next few weeks walking around, tape crisscrossed over my face, looking like an escaped Egyptian mummy). What could have been a disaster actually turned into a wonderful—if painful!—experience.

Mateship has, at different points in Australia's history, symbolized everything from solidarity among convicts transported from the U.K., to comradeship shown by Australian soldiers in war, in conflicts that have left a deep imprint on the national memory. Mateship is the core of the Anzac spirit that is central to Australian identity, immortalized by the famous photo of an Australian soldier carrying his injured mate across the beaches of Gallipoli in 1915.

Still, it has been a sometimes controversial issue. As with many fundamental national values, people often ask whether it still exists and has relevance in the modern world. For some it is too male a concept to be inclusive, while others have been put off by how politicians have sought to appropriate the idea. Liberal prime minister John Howard even sought to have it included in the Australian constitution in the 1990s.

But hijacked for commercial and political reasons as it may have often been, mateship still represents something fundamental in the Australian psyche. "For better or worse, mateship is part of our cultural DNA," the historian Nick Dyrenfurth wrote in a book on the subject. "In a nation supposedly hostile towards spiritual or ideological dogma, mateship has acted the part of a de facto religion." Mateship is about being more than a good friend. It's about the essential values that hold together an egalitarian society: trust, loyalty, commitment, and self-sacrifice. You'll always do what's needed to help out a mate, whether you've known them all your life or only just met. How much better would all our personal and professional relationships be if we took the same attitude?

Politeness

A voodoo ceremony in Ouidah, Benin.

In Benin, a quick question can lead to a long conversation. Ask someone on the street where you can find the post office, and you will get not just directions in return, but a full conversation: "How are you, what's going on, what are you doing today?" Total strangers will chat like long-lost friends.

Politeness in Benin does not begin and end with a perfunctory greeting. There is a warmth, an essential friendliness, and a desire to engage with people that becomes clear in almost every interaction. People quiz you about everything from your family and your job to your pets and hobbies, in search of common ground. In Benin people want to know, and they want to talk.

To the Western visitor, your first response may be that this all feels like a bit of a waste of time. Not to mention a culture shock. If a stranger stops you for a chat on the streets of London or New York, you're generally going to try and shut it down pretty quickly. You're in a rush, you don't really have the time. And anyway, why bother to get to know someone you will almost certainly never see again, and does it really have to be the case that we find something in common with everyone we encounter?

But the more time I spent in Benin, the more I realized that I was completely missing the point with this attitude. It costs you nothing to give people the time of day, to show some basic human empathy, and treat people with respect rather than as a means to an end. More than that, politeness spreads positivity and good feelings. It's about a society where people go out of their way to help you, and you would do the same for them.

Many of us use our busy lives, our lack of time, and our need to get from A to B as quickly as possible as an excuse to be impolite to the people around us. In Benin, people would tell me (politely, but with a playful smile) that though I might be the one wearing a wristwatch, they had the time. And they were right—they don't count every minute as it ticks by, they actually have all the time in the world. And what they might lose in efficiency, they gain from the kindness, openness, and serendipity of taking the time to be polite to people, even complete strangers.

I experienced this time and time again, where doors opened and opportunities emerged through chance interactions, simply because people give each other the time of day, stop to have a chat, and find out about each other. Asking for directions, I would often find myself directly escorted to the place I was headed to. And in the conversations that ensued, we would learn about each other, I would find out about new things to do and explore, and at the very least a friendship would be struck up that could simply not have occurred otherwise. The openness that is fundamental to Beninese culture feeds one of our most basic human needs, to relate to others and feel a connection. Everyone's day is brightened by these small acts of politeness and human warmth.

What's more, they can also lead you to all sorts of hidden gems that you would never otherwise discover. Just by being open and getting comfortable striking up conversations with strangers, I was taken everywhere from the voodoo temples of Ouidah (closed to the public) to a pioneering research center developing treatments for E. coli and diarrhea in the town of Grand Popo (excuse the pun). My experience of Benin was shaped and enriched by the people I met, the consistent politeness I encountered, and the knowledge and goodwill that emerged as a result.

It is too easy to live a life and pursue a career where you are closed off to new ideas, new ways of thinking, and new relationships. In the busy rush of everyday life, the importance of new interactions and inspirations can get lost. Benin teaches us how much we can benefit from simply stopping to speak to people, showing politeness and common courtesy. Through something as simple as the words you use and the way you interact with others, you open up a whole world of people, places, and potential that you might otherwise have never even noticed, let alone explored.

Love

Carnival, Rio de Janeiro, Brazil.

With its golden beaches, famously good-looking people, and expressive music and dance, Brazil is often seen as one of the world's romance capitals. In Brazilian Portuguese, there are twelve different ways to say "I love you." The phrase *Mais amor por favor*—More love, please—is printed on T-shirts, displayed on signs and posters, and painted on walls all over the country. But love in Brazil isn't just about romance (much as Brazilian men may be known as some of the world's most accomplished lotharios). It's also about how people show love to those around them, and how loved is shared on a communal as well as a personal basis.

If you want to know what Brazilian love looks and feels like, then there is only one place to go. Rio's Carnival, the world's biggest street festival, is an entire day of celebration with love at its core. For over fifteen hours nearly two million people eat, dance, and travel together;

a massive crowd comes together as one to celebrate, share love, and be in the moment. Attending with my sister Rajdeep, I noticed how people show love by looking after each other, making sure those around them have enough to drink, take shade from the sun, and have a break every now and then. Carnival-goers will even massage each other to help boost energy levels: it's about the experience of people around you, whether friends or total strangers, as much as your own. Brazilians show love instinctively and regardless of who the person is. The occasion reminds us to find joy in life—not for nothing, Brazilians are known as a nation of dancers and partygoers—but it is also about looking out for your friends and family during the tough times, of which Brazil has had its fair share.

My friend Adriana explained that, under the military dictatorship that ruled Brazil between 1964 and 1985, people would band together to help those targeted by the regime. When her friend's husband was incarcerated for seditious publication, she and a group of others got together to support his wife, provide child care, and bring food to him in prison. "We consider ourselves as very warm, open, loving people and we want to continue this way," she told me.

In Brazil, especially in the favelas I visited as a reporter, you feel powerfully the proximity between life and death. As part of my feature, I was invited to wring the neck of a chicken, something I could not bring myself to do. You can know full well where meat comes from, and about the realities of animal slaughter; but until you are actually asked to kill a living being yourself, you don't feel the compassion I felt for the chicken I found myself unable to kill.

Brazilians also see love as a way to overcome some of the political and economic challenges they face, having experienced the worst economic recession in its history between 2015 and 2017, and with a massive bribery and corruption scandal having seen one ex-president imprisoned and another arrested. Many worry about what the rising tide of social conservatism and evangelical Christianity, epitomized by the election of Jair Bolsonaro as president in 2018, will mean for equality. But they believe the Brazilian capacity for love can help overcome these threats. "We are all about love and empathy, particularly in the face of intolerance, whether that is toward homosexuals, women, religions, or any member of society," said my dear friend Flavia.

Love is such an important part of every life, from the love shown to us by our families to that we find for ourselves with the people we choose to spend our lives with. Love is perhaps the most powerful emotion we can feel—the bond that will never be broken, the thing that ultimately gives us meaning in life. Yet it can be hard to express the love we feel. Brazilians, for the most part, don't have this problem. Whether they are trying to seduce or support, love is freely shown and shared. They are comfortable with and love themselves, wearing what they want, dancing how they want, not feeling a shred of self-consciousness; and this allows them to love others more easily too. We would all be happier, freer, and more relaxed if we did more of the same. *Mais amor por favor!*

Informality

Fally Ipupa (Congolese music artist) and Samuel Eto'o (Camer-oonian footballer) come to relax in Assinie, Côte d'Ivoire.

Eating out in Côte d'Ivoire, you will likely dine not in a formal restaurant but a *maquis*, one of the roadside kiosks found every-where in Ivorian cities, also known as *cul par terre* (bum on the ground). You'll sit on the floor or near it, only eating with cutlery if you insist. All walks of life mix easily together in the ultimate informal setting, which might be little more than an awning and an open grill. It is, quite literally, a down-to-earth experience.

This typifies the informal ethos of Côte d'Ivoire, where life is easy-going, relationships are quickly formed, and pretensions are few and far between. As you sit and eat your *poulet* and peanut soup (skipping over *agouti*—rat), you will experience another aspect of Ivorian informality: people's willingness to approach you and strike up a conversation.

"*Tu as empoché?*"—Is there something in your pocket? This could be a request to share some food, to bum a cigarette, or even for a little money. It's not about the person asking being a freeloader, but an invitation to show generosity, and to establish friendship.

It's symptomatic of how relationships are conjured almost from thin air, without preamble or prevarication. Someone you may have met twice, and been friendly with, can become your brother. You are now within your rights to ask to share what's his, and vice versa. It's not seen as manipulative or cheeky inviting yourself to someone else's party, but as an extension of a fundamental sense of brotherhood. This is relationship building the Ivorian way: immediate, instinctive, and informal.

This informality extends from how people behave together to the way they speak. The official language of Côte d'Ivoire may be French, but many Ivorians rely on their own dialect, a rapid-fire, constantly changing version that draws inspiration from an eclectic mix of other languages: Spanish, Dioula, and English among them. Nouchi (literally: nose hair), a street language that emerged in the 1970s, has become increasingly prevalent in pop culture over the last decade. Some research suggests it may even now be the first language of Ivorians between the ages of ten and thirty. Nouchi is wholeheartedly Ivorian: fluid, creative, eclectic, and never standing still. New words are added all the time: it is an informal, grassroots product, not something governed by any central authority. Nouchi is language not as a fixed construct to be learned, but something to be played with: you can invent new words, join them together, bending and breaking the rules as you please. It reflects the Ivorian urge for informality, as well as the mix of French influence (from its near seven decades as a colony until 1960) and Ivorian tradition that is prevalent across popular culture.

The informality of language and relationships extends to how some famous figures conduct themselves in Côte d'Ivoire. On New Year's Eve, at a beach party in Assinie, I saw the president, Alassane Ouattara, dancing along with everyone else; and Samuel Eto'o, the famous Cameroonian footballer, enjoying a game of beach football with his son, the famous Ivorian rapper Fally Ipupa, and others he had probably just met. No velvet ropes here. The president, Alassane Ouattara, is accessible in more ways than one. When, in 2014, he returned from medical treatment in France carrying a walking stick, it spawned a whole craze. Comedy sketches abounded and young people started walking around with sticks, "doing an Ado" (ADO being his initials). The meme spread so widely that even the president could not help but laugh at himself.

Côte d'Ivoire's informality, however, has not held it back from becoming one of Africa's economic powerhouses. The world's largest cocoa exporter, it has been investing heavily in infrastructure in recent years and sought to diversify an economy that had boomed in the decades following independence but stalled amid political turmoil and civil war in the early 2000s. Those efforts have been rewarded with its status as one of the continent's fastest growing economies.

Especially in our professional lives, it is easy to get sucked into the idea that process and formality are prerequisites to making progress—when you have come from a more serious, straitlaced culture, there is something wonderfully liberating about spending time in Côte d'Ivoire. The Ivorian approach to life can be hugely powerful in putting things into perspective, fostering friendship and brotherhood, and—most importantly of all—letting you have a great time. There is a deep creativity and camaraderie that arises from the informality. With less inclination to follow the rules, there is more scope to innovate and do things differently, and a different mind-set emerges: one where breaking down the barriers of language, relationships, and culture can unlock both goodwill and success. Sometimes we need to throw the rules of engagement out the window, and invent our own.

Friendship

In Croatia, a friend in need will always find help.

Most people react anything but calmly when they are woken by a phone call at 4 a.m., let alone when it's about someone they hardly know. But when my Croatian friend Ivan was called by one of his friends about her sister, who was stranded and in urgent need of a lift home, he just got on with it. He got out of bed, into his car, and drove to help without question. In Croatia, that is what you do for your friends. Even if they're not actually your friend.

Whether you're financially in need or have just suffered a blow, Croats guarantee that your friends will be there for you with whatever monetary or moral support you need. In most countries, you might write a letter, make a phone call, or pay a short visit to someone who has recently suffered a loss in the family. Croats go and stay for a couple of days or weeks and do everything for the bereaved, giving them what they need to get back on their feet.

This is partly the product of a turbulent recent history. From the fascist dictatorship of Ante Pavelić, to the years of communist rule, the decades of Tito's dictatorship, and the Balkan wars that followed independence, Croats have learned to stick together and look after each other, through the bad times and the good, because the state will not.

Your friends are a network who support you through all stages of your life. Where most people have the godparents that are chosen for them at birth, Croats keep on acquiring them: at confirmation, and then those you choose for yourself when you get married, and those you select for your own children. Of course family matters, but you also create your own tribe, starting with the friends you make at school who stick with you through thick and thin. These are the people you can talk to about anything, and for whom you will drop everything to help in a time of need.

Friendship also dictates the creation of common bonds such as religious affiliation. Even though the state is secular, Croatia is one of the most Catholic countries in the world, with over 86 percent of the population members of the Church. In a Pew survey, a majority of Croatians (58 percent) said that being Catholic was an important part of national identity. Where you call home plays a role as well; there is much playful stereotyping of Croatia's different regions, from the temperamental, very Italianate Dalmatians, to the urbanite Zagrebians, the reserved Istrians, and the garrulous, gourmand Slavonians. All serve to reinforce local identity and relationships.

In parallel, friendship exists on an international level. As a socialist country Croatia has actively pursued an inclusive path, and worked hard to establish friendly ties with countries including India, with programs such as student exchanges. But the Croat culture of friendship can extend in unhelpful ways. Corruption and nepotism are widespread within the workplace, with people doling out jobs and benefits to their network. A specific term, *uhljeb*, has even been coined to describe the incompetent workers who are the product of this system, and who hold their jobs through personal or political patronage.

While some Croats might be doing their friends too many favors, the Croatian culture of friendship is on the whole a power for good. Think how often you actually see your friends, carve out time to spend with them, or simply just drop them a message to say that you are thinking of them. In Croatia it would be unthinkable to let friendships fall by the wayside as they can elsewhere through inertia. Friendship is prized as the hugely valuable thing that it is: a lasting bond that allows us to celebrate the best things in our lives, and to survive the worst. Our friends matter more than we often realize or recognize through how we spend our time. The Croatian example points to the need for a welcome rethink.

Appreciation

Looking out onto the Mediterranean Sea, near Paphos, Cyprus.

How many times a day do you stop to show appreciation for someone, at work or at home? Small gestures of thanks can brighten people's day and lift their mood, but too often such sentiments fall by the wayside because we feel too busy to stop and say thank you.

This would never happen in Cyprus, where showing appreciation is a deeply ingrained habit. I first noticed this when taking my car to the gas station. A queue of vehicles was being filled up by the *pappou* (patriarch). The convoy was proceeding quite slowly because, rather than offering a monetary tip to the *pappou*, people had stepped out of their car to share a laugh or a chat with him. This was their way of showing appreciation: stopping and taking the time to have a proper conversation. Not just sharing money, but sharing their heart.

It's the same in Cypriot restaurants, where service isn't just a matter of bringing food to the table, but proprietors showing appreciation for their customers in a more meaningful way. That's why, while the younger generation does the heavy lifting, the elders are at the front of the house, touring the tables and having friendly conversations with customers both old and new. Again, appreciation is shown in a very human, personal way: shared rather than transacted. You see the same in how people communicate. When you pick up the phone, rather than saying your own name, you might say "Vincent's dad speaking" or "Maria's partner here": another small way of conveying appreciation for loved ones.

Older people are the cornerstone of Cyprus's culture of appreciation. Grandparents hold a special place in society, revered for their experience and knowledge. There is no generational divide where older members of the family are distant from the youngest, who are just desperate to go out and do their own thing. There wasn't one meal with a Cypriot family I attended where grandparents weren't both present and the center of attention. The older generation are looked after and appreciated for their wisdom. And when you are all out for a meal and it's 11 p.m. and time to go dancing, then you take them home and make sure they are comfortable before you set off yourself.

The appreciation shown by Cypriots is about not just individuals, but also heritage and identity in a broader sense. When people introduce themselves, they will often tell you more than their name, also mentioning the place they come from and where they live now. There is an appreciation for the importance of roots and identity, and how the places where we grew up and live now shape us as people. The same is reflected in Cypriots' approach toward national memorials and sites of historical importance. You won't pass a ruin that isn't being studied and looked after in some way. The nation's heritage is maintained and nurtured in a way that shows appreciation for its meaning and significance.

Appreciation is so important because it promotes greater understanding for the needs of other people. I encountered this very vividly, touring around with my newborn, Saiyan. I wandered into the courtyard of what looked like a café and sat down, and when a woman approached me I asked if we could have some milk, ordering as if I had sat down in a restaurant. But even though it looked like one, it wasn't a café at all, just the garden of this woman's home. At that point she could have kicked us out, but in fact we were welcomed and looked after. Milk was fetched, and we ended up being given a tour of the garden to collect herbs to use in our evening meal. Only in a society where appreciation for those around you is so entrenched could something like this have occurred.

Cypriots understand that there are many different ways of showing appreciation, and that the greatest failing is not taking the time to do so. Technology can often make life feel rushed and impersonal, and in that context the value of appreciation is becoming ever more important. Time is the most valuable commodity we all have, and also the great equalizer: all the power and riches in the world cannot give you more than twenty-four hours in a day. That means the way we can most appreciate people is to share or give of our precious time. By showing appreciation you make yourself, and the person you are thanking, feel uplifted. It's a simple social courtesy that is also fundamental to our well-being, and that of society as a whole. Appreciation oils the wheels, it lifts the mood, and it conveys our gratitude to those around us. Showing it is one of the most authentic, and important, things we can ever do.

Helpfulness

In the Wadi Rum desert of Jordan.

I n Jordan, if someone asks you for help, you don't pause to ask why, who, or when. There is no weighing up of who this person is or what their ulterior motive might be. Helpfulness is instinctive, immediate, and unquestioning. As my friend Hiba puts it, "When someone is in need of help, they don't need to be further traumatized with questions and interrogation, they just need help."

I remember her sharing the example of her grandmother, who lived in a rural village. One evening, there was a knock at the door, which she opened to find three men in uniform. Could she lend three mattresses? Without asking why she did so, and a few days later they were duly returned. When she asked if the men had slept well, they said they had, and were grateful, as was the king of Jordan, who had been visiting a neighboring home and whose bodyguards they were. Her unquestioning offer of help was based on a fundamental Islamic teaching that, if a stranger comes to your house, you give them what they need and don't even ask their name for the first three days, out of respect for what they may have been through.

This kind of instinctive helpfulness does not just happen person to person. It is also seen in how communities come together to help those in need. I witnessed this transpire for a colleague who needed her house to be painted. She asked her grandchildren if they could help. Their response was not just to turn up with buckets of paint and paintbrushes, but also to ask their friends. A small army of helpers turned a chore into a day of music, food, and communal enjoyment. The house looked brand-new, and friendships were deepened. You never sleep while your neighbor goes hungry, only ever give a plate that is full, and never return one that is empty. People readily give up what is theirs so that they can help others.

Helpfulness is a universal value in Jordan, encountered everywhere and regardless of wealth or social standing. In the car with my friend and her father, journeys would take unexpected turns when a stranger asked for directions, and would be personally escorted to their destination. The same generosity of spirit can mean competitive bargaining over the check in restaurants, where other people's offers to pay will be vigorously protested.

That does not mean sweetness and light surround you everywhere you turn in Jordan. In fact, Jordanians are well known for being taciturn and their unwillingness to smile. Much has been written about the "Jordanian frown" as the default expression and state of mind. But if you can get past that exterior, you will find Jordanians among the world's most forthcoming and helpful people. As so often, first impressions can be misleading.

Jordanian helpfulness and generosity have been demonstrated in recent years as Jordan has opened its doors to hundreds of thousands of refugees from the civil war in Syria. Over 650,000 Syrian refugees are estimated to have resettled in Jordan, the vast majority in communities rather than refugee camps. The Jordanian government has put the figure at 1.3 million, including those not formally registered as refugees. This is in keeping with Jordan's record of hosting refugees from across the Middle East stretching back decades, and Amman's status as a hub for humanitarian agencies and support.

While this has put a significant strain on Jordan's already struggling economy, and infrastructure from the school system to social security, and though Jordan has been criticized for deporting some refugees, I believe it still speaks to something fundamental in Jordanian culture: you do not avert your gaze when you see someone in need, but actively reach out to help them.

In Jordan you learn to look past what you initially see; people may not be readily smiling and laughing, but there is a warmth and generosity that quickly comes to the surface when you ask for help. And you learn too that there is a cost to not asking to help and to weighing every interaction as a transaction, where you carefully judge the help you want to offer depending on who the person is and what they need. Jordanians don't go in for that, they just do what they can to help. If we could all be so instinctively, unquestioningly helpful, our society would heal faster and we would feel better—nourished by the culture of unwavering support that many small acts of helpfulness create.

Harmony

Hindu Sri Subramaniam Temple nestled in the limestone
hills of the Batu Caves, Selangor, Malaysia.

Growing up as a British Indian in Gloucestershire, in England's south-
west, I was used to a world in which almost every face was white.
At my school, one of the only exceptions was Louise, a half-Malaysian,
half-British girl who became and remains one of my closest friends.

Visiting her family in Malaysia opened my eyes to what a soci-
ety looks like when races readily mix. I remember arriving in Kuala
Lumpur and being taken the same day by Louise's family to their ex-
British country club, and watching in amazement at how the Malays,
Indians, and Chinese interacted with each other. It was a new world,
one confirmed when I visited some family of my own at a wedding

in Penang; the bride was surrounded by friends who represented a complete fusion of Malaysia's three main ethnic groups. The Malay and Chinese understood how to join in with the customs of an Indian wedding, as if they were their own. The different cultures felt in balance, comfortable with one another, none dominating.

Such harmony is the cornerstone of culture in Malaysia, where co-existence between the Malay population, and the large Chinese and Indian communities—introduced by British colonial rulers—has long been a political and social priority. This has been the case since the race riots of 1969 between the Malay and Chinese, which remain in the forefront of the national memory, having occurred little more than a decade after Malaysia became independent.

It is important to understand the nature of Malaysian harmony between races, which is distinctive and not focused on the wholesale integration of the races that is often prioritized in the West. There is positive discrimination in favor of Malays, affording them protected access to everything from affordable housing to government jobs, share ownership, and university scholarships. This has succeeded to some extent in narrowing the stark economic gap that existed between Malays and the minority Chinese community in particular (though there has also been criticism for its role in concentrating wealth in relatively few hands).

Education too runs on ethnic grounds, with separate systems for the Malay, Chinese, and Indian populations. The Malaysian constitution also protects the right to religious freedom, though all ethnic Malays must be Muslim. In politics, until the landmark election of 2018, government had been dominated for decades by the United Malays National Organisation, a party that frequently made political capital out of protecting the needs and interest of Malays, and scaremongering over the threat posed by the prosperous Chinese population.

On the surface, this combination of policy and politics might appear to be a recipe for entrenching divisions: prioritizing the native population and declining to integrate different groups from a young age in a way that can forge collective identity. But in Malaysia, it is the very preservation of unique identity that provides the basis for harmonious relations between the different ethnic groups. Malaysia allows its predominant groups to retain their language, customs, and religious freedoms. It understands that you can best help people to come together by enabling them to—in some ways—remain different and keep hold of the traditions that are their own. There is not equality between the different populations, but there is a tacit understanding that each group has its own place of advantage: the Chinese are the most entrepreneurial and prosperous; Indians dominate in the professions; while Malays often hold government jobs.

Politics in Malaysia remains racially charged, but people are focused on their everyday lives and being friendly with those around them. The principle of *muhibbah*, living in harmony, is fundamental in interpersonal and community relations. According to the University of Malaysia's Dr. Kamar Oniah Kamarul Zaman, this "is a spirit of togetherness, a culture of sincere and appreciative coexistence with sensitivity toward fellow citizens and fellow beings." The bonds of *muhibbah* are reinforced by long hours spent together in "Mama's place" eateries: twenty-four-hour restaurants that span the three cultures. In food, music, culture, and friendship, Malaysians of all ethnicities enjoy harmonious relationships and shared experiences. In a poll conducted as part of the government's 2050 transformation plan, almost three quarters of Malaysians opposed the suggestion that "your neighbors should be the same race as you."

Division is everywhere in our societies—whether ethnic, religious, political, or otherwise—which means the search for harmony has become one of the defining needs of our age. Malaysia offers a model that is not perfect, but that shows the importance of what happens on the ground between people, and underlines the necessity of understanding and celebrating differences if harmonious relations are to be achieved.

Directness

The lowlands of Ransdorp, Netherlands.

"If you want a better planet, conduct your meetings in a naked Dutch spa." This was the unlikely advice offered to me when I interned at the European Commission in my early twenties. When I later got the chance to visit one in Amsterdam, I understood what it meant. At first it's a disconcerting experience to be in a room full of other naked people. But once you get over yourself and literally start to immerse yourself—from the piping hot water of the steam room to the freezing bath of the plunge pool—it becomes empowering. With your clothes off there is nothing to hide or hold back. It is the perfect environment for deal making.

The Dutch love for the nude spa tells you something about their culture, which is as free from doublespeak and circumlocution as the plunge pools are from bathing suits. Sorry, let me be a bit more Dutch about it. They're incredibly direct. In every way, all of the time. They believe in *bespreekbaarheid* (literally, speakability): the idea that no topic or idea is out-of-bounds.

To explain the source of Dutch directness, we need to look both to Dutch geography and history. The culture partly reflects the land: the flat topography, with almost a quarter of the country at or below sea level, means you can see for miles around; making the land as transparent and unguarded as its people. It matters too that the modern Netherlands emerged not from aristocracy rule, but the mercantile power and trading prowess that defined its sixteenth-century Golden Age. The Netherlands retains its monarchy, but Dutch directness means they are in no way insulated from criticism. Willem-Alexander, now king and then prince of Orange, had to abandon plans to build a luxury villa in Mozambique in 2009 after a sustained public and political outcry.

The Dutch will never hold back on what they think out of concern about how others might react. They don't dance around people's feelings and war-game their likely reactions. They just dive straight in, make the point, and move on. They will have no qualms about saying their girlfriend just left them, they got fired, or that someone's idea in a work meeting was a stupid one. You always know exactly what people think, and that means you are never second-guessing or watching your back. To the Dutch this isn't brusque or rude. It's just a sensible way of communicating, without ambiguity or double meaning. If someone says you're doing a good job, you know they actually mean it. Dutch directness has no fear of hierarchy either. An intern will be asked for their opinion, and a subordinate can criticize their boss if they disagree with them, without fear of reprisal. That is unique and valuable.

For the same reason, a meeting in a Dutch company won't go through endless circles of small talk. It gets straight to the point. Everything else is seen as a waste of time. It's a more efficient, and curiously more relaxed, way of doing business.

Dutch directness is also an essential part of how the government shapes policy and tackles problems. Drug policy is one obvious example. While the Netherlands, and Amsterdam in particular, is famous for its pot-smoking coffeehouses, the country actually has one of the lowest drug abuse rates in Europe. That is often credited to Dutch policies that have been considered excessively permissive elsewhere, but which have directly attacked various root causes of what had been a major problem in the 1970s: the separation of legalized cannabis from prohibited harder drugs, minimizing the gateway effect prevalent elsewhere; the widespread provision of treatment services and needle exchanges; and a tolerant approach toward offenders.

As a result, the Netherlands sees far fewer people who use cannabis progressing to drugs such as heroin, and experiences negligible instances of HIV transmission through needles. A drug policy that was focused on preventing harm rather than criminalizing behavior has been decades ahead of the rest of the world: a testament to the power of Dutch directness in identifying problems as they really are, not as society might think them to be.

When you experience it for the first time, Dutch directness can be bracing, and even a little uncomfortable. If you are not used to people speaking their mind without much of a filter, it can catch you off guard. But once you have gathered your senses, you realize it is also a very refreshing approach—whether at work or simply among family and friends. Directness means less ambiguity, fewer frustrations at not being able to put forward your view, and ultimately more genuine dialogue.

We might not want to conduct all our meetings without clothes, but we could certainly benefit from casting off some of the restrictions that hold us back from speaking our minds. The Dutch example shows that directness does not have to mean rudeness: often, instead, it is simply the language of getting things done.

Loyalty

Kumsusan Palace of the Sun (Kim Il-sung Mausoleum), Pyongyang, North Korea.

"Don't you dare look back." At Pyongyang airport a cluster of soldiers surrounded us and a gun was pointed at me. I was seven months pregnant and terrified, not for myself and my unborn child nor for my younger brother, Manreshpal, who was with me, but for our guide, Yo-han, who had just been violently arrested by the army.

I had bought a propaganda poster, in one of the few (state-owned) shops we had been taken to, but I hadn't kept the receipt. Yo-han had forgotten to tell me I should, and so—without my having said a word—my crime was instantaneously transferred to him. This breach of regulations, discovered as we were going through airport security, meant he was dragged away to a fate I would never discover and often think about, and Manreshpal and I were escorted onto our plane at gunpoint.

It was the starkest possible reminder that North Korea is a country where loyalty is a life-or-death issue. Those who commit the slightest infraction of the loyalty expected to the Kim regime can pay with their lives. In a country where everything you say and do can be subject to surveillance, loyalty between people is essential for survival: knowing who is really loyal to you, and who will give you up out of loyalty to the state.

When you spend time in North Korea, the extent to which fealty to the regime is demanded quickly becomes clear. Everyone you meet will be wearing a badge with a picture of the "Great Leader," Kim Il-sung, grandfather of the current ruler. Switch on a TV or radio and you will hear nationalist and martial songs blaring out. Workers, at the end of a long day of mandatory labor, might be treated to a school band singing in allegiance to the Kim family, or visitors might be required to pay homage to the embalmed body of Kim Il-sung, frighteningly lifelike in its glass-fronted sarcophagus.

Loyalty to the regime is, of course, not earned but enforced by a brutally oppressive government machine. According to a U.N. report, between 80,000 and 120,000 political prisoners are held in huge prison camps across the country, where according to witness testimonies murder, severe beatings, and rape are commonplace. One estimate suggests that over 10,000 North Koreans die in these camps every year.

Those the regime are not actively punishing are being watched. I was told that the state profiles every family according to its loyalty to the Kim family. All are classed as either "loyal," "wavering," or "hostile." Those who are perceived to be loyal are given preferential access to food, housing, and jobs; while those deemed hostile are exiled to the poorest parts of the country, and consigned to hard labor in the fields or mines.

This is one level on which loyalty exists in North Korean society, as a necessity for survival in a violent and repressive environment. Another is the loyalty that exists between person to person, comrade to comrade, family member to family member.

When you are living in an environment of state surveillance and violence, your every move scrutinized for any evidence of loyalty or disloyalty, the bonds between people have to be stronger than in a free society. There are many people you cannot trust, to whom a stray admission or attempt at a joke could easily see you reported and disappeared. Conversely, with those closest to you, your sense of loyalty is absolute. You know that any misstep on your part could see friends and family punished. So you go further to protect them. A parent, for instance, might shield certain information from their children because it would put them in danger to even know about it. They might be listening to a prohibited foreign news service, but will tell their kids they're just learning English: a lie motivated by loyalty to their best interests.

In North Korea, you are responsible not only for your own actions and safety, but also for those of the people around you. Because it is not just by demonstrating loyalty to the state that you stay alive amid a lottery of risks; it is by showing loyalty to others, and relying on receiving the same in return. Loyalty is something that is important in all of our lives: the cornerstone of trust and as such the foundation of both personal and professional relationships. Our loyalties—to family, friends, employers, teams—define us as people. So, if you are someone to whom loyalty is important, reflect on North Korea: a place where it is not just an admirable quality that underpins personal relationships, but truly something that can make the difference between life and death.

Connectivity

Cargo ship in Miraflores Locks, Panama Canal, Panama.

Over two decades ago, before I had been to most of the places I have written about in this book, Panama was the first Central American country I visited. Then an inexperienced traveler, wandering around Panama City, I felt out of my depth, even a little lost. These were the thoughts going through my head as I found myself in a supermarket, getting out my purse to pay for shopping. Wearing my *kara* (an iron bracelet worn by Sikhs), I suddenly noticed the person ahead of me in the queue also had one around his wrist. A few years later, I would meet my Sikh spiritual advisor, Bhai Sahib Mohinder Singh, in the same way, but that was at the United Nations in New York and this was Panama, the most unlikely of places to meet a fellow Sikh. That one small thing helped jolt me out of my loneliness. Here was a familiar thing, a shared culture and symbol in an unfamiliar place. A chink of light. A connection out of nowhere. It was later that I realized this small episode was symbolic of Panama as a country that is defined by the connections it makes: between people, between countries, and as an entrepôt for global flows of trade.

By its geography alone Panama represents connectivity: a strip of land, just sixty kilometers wide in places, that links Costa Rica and Colombia, tying together Central and South America. One of the smallest countries in the region is also the most strategically important, a trade route that unlocks the economic potential of continents. Panama's connectivity explains why mighty China has courted this tiny isthmus as part of its plans to scale up trading links with Latin America.

Of course the defining fact and symbol of Panama's connectivity is the Canal. As a nexus that, following its recent expansion, connects over 140 trade routes to 80 countries and approximately 1,700 ports, the Panama Canal is one of the great forces for global connection and trade. But the Canal has done more than help create a global infrastructure for trade. It has also been a substantial force for connecting people, from those who came to build it in the first place to the many who continue to earn a living through it today.

While the U.S. has been most associated with construction of the canal, the 75,000-strong workforce that built it over a ten-year period came from across the world: from the Caribbean, China, India, France, Spain, Italy, Greece, and Costa Rica. Today Panama remains a place where the world comes together, especially in the capital, where over half the population lives. Panama City has been described as the most cosmopolitan metropolis in Central America, home to workers and visitors from around the world. Immigration has underpinned an economy that grew at twice the speed of the regional average between 2001 and 2013, and which is ranked the second most competitive in Latin America and the Caribbean.

The Panamanian government has recognized the importance of this global connectivity to the country's success, with a *crisol de razas* (melting pot) program that has provided legal status to tens of thousands of foreign workers through large-scale amnesties. These have continued despite some opposition, because of the significant economic benefit that immigrant labor provides.

Connectivity matters for nations and economies, and the same is true for people. We all have a choice about whether to be more or less connected: to meet new people in our personal or professional worlds, to improve our understanding and empathy, and to bring together individuals and organizations who might have something in common. People and companies thrive on connectivity: the intangible power of a network of people, ideas, and experiences. And we become better people by being more connected: more knowledgeable, more informed, and above all more compassionate to the people and world around us. It is hard to succeed in life as an island; only by creating connections, for ourselves and between other people, can we truly thrive.

Qatar

Trust

A familiar laugh between friends, Souq Waqif, Doha, Qatar.

magine there are two of you in the car. One of you is pregnant, the other has a three-month-old child. At a busy roundabout, the engine suddenly gives out and the car is immobilized. What happens next? You expect a hail of horns, frustrated shouting, people rushing to the window to remonstrate with you about delaying their journey and ruining their day.

However, in Qatar, where this happened to me while I was traveling with my son Naryan and friend Sherine, the response was quite different. A man approached us, not angrily but supportively. "I can see you're in difficulty," he said. "You take my car, and I will take yours to be fixed. Just give me your number and address, and I'll make sure it's delivered back to you."

And that is exactly how it turned out. A complete stranger rescued us, he trusted us—two people he knew nothing about—with his car, and we trusted that he would do as he said. Everything happened exactly as had been promised.

Imagine if someone approached you in this way on the streets of Los Angeles, Lagos, or London. For one, it would just never happen. And if it by some chance did, you would be very unlikely to trust your car or safety to a complete stranger. Our first instinct is to assume a malign motive or hidden agenda. Trust does not come easily among strangers.

But in Qatar I found the opposite to be true, because this is a place where trust is offered and received unconditionally. You don't lock your door at night. You can leave your keys in the ignition when you park your car. You do business—at least between Qataris—based on a handshake and a verbal agreement.

Before I arrived, a Qatari friend Khalid had given me a package to be delivered to a family member. Rather than committing it to air mail, he simply told me to hand it to anyone—*anyone*—at the airport who was a Qatari and ask if they would deliver it for him. In their hands, he said, the package was sure to be safe. It duly arrived.

This culture of trust is rooted in the small, tightly knit population of ethnic Qataris, who today comprise only 12 percent of the national population. As Qatar developed into what would eventually become a prosperous, independent nation, it faced periods of severe economic hardship, especially in the 1930s when it suffered from the decline of the pearl trade and the effects of the Great Depression. Trust has arisen from a national culture in which resources were historically scarce, and the bonds among this small group of people became all-important. "We are from one cloth," Khalid said to me.

The tightly knit ethos remains today. Qatari citizenship is closely guarded: to be eligible you must have lived in Qatar for twenty-five years, or fifteen if you are the citizen of another Arab country. There is no recognized dual citizenship, and acquiring another will generally lead to Qatari citizenship being lost. Moreover, as the Arab world puts Qatar under diplomatic and economic sanctions, and a siege mentality sets in, the internal bonds of trust become ever more important. Surrounded by countries that don't trust them, Qataris have no recourse but to tap into the deep well of trust that exists among them as a people.

Because trust is so widely relied upon, the cost of breaching it is significant. Breaking an agreement damages not just an individual's reputation, but also undermines the trust that has been built up over time between different families, tribes, communities, and places. It is something that most Qataris will do anything in their power to avoid, because generally there are no second chances. Break trust once and you will be ostracized, probably for good.

Qatar is one of the most trust-based places in the world, and there are few values more fundamental to how we live and interact together as people. Without it, no business can be done, no friendships formed, and no disputes ever resolved. As the Sheikha, Alanoud bint Hamad Al-Thani, who manages business development for the Qatar Financial Centre, told me, without trust Qatar cannot attract the foreign direct investment that is such an important part of its economic future.

From individual companies to national governments and international organizations, trust is the fuel that keeps things moving. Without trust nothing can move: relationships can't be formed, deals can't be struck, and progress can't be made. Let the tank of trust run dry and, just like my car in Qatar, you will grind to a sudden halt.

Cooperation

Artic huskies, near Kiruna, Sweden.

Sweden is a country with a population below 10 million, smaller than that of some major cities. By GDP it is not in the top twenty largest economies, and only six countries spend a higher proportion of national income on social security. So how can a country that is so demographically small, and state dominant, be ranked as one of the world's most innovative countries? Sweden has produced more billion-dollar tech companies—Spotify being the most notable—per capita than anywhere in the world bar Silicon Valley. There is clearly something distinctly innovative in Swedish waters, but what?

Sweden does not fit the traditional vision of innovation, the lone founder or business taking on and changing the world—that is the hyper-capitalist, American ideal of winner takes all, the individual business triumphing over the system. In Sweden, the exact opposite is true. Its innovation economy is based on a deeply rooted culture— one that stretches from the primary school classroom to the corporate boardroom—of consensus and cooperation.

Swedish innovation rests on a cooperation between industry, state, and academia, defined as the Triple Helix model by social scientists Henry Etzkowitz and Loet Leydesdorff in the early 1990s. In many countries, industry complains that it can't access the talent to meet its needs, and that commercializing academic research is troublesome. In Sweden, where there is a strong stress on vocational education, companies spend more time working with schools and young people, and universities such as Linköping and Blekinge have made knowledge transfer a core part of their purpose, so the same skills gaps do not arise. The national innovation culture rests on the effective cooperation of the different institutions required to make it happen. Companies need universities, which provide them with talent and ideas that can be commercialized. Universities need support from government, government relies on the taxes generated by industry, and must also work with it to devise an appropriate regulatory environment. The better the overlapping cooperation among all three parties, the more effective, forward-thinking, and innovative an ecosystem can become.

The same spirit of cooperation informs everything from how schools are run to the way companies are managed. In a Swedish classroom the approach is much less didactic than a traditional curriculum-based model found elsewhere. Instead, pupils are taught based on their interests, and teachers have the flexibility to adapt to the needs of a particular class. The focus is on feeding children's curiosity, helped by the fact that there is no formal learning until the age of six, uniforms do not exist, and much more time is spent outside. The education system is also set up to encourage independence, with most children traveling to school on their own by the age of eight. What is taught from a young age carries on throughout life, and Swedes are always respectful of your time and theirs. When we hosted a party and invited people for 7 p.m., the doorbell rang at 6:59, and eight people were already waiting outside.

In business, the Swedish management ethos is similarly cooperative and based on flexibility rather than hierarchy. Decisions get made not by a boss who tells the team what to do, but through a collaborative process: a series of meetings that only produces a decision once all aspects have been considered and everyone has had the chance to have their say. To some this might seem inefficient, but it means that once something has been decided, it tends to stick. This democratic ethos has helped Swedish entrepreneurs become trailblazers of the internet era, from Skype cofounder Niklas Zennström, who explained the team-first approach to me when I interviewed him in the company's early days, to Spotify's Daniel Ek, who has led the creation of Europe's most successful internet start-up.

Cooperation is the root of effective teamwork—the value that shows us how to listen to each other, support one another's needs, and work more effectively as a group than we ever can alone. It is cooperation that creates stronger, happier, and healthier institutions, from school to the workplace. And as Sweden shows, it encourages innovation and provides the catalyst for outsize commercial success. As polarized political systems around the world are finding, without cooperation everything can grind to a halt and acrimony rules. Sweden points to a better, more mutual way forward.

Consideration

My home for eleven days, Chiang Mai, Thailand.

"You don't negotiate with a monk!"

This was my first real experience of the distinctly Thai concept of Kreng Jai, the importance of respect and deference toward others, and it came in the most public of settings.

In front of several hundred people in a Buddhist temple in the southeast of Thailand, the presiding monk had somehow picked me out from the crowd and called me into his presence. Having fought my way to the front to sit at his feet, I was left listening to a conversation in Thai that was clearly about me, but whose meaning I could only guess at.

Once they had finished talking, it was translated for me. The monk was asking that I spend twenty-one days in a silent monastery in Chiang Mai, north Thailand.

Twenty-one days? It was longer than I had planned for the rest of my trip. Still an undergraduate, I had to be back at university for the start of term by then. At best I had fifteen days left, and I was meant to be having a holiday.

"Can I do less?" I offered in what I thought was a polite tone, but which judging by the response of those around me clearly fell short of the standards of Kreng Jai. That drew the admonishment.

"You are extremely lucky that he has even registered your existence, let alone spoken to you, and then recommended something!"

As I scrambled to recover, the monk spoke again. "She needs to know," he said in Thai, "that if she doesn't meditate she will either commit suicide or go mad." The room, which had been humming with quiet conversations, suddenly fell silent.

"I can come for seven days," I said, breaking the silence.

"Fifteen I could accept," he replied.

"I just can't, I have to go back to university."

"It must be an odd number."

"Seven?"

"Is too few. Double digits and preferably with the number one."

"So you will only accept eleven?"

"Even that is too few," the most esteemed replied.

By now my exasperation was showing. "I have to get back. I cannot spend the rest of my time here in pursuit of I know not what."

"It's few, but enough. Eleven it will be."

The monk was beaming in blessing and my holiday plans had taken a sudden twist. I was sent to the market to purchase all I would need for life at the monastery: plain white clothes, a plastic alarm clock I would live by, and a bar of soap. All my other possessions were taken off me.

A train journey and tuk-tuk ride later I was in Chiang Mai. I was shown to my solitary hut, told I could meet the group in silence twice a day (6 a.m. and 11 a.m.) for our two meals, and would have access to a meditation teacher for ten minutes every other day, the only time talking was allowed. That was my entire life for the next eleven days.

If you want a feeling of what that was like, try spending even a few hours on your own, without access to any technology, any books, or indeed any kind of distraction. Just focus on your breath: in and out. Soon, thoughts, memories, and emotions that may have been latent all come rushing to the surface. Altogether, this was the single hardest thing I have ever done, and there was a time when I thought it was the meditation that was going to send me into madness. However, by the eighth or ninth day, it had settled the turbulence of my mind. As sand falls to the bottom of the ocean floor, my anxieties settled and my mind gradually became clearer. I walked out of the monastery eleven days later, the lightest and happiest I have ever been in my life. It was as a result of that experience that I learned the true meaning of Kreng Jai, a uniquely Thai idea that literally means "awe of heart," as in I am afraid of hurting your heart.

Practically this means to walk in the other's shoes and to assess constantly how your actions will affect them. It is a very deep, all-encompassing form of empathy, one that manifests itself in consideration for how everything you do will affect those around you. With Kreng Jai, you are thinking about other people and how they will respond before you do or say anything. It means properly listening to other people, even if they are boring you; not leaving an event or performance before it is over, to avoid disrespecting those onstage or disturbing people in the audience; not backing out of commitments you have made at the last minute; not complaining about things like the food not being to your liking in a restaurant; not, as a child, asking your parents to buy something they cannot afford.

Most of us probably think we know what it is to be considerate of others, looking after their feelings and trying to avoid any offense or disturbance. Kreng Jai takes this to an entirely new level; it creates a different perspective on everything you say and do, forcing you to think beyond your own instincts and to consider any possible way in which you might infringe on someone's equilibrium, happiness, or feelings.

I had heard a lot about Kreng Jai during my time in Thailand, but it was only my encounter with the monk, and the eleven days of solitude that followed, that helped me to really understand what it meant. I realized that the monk had shown Kreng Jai toward me, understanding instinctively how much I would benefit from the period of silent meditation. In the solitude that followed, I had the chance to think over every aspect of my life, and of the real meaning of what people had been telling me about Kreng Jai. When you are on your own for what feels like forever, you think a lot about other people, your relationships, and the company that you have been temporarily deprived of.

When you embrace Kreng Jai in this way, it helps you to understand that by putting other people first, and thinking about their needs proactively, you contribute to everyone's happiness and well-being, especially your own. It allows you to go beyond your own needs and agenda, to live completely in the moment, and to find a greater harmony between your life and those of others. A little consideration, in other words, can unlock a great deal of self-knowledge.

Welcome

Flags Promenade, Lomé, Togo.

As a journalist traveling the world, you learn to tell a lot from the welcome you receive. Are people open, approachable, and eager to talk? Or are they suspicious, afraid, and liable to give you as little as possible? From the moment you go through immigration at the airport, you start to get a feel for how difficult or not your job is going to be in getting people to share their stories, introduce you to their friends, and point you toward the unreported places and people.

Togo is a country that opens its arms to visitors and provides the warmest possible welcome. As soon as you arrive, you become part of the family. I flew in on Christmas Eve, and was immediately welcomed into the home of my friend Tessia's uncle, a former ambassador. I entered to find a party already in full swing. For the duration of my stay, I was treated like a long-lost friend. As the head of the family said to me: "a foreigner always has a place in our house."

Wherever you look in Togo, a warm welcome is usually being extended. A friend told me how she moved into a new apartment to find the landlord had already covered the bills up until the end of the month, to help her with moving costs. This is not rare. People make it their responsibility to be a good and welcoming host to all comers. The same ethos is baked into its immigration system, and it has been ranked fifth out of all African countries for visa openness, where people can travel without papers or by securing one on arrival. It ranks highly on the Gallup list of the countries that are most accepting of immigrants.

The Togolese culture of welcome also extends into the practice of ancestor worship, recognizing and calling upon the spirits believed to be inherent in all things: animals, plants, and every part of the landscape around us. The priest Godfried Agbezudor introduced me to the idea that there should be no boundaries to our consciousness, that we must welcome in every spirit that surrounds us. The ceremonies that seek to achieve this with drums, music, and the invocation of spirits that go on deep into the night, were like nothing else I had ever seen or been a part of.

Among the smallest of West Africa's countries, Togo has nevertheless been a strategically important route for trade throughout its history. It was contested territory among colonial powers, passing from Portugal to Germany, the U.K., and finally France before achieving independence in 1960. Togo's history at the center of the colonial slave trade is reflected in the widespread prevalence of Brazilian names, among families descended from Afro-Brazilian slaves who returned to West Africa in large numbers during the nineteenth century. Today, it remains an important trading hub for the West African economy, and the diverse heritage of its people is clear to see.

There is so much to be gained, both personally and professionally, by being welcoming to new people and ideas, rather than defaulting to the standard instinct to avoid the unknown and the untested. Unless we welcome in the new, we get stuck in a rut, stay in the past, and lose the ability to learn and develop. That stands for people, businesses, and communities as a whole. An unwelcoming institution is one that is closed off to the benefits of change. By contrast, a warm welcome opens the door to boundless opportunity.

Hospitality

Cappadocia, Central Anatolia, Turkey.

Hospitality is something you encounter all over the world, often in ways that go well beyond the everyday courtesy you might expect as a stranger in an unfamiliar place. But of all the countries I have visited and am writing about, there are none that quite do hospitality like the Turks. Here, the unexpected visitor is not only welcomed, but also honored as *tanri misafiri*: a guest of God.

What comes to mind is an almost identical scenario that I experienced on the streets of Istanbul and New York. In both cases, I had got myself lost on the way to my hotel. In New York, the pedestrian I tried to flag down did not even break stride. "What do I look like," he drawled over his shoulder to me, sunglasses firmly in place. "A mother-f****ng map?" In Turkey, a stranger not only set me right and guided me right to the doorstep of the hotel; but, having taken one look at it, declared that he would prefer to put me up in his own home.

While Turkish hospitality is encountered all over, it is of course at its strongest within the home, so much so that it's taken into consideration when designing one; every self-respecting Turk will look for a guest room when buying or renting. Most will have grown up in a house with two living rooms, one for everyday use and another for guests only, which otherwise remains untouched, clean and tidy and waiting for its next visitor. Similarly, there will be biscuits, nuts, and coffee of a superior quality held back for guests, even by families who generally struggle to make ends meet. Even if you are facing hardships, through your hospitality you seek to conceal these, and present your best possible self to your guests.

I experienced this visiting a village in eastern Turkey, which was still recovering from the aftereffects of a serious blizzard, with many people living in makeshift houses. Despite all of this, the local official, Serge, insisted on putting us up and that we dine with them. Amid severe food shortages, a feast was prepared and served. Nothing was going to get in the way of providing the best hospitality that the village could offer.

For Turks, offering hospitality is not just about providing a place to stay. It is also an almost competitive activity to prove that you are doing everything within your power to make others feel at home. To a Turk, the failure to be a good host erodes your sense of self. It's disgraceful to not be willing to share your last meal, so Turkish families go above and beyond to provide the best experience they possibly can, even if it stretches them financially. In a country where many communities coexist, legacy of the wide-reaching and multiethnic Ottoman Empire, there is a fierce pride in the home as a representation of your family and community. Hospitality is not just about making guests feel welcome; it is also about people restating their own sense of belonging and identity.

What that contributes to is a society that is more connected, one where people look out for each other, and there are shared expectations that lead to stronger communities. There are so many gifts from being a giver: by welcoming guests into your home, you fill it up with conversation and laughter, benefit from new perspectives, and contribute to a society in which people's first instinct is to open doors and not shut them. As the saying goes, "if you knew the power of giving, you would never let another meal go unshared." When bread is broken together, new ideas, passions, interests, and experiences are shared, leaving us all richer.

Turkish hospitality is about so much more than the experience of the individual guest. It is also about the collective ethos and bonds of community that it helps to create.

Part IV: Communal Values

There are some values I encountered that were so powerful, they seemed to set the terms of how a whole community behaves. These are the values that dictate how people come together in times of need, support each other in everyday life, and make their contribution to communal life. They are the communal mores and behaviors that have been passed down from one generation to the next, and represent an unspoken moral code for the role people should play in the society of which they are a part.

Openness

Expansive Niagara Falls, Ontario, Canada.

"Canada in many ways is an extension of Punjab," Prime Minister Justin Trudeau joked with me during an interview. Not the kind of prime ministerial quip you necessarily expect, but one that perfectly captures the openness that is Canada's national DNA, and which provides the foundation for its determinedly multicultural society, one that travels across politics, music, food, and lifestyle.

Four generations of my family have lived in Canada, which I visited for the first time at age seventeen, and whose open arms have always called me back. Sikhs, like so many peoples, have found Canada to be one of the world's most open countries to those from different places and faiths, so much so that three—Harjit Singh Sajjan (Defense), Navdeep Singh Bains (Innovation, Science, and Economic Development), and Jagmeet Singh (New Democratic Party)—have ascended to high political positions in recent years.

In a survey conducted to mark the 150th anniversary of Canada's independence, people were asked what makes them most proud of their country. "Open-mindedness toward people who are different," was one of the most popular, ranking ahead of the Rocky Mountains, Céline Dion, and even Canada's most famous export, maple syrup. This is a trend that is only set to continue, with people younger than forty-five considerably more likely to express pride in Canada's open-mindedness and its multiculturalism than the older generation.

It is a value that has transformed itself into law. As far back as 1971, then–Prime Minister Pierre Trudeau declared an official policy of multiculturalism, making it the first country in the world to adopt it as government policy. Where so many countries pursue policies of assimilation, Canada is defined by a stated ambition to embrace difference— to be open to multiple religions, customs, and nationalities. It not only offers legal protection for minorities, as has become the norm, but actively seeks to promote multiculturalism as essential to the social and cultural good of the nation. Multiculturalism is also enshrined in Canada's Charter of Rights and Freedoms, part of the constitution. Today, over a fifth of the Canadian population is immigrant, and that share is expected to rise to as high as 30 percent by the 2030s. Toronto and Vancouver have frequently been ranked as two of the world's most multicultural cities, and consistently voted as among the most desirable places to live.

Canada also has a long history of being open to refugees from the world's war zones, from those fleeing the Hungarian Revolution in 1956–57 to the Vietnamese boat people and Ugandan Asians in the 1970s, Kosovans in the 1990s, and most recently those displaced by the Syrian civil war. It is not just that Canada opens its doors to refugees—it also in many cases offers a platform for them to prosper. A study of those who arrived as refugees in the late 1980s and early 1990s found that they now typically earn around $5,000 more than the average Canadian.

Openness is as much a geographical feature of Canada as it is a historic foundation and cultural pillar. The vast majority of the population lives near the southern border, while huge swaths of what is the world's second largest country by landmass are uninhabited. More than 80 percent of the nation lies empty of people.

And where people do live, there is no shortage of space either. The typical Canadian home will be a large one, big enough to house an extended family across several generations. The grandparents might live in the basement, and the children in the loft conversion. Big backyards, for frequent family barbecues, are another consistent feature. Canadians also love to spend time in the country's vast open spaces—enjoyment of the outdoors ranked highly in the list of reasons to feel proud of Canada.

On my first visit, I remember vividly both the beauty and the amazing diversity of the Canadian landscape: from the beaches to the mountains, the forests to the ice floes, all within a thirty-minute radius of British Columbia.

As a country that has welcomed people from around the world with open arms, Canada admits it has too often failed to look after the needs of its indigenous peoples. Indigenous Canadians have a markedly lower life expectancy, while four out of five First Nations communities have a median income below the poverty line. Prime Minister Justin Trudeau has committed to tackling these inequalities. He has spoken of the "shame" of how indigenous Canadians have been treated, and the "sacred obligation" of ensuring their rights are protected, as well as making moves toward helping ensure greater self-determination, reviewing federal laws and policies.

Yet if Canada's record of being open and accepting to all is not flawless, it nevertheless offers an important lesson. Whether it is in politics, in business, or in local communities, only by being open can we grow as people, think outside the box, and become easier on ourselves and others. Only by being open can we learn about different people, cultures, perspectives, and beliefs. Only by being open can we breed tolerance, heal ignorance, and create healthy institutions and societies. So much of the human instinct is to close ourselves off from things we don't understand or recognize. But progress—whether it is social, economic, or technological—has only ever come from being open to new ideas, experiences, and choices. By being open, both collectively and as individuals, we broaden our understanding of the world, the lives we are able to lead, and the people we can become.

Competitiveness

The aspirational spires of Budapest, Hungary.

Of all the weird and wonderful things that competitions exist for around the world, is there anything stranger than Hungary's national championship for gravediggers? It's not every day that people are judged on who can dig the fastest and neatest grave (a bit over half an hour was the winning time).

This competition had a serious purpose—to promote an industry that was struggling to find new recruits—and is also indicative of a wider truth about Hungary. It is quite simply one of the most competitive places on the planet. From tech start-ups competing for funding, to riders who face off in traditional horseback archery competition (it hosts the world championship), Hungary is full of people and organizations who are battling to finish first. How else to explain that only two countries in the world have won more Olympic gold medals per capita than Hungary, which also has the most medals of any country not to have hosted the summer games.

Inherent competitiveness means Hungarians have been driven throughout history to go out into the world and make their mark on science, technology, and medicine. The list of those who have emigrated and gone on to great things is significant, spanning individuals whose legacy can be summed up by their name alone—Pulitzer, Rubik, Bíró; major contributors to modern computer science, from John von Neumann, who helped pioneer the computer, to Charles Simonyi, who led the development of Microsoft Word and Excel software; and medical innovators including Albert Szent-Györgyi, who discovered vitamin C. So many Hungarians who went on to become notable scientists emigrated during the 1930s and 1940s that they acquired a collective nickname: the Martians. This was coined by one of their number, the nuclear physics pioneer Leo Szilard, who responded to a question about extraterrestrial life with the quip: "They are here among us, but they call themselves Hungarians."

This legacy cannot be explained without understanding the powerful sense of injustice that lies at the root of modern Hungarian society, even a century after the event that did most to inspire it, the 1920 Treaty of Trianon. One of the agreements that brought the First World War to an end, Trianon effectively dismembered what was then the Kingdom of Hungary. More than two thirds of the country's landmass was handed over to six different nations, taking more than half the population along with it. The legacy of Trianon, often characterized as "Trianon Syndrome," has continued to loom large, not least with the far-right government of Viktor Orbán turning the anniversary of the signing into a day of national memorial. A tendency toward lamentation is nothing new in Hungarian culture and national identity. "We are the most forsaken of all peoples on this earth," the Magyar poet Petőfi once wrote.

The sense that Hungary has been at the mercy of great geopolitical powers surrounding it—a constant through its history, from the thirteenth-century Mongol invaders to the Soviet Union—has also helped to mold this competitive spirit. If Hungary has often struggled to shape its destiny as a nation, no one can stop its people from excelling in their chosen fields and leading the world in everything from science to sports. Parents raise their children to compete with each other over the smallest things early in life, and later, in business. Competition is simply a fact of life because of the brain drain and the talent shortage. More than half of Hungarian companies report difficulty filling vacancies, meaning the competition for skilled workers is fierce.

Hungary is neither one of Europe's largest, richest, or most influential nations—but it nevertheless has a long and proud history of being one of its scientific, technological, and sporting powerhouses. It makes up in competition what it lacks in demographics and capital.

We should all understand the power of competitiveness so well. After all, what is it that makes the difference between the person who gets the opportunity and the one who doesn't? It might be talent. It can be luck. But more often that not, it is the innate competitiveness that drives that person to be the hardest worker, and someone who earns the opportunities that come their way. We all have to learn to fight for the things we want, because one certainty in life is that the competition always wants to get there first.

Support

Balinese rice fields, Indonesia.

Everyone in the village was being absorbed by the procession, and soon my friend Mustafa and I were too. Incense wafted over our heads, bells chimed in rhythm, and flowers fluttered ahead of each step taken by the hundreds of mourners. A beautiful, haunting melody accompanied the transition of this village elder into the next life.

Perhaps the most notable aspect of this funeral was how it had brought the entire village to a standstill. Everything else stopped and everyone was outside to participate. But in Indonesia, taking part means more than just showing up. The principle of *gotong royong* (mutual assistance) means that an event such as a funeral will be the work not just of the bereaved family, but also of the entire community. People will give support in every conceivable way: from providing food to arranging the burial, meeting costs, and attending for the full seven days of memorial.

Gotong royong was a term created, and an idea popularized, by Indonesia's founding president, Sukarno. "The state of Indonesia, which we are to establish, should be a state of mutual cooperation," he said in his inauguration day speech. "How fine that is! A *gotong royong* state!"

This uniquely mutual, supportive culture makes Indonesia the polar opposite of an individualistic society. It means your problem is my problem, your pain is my pain, and your success is my success. Everyone comes together to make sure the needs of others are looked after: from the personal to the communal. This supportive, communal culture has its roots in Islam, which arrived in Indonesia from India in the seventh century. Today, Indonesia has the largest Muslim population of any country in the world. Its Islam is one with tinges of Hinduism and Buddhism, reflecting its Indian roots. It is a faith that follows directly from a teaching of the Prophet: "the best people are those who benefit others." Supporting those around you, in whatever way they need, is done without pause or question. It's simply what is expected.

This is something taught from a young age in Indonesian schools, and which is organized by a specific village elder who convenes community meetings to agree on what projects need organizing and supporting. It might be repairing a road, safeguarding the water supply, or helping a family meet emergency costs. These communal efforts are needed in a country that experiences some of the worst income inequality in the world: according to Oxfam, Indonesia's four richest men are wealthier together than the nation's 100 million poorest. I visited in the aftermath of the Asian financial crisis of the late 1990s, when economic pain was being widely felt. There was a palpable sense that people would not feel back on their feet until all those around them were too.

Indonesia is far from the only country where strong, mutual ties bind families and communities. But the distinctive feature of *gotong royong* is the lengths to which people will go to support those around them. It isn't just about raising money and leaving it there.

In a world where many people say they don't even know who their neighbors are, and technology promotes both individualism and isolation, Indonesia shows the value of a more communal approach to life. Imagine knowing for certain that the people around you have your back; that you can call on anyone in your community during a time of need. Imagine how safe and secure that would make you feel. That is the power of Indonesia's *gotong royong* culture. It shows that more can be achieved by working together than living purely as individuals. And what you put in to support others, you will see back in your own time of need.

Discipline

Blue Lagoon, Port Antonio, Jamaica.

Think of Jamaica and you think relaxed, laid-back, carefree. But this widespread perception is at odds with the real culture of the island, where discipline is the prevalent value: as predictable a part of life as rice and peas or the rainy season.

I remember being on a bus in the capital, Kingston, watching an elderly woman come on board. There were no seats available, and eyes started to move to a young man who had remained seated. At first some heads turned and eyebrows raised. When that did not achieve the desired effect, someone called out to him: "I think you should get up bawy." Which he finally did, muttering a "whatever" under his breath, and you might have expected that to be the end of it.

But the bus was not appeased and one woman decided she would go further. "Did your parents forget to teach you how to behave properly?" she scolded. And then the killer blow: "Ask yourself, how would you want your grandmother to be treated on a public bus?" By this point there wasn't a single person on the bus who wasn't watching the incident unfold. It was as if all the bus were acting as a member of his family—disciplining him as his parents, grandparents, aunts, and uncles would have.

The bravado had quickly disappeared, and the boy was blushing. My mouth was dry and I felt nervous for him. Given I remember the incident so clearly, I can only imagine how much of an impact it must have left on him.

The question about the boy's grandmother was particularly telling, because of the central role that family plays in Jamaican life and especially in creating a collective culture of discipline.

Visiting a university friend of mine, and his young family, you couldn't miss the very structured and strict routine that everyone followed. The children would wake up early on Monday morning, completing all their assigned chores before going to school. After making their bed, one would lay the table, the other helped prepare the breakfast, and the third would help with the washing up. They would depart for school looking pristine—uniforms ironed, ribbons in the girl's hair, skirt at the mandated length.

Education is highly prized in Jamaica, but children are also expected to support their family in whatever their work may be, from helping with the animals if they are farmers, to helping sell goods if they are traders. In the summer, children might spend time with their grandparents, clearing the apple trees in the large orchards, and doing the same in neighboring orchards in return for a few apples to sell for pocket money. From a young age, you are taught about pulling your weight and picking up your responsibilities. As the Mama of the house where I stayed put it to me, in a very matter-of-fact way, "They have to help out, and do stuff—and if they cannot think of anything to do, then they should go and find something." That disciplined attitude toward work and time management is one that, despite Jamaica's laid-back reputation, continues for most throughout life.

Discipline is not just something that exists in the family context. It is also integral to Rastafari, the religious movement that began in 1930s Jamaica, and its concept of Livity: a natural way of living thought to enhance your inner energy and life force. This includes the Ital diet, one that scorns meat, alcohol, and processed foods and which in some cases is entirely vegan; letting the hair grow long and natural; and avoiding any piercings or tattoos, keeping the body in its natural form. Again, the cliché of the laid-back, freewheeling Rastaman is at odds with the reality of a culture that is highly disciplined and has strict rules about how to live. It is this core of discipline that underpins the free-spirited creativity that has made Rastafarians like Bob Marley, and reggae music, famous around the world.

The Jamaican culture of discipline is so powerful because of how widely it is enforced. As I witnessed on that bus ride, complete strangers will make a point of pulling back into line people who are not showing the expected discipline, especially youngsters. Although the immediate family unit is where children are taught the value of discipline, there is a society-wide embrace of the responsibility to ensure discipline is upheld. "I would look out for all the children on this island as if they were mine," someone told me. "Many times that means to talk to them and discipline them as if they were my own, because I would want my children to receive the benefit of this from others also."

When fairly enforced, there is a huge amount that Jamaica can teach us about the importance of discipline, and principally the way in which it shapes behavior. When you know there are going to be no consequences, it becomes easy to start ignoring or bending society's rules, whether that is dropping litter or refusing to give up your seat on public transportation to someone who needs it. But when people around you will not tolerate such infringements, your behavior quickly changes. You start to self-police, to become more conscious of how you are acting and how others perceive you. Above all, you do not forget that, in everything you do, at all times, you represent not just yourself as a person but also the family that raised you.

Respect

Inside the temples of Kyoto, Japan.

From the moment you arrive in Japan, before you have even gotten off the plane, you encounter respect. A hot hand towel is provided so you can wipe your hands, refreshing you and protecting everyone else against any germs you might be carrying. This is the foundation of Japanese respect: improving the "me" because you are mindful of the "we."

The more you travel around the country, meet people, and witness Japanese culture, the more you see respect all around you. You see it in the immaculately clean streets and public spaces, in the design of everything from newspapers (neatly foldable) to public toilets (with thermostatically controlled seats), and in how people move in what feels almost like a choreographed dance. Tokyo is the world's most populous city, but it is one of the easiest places to get around. There is no pushing past people, blocking the road, or dawdling. People wait for traffic lights. Only tourists jaywalk.

People are deeply respectful to one another; objects and spaces are both designed and treated respectfully; the famously healthy diet is one that respects the needs of the body; and there is a deep respect, even reverence, for age and experience. There is a respect for time, shown in the faultless punctuality of everything from public transport to people's attendance at meetings. And there is even respect in things that, to the visitor's eye, do not necessarily seem respectful: when people crowd close to you on a train, it is not because they are invading your personal space, but to respect others' need to get on and make their journey. Face masks and linen gloves, which are common sights, are worn as much to protect others from your germs as the other way around. They will often use very humble expressions to refer to themselves, and honorific ones for the person they are talking to.

Cycling home late from the office, I would see groups of salary-men bidding each other farewell outside an *izakaya* (watering hole), with an elaborate series of bows, each deeper than the one before. Bowing is a complex ceremonial art form in itself, where the duration and inclination of your bow will increase in respect to the seniority of the person you are addressing.

The importance of respect is established in the earliest possible years of a child's life. In *youchien* (kindergarten) children will arrive equipped with multiple sets of shoes, and towels for both the hands and face. They are taught to change to indoor shoes before entering the classroom, to wash their hands as soon as they sit down, and to neatly store their things in the appropriate place. When visiting someone's home, you will be presented at the door with a set of indoor slippers to change into. Going to the bathroom, you will sometimes find a second set of shoes waiting for you, for this specific purpose alone. Your comfort is being respected, but above all, so is the cleanliness and order of the home.

To an outsider, the culture of respect can sometimes cause confusion. On visiting the home of a friend, meeting his family, and being invited to participate in a tea ceremony, it only slowly dawned on me that marriage was being proposed to me. The proposal was made in such an indirect, respectful, and allusive way that it took me some time to realize what was happening.

But as a whole, I found the Japanese way of life invigorating. I had a lot more energy, I thought more about my well-being and lifestyle, and I became more conscious about how I interact with other people.

We are so used to living busy lives where everything is done in a rush. Respect goes out the window, and it is easy to get consumed by your own needs to the exclusion of all else. In Japan it is different. Respect and consideration for other people direct everything you do. You pause to think about how your actions will affect other people. And you reciprocate the respect that is given both to you and the spaces you live in and move through.

I found myself thinking more, listening more, and appreciating more the value of taking time to do things properly, rather than just seeking to do them quickly. It is an approach to life that is both more mindful of the world around you, and more beneficial to personal growth and well-being.

And in Japanese society, the positive effects are clear to see. Japan has the highest life expectancy of any major country in the world, which is often put down to the very healthful diet—heavy in fish, grains, and vegetables and low on fats, dairy, and processed foods—but which I think also reflects the honored place that age holds in Japanese society. Crime rates are also extremely low and, wherever you go and whatever time of day, you feel safe.

That is not to say that the Japanese culture does not have its controversies and drawbacks, for instance when respect for authority can become blind obedience. There are well-established social and economic problems, from high rates of poverty among single mothers, to low levels of consumer spending and a lack of confidence and social interaction among Japanese millennials.

But Japan still has a huge amount to teach us, especially those who come from more individualistic cultures. When you spend time in a place that genuinely cares about its people, and where the prevailing focus is on "we" not "me," you start to both think and behave differently. You take a more holistic view of the world around you, and your place in it. You are more considered, and considerate, in your decision making. By thinking more about your impact on the people and places you interact with, you get to know yourself better, unlocking the ability for significant self-improvement. Respect costs you nothing except a little time and conscious thought; but by choosing to be respectful, you open the way to a whole world of personal development and growth.

Togetherness

Wangari Maathai, the first African woman to win a
Nobel Peace Prize, whose efforts in sustainable development
were based on the principles of harambee. Nairobi, Kenya.

"Can you come and help me pick the harvest tomorrow?"

I have to admit I was a bit surprised when I was asked this by a Kenyan colleague. In many cultures, a request like this might be seen as presumptuous, or even rude. But in Kenya, it's fun, it's important, and it's expected. Whether it is help with the harvest, paying for a wedding, or rebuilding someone's house, there is an assumption that everyone will chip in, and that in their hour of need the same help will be available to them. Given that major expenses such as medical, school, or funeral costs can rarely be met by one family alone, this is not considered charity, but instead pooling collective resources to go further and achieve more.

When the call to help comes, people generally don't make excuses about being too busy or a bit short of cash. Most throw themselves into the task, whether it is helping one family, or banding together to do something the local community needs, such as building a school. Everyone works together to make sure the job gets done and the cost is met. Blue or red envelopes will go around the office on a regular basis, collecting contributions: for your neighbor's child who's just gotten into one of the country's best schools; to rebuild your colleague's roof, which fell down last night.

The philosophy that underpins this spirit of togetherness is harambee (pull together), the founding national value, with which every Kenyan is familiar. It even features on the country's flag. Harambee is a term that was originally coined in the 1890s, as a symbol of solidarity among the Indian workers who built the Kenya–Uganda railway, the so-called lunatic line, whose construction cost the lives of around 2,500 laborers, as a result of oppressive working conditions, malaria, and black fever.

Latterly, harambee was an idea popularized by Kenya's inaugural president, Jomo Kenyatta, who made the idea central to his Independence Day speech in 1963. "You must know that Kenyatta alone cannot give you everything," he said. "All things we must do together to develop our country, to get education for our children, to have doctors, to build roads, to improve or provide all day-to-day essentials."

What began under Kenyatta as a socialist platform to work toward national unity and self-sufficiency has become a ubiquitous symbol in Kenyan society. The presidential plane? Harambee One. The national football team? The Harambee Stars.

The idea of harambee may have had political origins, but it has been taken to heart by Kenyans who want to solve their problems locally rather than relying on government intervention. In a nation that can often divide along tribal and ethnic lines (especially when it comes to politics), harambee can unify communities around a common cause, one that will be to the benefit of all. Without harambee, there would be many more places without the roads, schools, and infrastructure that collective investment and labor have helped to build. It's a form of insurance that operates as a philosophy: powered by people and embedded in the community, something lasting, sustainable, and that will never let you down. It's a principle that underpins the prevalent institution of the *chama*, local cooperatives into which people pay a monthly amount to pool resources and help members one by one in their time of need.

While harambee has its critics, from an uneven impact on economic development to politicians who have sought to exploit the concept, it remains an integral part of Kenyan society, especially as its influence spreads into the digital world. The outstanding example is M-Pesa, the mobile money network that was launched in 2007 and counts around 55 percent of the Kenyan population as customers. Today there are endless apps that deliver the same kind of service, but few started so early and have achieved as much as M-Pesa (which is now used all over the world). Designed to help Kenyans overcome the country's weak infrastructure for moving money, it has become an essential tool for city-dwellers wanting to send money back to their families in remote villages, and to local communities in pooling resources to deliver harambee projects.

A culture in which fund-raising drives can be supported by the effortless transfer of money, and activities quickly shared over Facebook or WhatsApp, is one where harambee can happen more easily and quickly than ever before. In a country where access to mobile phones is more common than access to clean toilets, digital networks are services helping people work together in a new way, in the long-standing tradition of harambee.

Harambee is important not just because it helps support communities and build facilities. The experience of it is almost uniquely uplifting. The morning I helped out on the harvest showed me that working together in this way is not just valuable, but also joyful and invigorating. You can forget all the things on your mind and throw yourself into the task at hand, supported by others who are volunteering their time too, and driven by the sense of making a positive contribution. When you know that your problems will be shared, and that the community will stand with you in your time of need, you sleep easier at night. Togetherness is the ethos that drives everything from thriving communities to successful companies. More insular cultures (think how little you know even your next-door neighbors) should look to Kenya, and how the power of working together can bridge divides, boost local communities, and uplift the spirit.

Service

**The Laotian boy on the far right is the one who saved my life.
Vang Vieng, Laos.**

If you have visited Laos, you have probably gone tubing. This is white-water rafting without the raft: you quite literally plonk yourself in a rubber tube, bum as your security, and down the river you go. In recent years the practice has been curtailed and new regulations have been introduced. But over twenty years ago, no such protections existed. Tubing was dangerous, as I was to find out to my almost fatal cost.

It began in tranquillity, part of a group floating gently enough, nudging each other's tubes with our feet and generally messing around. The water was crystal pure, the scenery idyllic. Then things started to speed up. Some of my group were racing ahead, moving faster and faster. Quickly I found myself alone, swept into a deep ravine with steep banks on either side of me. By now the tube was gone and I was being tipped upside down and rolled around, at the mercy of the fierce current, as if being spun around in a washing machine.

I was pushed underwater. My glasses were gone and my ears were ringing, the rapids way too powerful to swim. Drowning is my ultimate nightmare, and I had a sudden vision of my mother being told about my death. For some reason, my main thought was that she wouldn't even know what Laos was, let alone be able to pinpoint it on a map.

Then I was jolted out of my reverie by something slamming into my shoulder: a tree root. I grabbed on to it and started to haul myself up. My head was above water and I could gulp in some air. I was alone, lost in the wilderness and only just clinging on.

I don't know how long I was stuck there, wedged between the roots of this tree, panicking that I would never be found. Then suddenly the face of a boy no older than ten appeared. He peered over the bank, and climbed down to my level. Digging himself into the soil he beckoned me to climb over him. When I did so, he climbed back over me and, as an alternating human ladder, we got out of the ravine together. I had stopped thinking, and was just doing: pushing my fingers and toes as deep into the soil as they could go, again and again.

My life had just been saved, and I had this amazing boy, and the Laotian value of service, to thank for it. Because in Laos, the greatest virtue is to be of service to other people, and to find ways to help. It's parallel to the Sikh value of *seva*, where help is offered unconditionally and without reservation.

Laotians are always looking out for others. Say hello and usually the response will be, "Have you eaten?" It's by no means unusual to be invited to join a group of strangers in a meal. I traveled on buses that would pull over and pause their journeys to help someone broken down on the highway. And in response to your profuse thanks there will come the laconic acknowledgment, *Boh penh yang* (It's nothing, don't worry). This culture is rooted in Laos's Theravada Buddhist majority, which makes up around three quarters of the population. The relationships between the monks and the laity reflect the service tradition, with the latter contributing *tak bat*—financial and comestible alms—on a daily basis.

In Western culture, the idea of service carries the connotation of servitude. But as Laos demonstrates, the true value of service is egalitarian—helping others without hesitation. Service encourages a selfless mind-set where the needs of others are always equal or superior to your own. It is hard not to be a better person, a happier person, and more rounded personality, when your first thought in any situation is not what you want and need, but how you can be of service to others.

Self-expression

Town Musicians of Bremen, Riga, Latvia.

As sing-alongs go, the Latvian Song and Dance Festival is one of the more vocal ones. Children from every school take part, among the thirty thousand performers who come together to celebrate the songs and culture that have been a cornerstone of Latvian identity through multiple eras of occupation and numerous battles for independence. Held every five years since 1873, it is both one of the world's biggest singing events, and a centerpiece of Latvian nationhood and self-expression.

To say that singing has been central to the culture and spirit of Lativa would be an understatement. In fact it is probably no exaggeration to say that the power of song helped create modern Latvia as an independent nation.

This value dates back to the mid-nineteenth century, when today's Latvia was part of the Russian Empire (as it would be until independence in 1918) and dominated by a Baltic German elite. A movement began to recapture the national identity, culture, and heritage. The Latvian language was repopularized, with the founding of a new national newspaper. Intellectuals, who organized under the banner of *jaunlatvieši* (Young Latvians, a term appropriated from opponents), started to define themselves as Latvian rather than German. And folk culture, especially songs, was studied and celebrated afresh. From the 1890s, this oral tradition was codified and published by Krišjānis Barons, who brought together hundreds of thousands of Latvian folk songs in six successive volumes. For this work he became a national hero, the only individual to feature on Latvian banknotes until the lats gave way to the euro in 2013.

"In many ways this coming together and singing led to the thought of Latvian independence, the creation of an independent Latvian nation," is how Vaira Vīķe-Freiberga, president of Latvia between 1999 and 2007, has summarized the importance of the folk tradition and song to what is now called the First Latvian Awakening: "The tradition that managed to survive through various foreign occupations . . . helped us to maintain our sense of roots, our link with the past, the sense of inheritance and entitlement that being Latvian meant to us."

From establishing their national identity, to fighting to maintain it under occupation, song and folk culture have been how Latvians have expressed themselves and their sense of nationhood. Singing played as much a part in establishing independence from the Soviet Union in 1991 as it had the Russian Empire in 1918. The singing revolution, which spanned Estonia, Lithuania, and Latvia, saw festivals of song become a central part of the protests that became famous for the Baltic Way demonstration, in which over two million Latvians, Estonians, and Lithuanians formed a human chain across three countries and over 675 kilometers, on the fiftieth anniversary of the Nazi-Soviet Pact.

It is through song that Latvians have resisted, persisted, and insisted on their identity and independence as a nation. The folk tradition does not just commemorate Latvian history and culture, but it has also been the primary vehicle for ensuring its survival and flourishing. The Latvian folk tradition is as richly diverse as it is culturally significant:

within Barons's giant anthology there are songs for hope, songs about identity and the countryside, songs to keep evil spirits away, to give people energy, and to inspire hope. "When singing together it is as if we all turn into angels and soar higher and higher together," my friend Kristine says.

Singing plays a central role in marking everything from Mother's Day to the summer solstice and the November 11 Independence Day celebrations, where Latvians around the world unite in singing and dancing, a third of the population is involved, and people sleep overnight in stadiums to reserve their place to watch performances. It is no surprise that Riga is full of purpose-built concert halls, or that singing plays a huge part in the Latvian education system from a young age. *The Economist* has described Latvia as "the superpower of choral singing." An estimated 10 percent of schoolchildren are members of a choir.

Just as singing is intrinsic to most religions—from gospel choirs to *kirtan* (Sikh devotional singing) or the Islamic call to prayer—in Latvia it has a galvanizing purpose: bringing people together both physically and spiritually, uniting them around a common history, and, often in Latvia's history, a common purpose for independence and nationhood. Latvia's singing tradition reminds us of the importance of the rituals and traditions that unite people, and of the joy and power of human expression. There is so much we draw from coming together to express ourselves, give voice to our heart and soul, and join a shared experience of the kind that can never be replicated alone. And there are physical and psychological benefits too: the deep breathing, posture improvement, and endorphin flow that singing as part of a choir allows. Self-expression of this kind has the power to uplift the individual and, as Latvia has shown, to liberate an entire nation.

Solidarity

Stronger together, Fianarantsoa, Madagascar.

Grief can be a lonely, isolating experience. But not in Madagascar, where no one is ever left to remember their loved ones alone.

I discovered this while seeking out Ange, the matriarch of the village where I was staying. Soon I had to abandon my car, because so many were parked on the streets, which were otherwise deserted. Where was everyone? Following the distant, soulful notes of horns, I soon found out. What seemed like the entire village had gathered together, around a tomb set at the top of the hill, by the side of the road. I had stumbled across a rare and very special event.

We were there, I was told, to disinter the bones of the dead and honor the endless cycle of life. This was *famadihana* (the turning of the bones), a ceremony that takes place every seven years, with its origins in the seventeenth century. It is a burial rite of the Malagasy, where the corpses of ancestors are removed from their crypts to be shrouded afresh. Madagascans believe that until their bones have completely disintegrated, the dead cannot pass peacefully into the next world. So until that time, they are pampered and cosseted more than the living. The tomb of Ange's ancestors was a concrete construction that looked built to last for all eternity, a far cry from her simple wooden house, which seemed ill suited to survive even a strong gust of wind. I watched as the men of the family carefully lifted shrouded skeletons from the crypt. Friends and family told stories of their adventures and achievements while they were being unwrapped for everyone to see. The bones of the dead were sprayed with expensive perfume and wrapped in costly silk. Then the band increased its tempo and the party began. The men danced with thighs, femurs, and ribs on their shoulders to reaffirm the unseen cord that ties the family together across the generations.

We are used to burial ceremonies where many people gather together for one person; but I had never encountered a collective ritual of this kind, where families were celebrating their ancestors together, in solidarity with each other.

"We all participate in this moment together. My family and my neighbors and my relatives from all over the island. The dead have gone through the door. We are here to share the grief of those left behind," Ange told me. It would be unthinkable to let a family grieve on its own.

From start to finish, *famadihana* is an act of community bonding and solidarity that reinforces a village's resilience to adversity. Families learn from those who have gone before and know that they will in turn teach those who have yet to come. In this they stand shoulder to shoulder with their neighbors offering emotional support in times of need. It comes in many forms—giving money to the family at the time of death, singing together, sharing food, gathering to tell stories, or to repair a house that has fallen down. The solidarity of family life spills over into the village and extends throughout the island.

Such solidarity is much needed in a country that has seen almost continuous political and economic instability since its independence from France in 1960. Having fought for years to obtain independence and seen multiple coups in the decades since, Madagascans rely on solidarity between families and communities to compensate for the lack of stability from government or the economy. Solidarity exists on an everyday basis, and it has come to the fore in moments of crisis, such as when farmers and students protested in unison in 1971, part of the *rotaka* movement that unseated Madagascar's first post-independence president, Philibert Tsiranana.

Our willingness to demonstrate solidarity, to stand by people even when the struggle is not our own, is one of the things that make us human: offering love, care, and support for no other reason than it is the right and humane thing to do. Without solidarity we are simply individuals plowing a lonely furrow, vulnerable and exposed. Solidarity is what keeps us safe, enriches our lives, and bonds us together.

Community

The streets of Valletta, Malta.

All my life, people have played a guessing game about where I am from: South America, southern Europe, the Middle East, South Asia. First they ask my name. This tells anyone who knows anything about India that my heritage is Sikh (because of the name Kaur, one shared by every Sikh woman) and likely Punjabi. Then, having learned where my family came from, they ask which village. And with a few questions they've gone from not knowing which part of the world I came from to pinpointing which five-kilometer corner of the world my ancestors lived in. It was these conversations I was reminded of when visiting Malta, a country that epitomizes the importance of community.

There may be fewer than half a million people living in Malta, but the island is also one of the most densely populated places in the world. And in a country where people are tightly packed, they are also tightly knit.

When the capital, Valletta, has a population of just 5,680 people, you realize that this is a country that truly embodies the village mentality. There is even an island, Comino, with a grand total of four people living on it. While, according to census data, there are over nineteen thousand different surnames in Malta, 75 percent of the population share the same one hundred names.

In a nation of villages, everyone seems to know everyone, and to know each other's business. I was staying with a friend whose grandmother had fallen ill and missed going to church a few times. That was enough to bring concerned people to her door inquiring after her well-being.

On an island with a colonial history stretching from the Phoenician occupation in 700 BC, to the end of British rule in 1964, people have learned to stick together. Even those who go on to find fame elsewhere never stray too far from their roots. The opera singer Joseph Calleja, regarded as one of the world's finest tenors, returns to Malta every year to perform a homecoming concert that is attended by thousands.

Community operates as an everyday part of life, visible in the interactions between friends and neighbors. And it exists at a more organized level, especially in the annual celebrations each village holds for its patron saint (or saints). This week-long *festa* takes place every summer and is complete with marching bands, fireworks funded by the community, the displaying of relics around the parish church, and the sharing of traditional foods such as *pastizz*, a ricotta-filled pastry. Band clubs (musical societies), with their roots in sixteenth-century religious processions, are central to the organization and celebration of the *festa*.

Malta's community spirit is most obviously seen at a local level, but it also exists nationwide. The country's biggest charitable foundation is the Community Chest Fund. With the president of Malta as its patron, it raises money to support local charities and help families with medical costs. An annual fund-raising event, L-Istrina, is televised across Malta and last year raised 7 million euros, or over 15 euros for every single member of the Maltese population.

I experienced the power of Malta's community spirit for myself when I was trying to get home from my visit. This was the spring of 2010, and what should have been a straightforward plane journey took another turn. There I was, like hundreds of thousands of others, suddenly grounded beneath the Icelandic volcanic ash cloud, with seemingly no way to travel.

My family was staying on, but I had to get back for a scheduled job interview, and I arrived at an airport that was full of frantic people trying to arrange their journeys home. In many places, you would have given up hope at this stage. But in Malta, the community instinct kicked in. Hotel and airport staff asked their friends and contacts to see if there was any route open. In the end a place was found for me on a boat, sharing a cabin, and I made it back to the U.K. by sea, rail, and road. That was only possible because of the Maltese approach to community: where people stick together, help each other out, and everyone knows everyone.

We are living at a time when loneliness has become an epidemic, with younger people isolated through overuse of technology, and many of the older generation marginalized because they don't have enough access to it. We need, more than ever, strong community bonds to tie people together in fractious times. Because where there is a tangible sense of community, people's well-being is improved, their identity is strengthened, and they stand to live longer and happier lives.

Celebration

El Baile de las Cintas, Chichén Itzá, Yucatán, Mexico.

The shades, the smells, the sounds, the sights, the celebration! I had just arrived in Mexico and been thrust into my first fiesta: the Guelaguetza, an annual event with its roots in a commemoration of the Aztec maize deity, Centeotl, praying for a strong harvest in the season to come. Today the Guelaguetza is a blend of indigenous and Christian traditions, and brings together people and religions from across the central state of Oaxaca in a festival of parades, dance, song, and food.

The festival, which is celebrated on the final two Mondays of July, completely dominates this city of over 300,000 people. It seems like every house is decorated, every street is taking part, and every family has its own particular style of celebratory dress. With little previous experience of Mexico, I congratulated myself on having hit lucky, inadvertently having timed my visit to experience this amazing event.

Except what I soon came to realize is the Guelaguetza, extraordinary as it is, is not the exception in Mexico but the rule. This is a country where, in almost any place, at almost any time, you can pretty much guarantee that someone is having a party. Forget people begging off social occasions or saying they feel too tired to go out after a long week at work. For Mexicans there are no excuses. The fiesta comes first, always. This is not just because Mexicans love having a good time, though they do, and they're better at it than almost anyone else. It's also about a deep-rooted culture of recognition and remembrance. It's about celebrating people both living and dead, commemorating traditions both indigenous and imported, and recognizing Mexico's rich cultural and ethnic diversity.

One of the most famous Mexican festivals, Día de Muertos (Day of the Dead) is all about commemorating ancestors. Families gather to remember those who have died and to build *ofrenda* (altars with offerings) in the home to welcome back the spirits of the dead into the world of the living, stocked with provisions and gifts such as a favorite meal or the favorite toy of a child who has died. In smaller towns and villages where ancestors may be buried nearby, marigolds are sometimes laid as a path to help spirits find their way home.

If the Día de Muertos is one of the most visible national holidays, there are also countless more local fiestas, especially those commemorating the saint who has been adopted by every village, town, and city district. These *fiestas patronales* happen annually and can be either a single day of celebrations or a full-blown *novenario*, where events happen across a nine-day period. Saints range from the more well known to the less pious, such as San Malverde, unofficial patron saint of drug dealers.

Whether national or local, Aztec or Christian in origin, or borrowed modern conventions such as baby showers and gender reveal parties, celebrations play a central role in Mexican life. It is not just events with religious roots, either: sporting events too, from soccer to baseball, boxing and the Olympics, are an excuse to throw massive parties. And of course there are widespread celebrations each year to mark the Grito de Dolores, independence from the Spanish.

A Mexican fiesta is not just about the event itself, but the preparations that take place in the weeks and days prior. Often these will involve the preparation of foods traditional for that particular event: *chiles en nogada*, chile poblano stuffed with a meat hash and topped with a walnut sauce, pomegranate seeds, and parsley (so representing the colors of the Mexican flag); *pan de muerto*, a sweet, anise-flavored bread roll to be eaten on Día de Muertos; or *rosca de reyes* (ring of kings), a circular, cheese-and-nut-decorated bread made specially for Epiphany. Flowers, decorations, and dresses are also agonized over and made to order for the specific fiesta. The whole family will get involved in these preparations: I remember sitting in the kitchen of the family I was staying with, making empanadas while watching the youngest child de-seed a pomegranate for *chile en nogada*. Whenever an event is happening, everyone will chip in: bringing food, arranging entertainment, and basically doing whatever they can to make life easy for the host.

The Mexican culture of celebration doesn't just make it an intoxicating place to visit. It is also a value that most of us could learn a great deal from. It is so easy to underestimate the importance of celebration, never taking the time to stop and think about why it's important to mark things, whether it is a new achievement or a remembrance of people no longer with us. The emphasis that Mexican culture puts on this is partly about taking more joy in life, but it's also about remembering what is really important. So many of us prioritize things that we won't see as important when we look back on our lives, like the next work deadline. Mexicans will never let that get in the way of an important fiesta, and there is a recognition that these things should take priority. What Mexico teaches us is that celebration is not a frivolous or unimportant thing, to be done only on special occasions, but a fundamental part of a life well lived. Given it ranks second on the global Happy Planet Index, it's safe to say that we could all take a leaf out of Mexico's book, and learn to party on.

Environmentalism

Rotorua zip line, North Island, New Zealand.

You don't usually expect to find a national celebrity walking casually down the street, much less doing so barefoot. Yet that is exactly how I once encountered the New Zealand film director Peter Jackson, wandering through Wellington without any shoes on. In most cities this would be madness: the combination of discarded cigarette butts, chewing gum, and broken glass would make the idea a nonstarter. But in New Zealand the streets are spotless, part of a national culture that puts the outdoors and the natural environment first.

In fact it was Jackson, through his *Lord of the Rings* trilogy, who helped fix the image of New Zealand as a land of outdoor wonder in the global mind. Filmed in New Zealand and showing off the country's extraordinary scenery, from green vistas to snow-topped mountains and luscious rivers, the films helped spark a visitor boom that meant the country's tourism industry doubled in size in the years that followed. It helped inspire the "green and clean" slogan that became the foundation of how New Zealand promoted itself to the world.

It was a good marketing slogan and, like the best, based on a substantial truth. For the strength of the environment in New Zealand is not just its compelling scenery, but also the deep commitment that people show to supporting and maintaining the rich natural world that surrounds them. In a 2017 survey of nine thousand New Zealanders, the environment came tied for first among the characteristics considered as "defining" to the nation, averaging 9.1 out of 10, the same score as "freedom, rights, and peace."

New Zealanders don't just talk about loving their environment; they look after it too. As part of their keen awareness of minimizing pollution, New Zealanders hold annual, nationwide clean-up efforts for seas, rivers, and forests. The social enterprise Keep New Zealand Beautiful estimates that it rallied almost eighty thousand volunteers during 2017, removing over 100 kilograms of litter. The environment is at the heart of political campaigning too: after Donald Trump's decision to withdraw the U.S. from the Paris Climate Accords, three friends from Christchurch began a crowdfunding campaign to plant "a global forest to offset Trump's monumental stupidity." Within a year, they had raised enough money to plant over a million trees.

For both city-dwellers and rural inhabitants, the outdoors is a shared space and a focal point of Kiwi life. From family trips to summer holidays, New Zealanders are more likely to head to the countryside than hop on a plane: hiking, camping, or barbecuing. Wherever you live, you are almost guaranteed to be just a short drive away from immersing yourself in the outdoors, whether your preference is forest, beach, or mountain. I found something magical about throwing myself into New Zealand's extraordinary natural world: from bungee jumping and zip lining to seeing volcano craters of many colors and stunning hot springs. There is a vividness and a vibrancy that speaks of a nation defined by its nature.

But New Zealand's commitment to the environment goes far beyond a widespread preference for spending time outdoors. It's also present in the country's rapid transition to clean energy, with 90 percent of its energy supply set to be renewable by 2025 (it was already at 82 percent as of 2017). The International Energy Agency (IEA) has praised New Zealand for being a "world class success story for renewables."

While much of the focus on the environment looks toward the future, and creating a nation that can truly wear the title of "green and clean," the national emphasis on the outdoors has much deeper roots, as one of the centerpieces of the indigenous Maori culture.

In Maori tradition, Papatuanuku (Mother Earth) is a central figure, said to be the source of all living things, and the force that continues to sustain all life. Maori deities descended from her almost all have a connection to nature: there are gods of forests and birds; fresh water; the ocean; fish; cultivated plants; the weather; and sharks, lizards, and rays.

For Maoris, the connection with all-powerful nature is fundamental, a part of *te ao Maori* (the Maori worldview) and something that begins at birth. For some, the tradition is for the placenta (*whenua*—also the Maori word for "land") to be buried on ancestral land, returning it to Papatuanuku, the original mother.

Many Maori also see themselves as *kaitiaki* (guardians) of New Zealand's land, sea, and sky, especially as the environment increasingly comes under threat. According to the New Zealand government, almost half of the Maori economy is vested in climate-sensitive industries from forestry to fisheries, agriculture, and tourism. A number of Maori rights concerning the natural environment and their stewardship over it are enshrined in New Zealand law. But recently, Maori communities have been seeking legal action against the government, which in its view has not done enough to limit carbon emissions and environmental damage.

They are not the only ones who question if New Zealand is doing enough to live up to its "green and clean" promise. In 2017, the OECD questioned if the country's fast-growing agriculture sector (especially in areas such as intensive dairy farming) is undermining its attempts to limit climate change. The focus on agriculture "may indicate that New Zealand's strong growth has come partly at the expense of environmental quality, a dynamic that puts the country's 'green' reputation at risk," its report commented.

Like any country, New Zealand faces its challenges when it comes to climate change. But as the natural world comes under increasing threat, New Zealand also symbolizes the importance of the environment: its role as a source of life, inspiration, and creativity; something that is truly worth fighting for.

Acceptance

Wahiba Sands desert, Jalan Bani Buhassan, Oman.

We're in a Jeep, driving through the desert out toward the coast. The windows are down. The sun is blazing. Childishly, we are amusing each other by accelerating fast over the undulating sand dunes. Then suddenly, something that might be glass flies through one of the open windows and into my eye. The pain is excruciating.

There is no question I have brought this upon myself. I wasn't wearing sunglasses, didn't have the windows shut, and had been driving too fast. I'm also a woman who doesn't wear the hijab, in a Muslim country. There would be every reason for bystanders to turn me away. Except when we flagged down the first person we could find, he took me home and with his wife tried to help us. Then I was taken to a doctor in the nearby village. My eye was patched up and the pain eventually subsided.

Not only that, but the couple insisted on us resting with them for a while. We got all the help we could have hoped for, and much more, because our new Omani friends were immediately and unhesitatingly accepting of these strangers who had stumbled onto their doorstep—despite who we were and how we looked. It is no exaggeration to say that I was welcomed and treated as if a daughter: not judged for who I was, but embraced as another human being in need of help.

This is the acceptance that is fundamental to modern Oman, one of the most peaceful and moderate Arab nations. Under the nearly five-decade rule of Sultan Qaboos bin Said al-Said, Oman has evolved from what was one of the poorest countries in the world to a prosperous nation in which life expectancy and literacy rates have steadily improved, and poverty has decreased. The U.N. declared Oman to be the "most improved" country of 135 it surveyed between 1970 and 2010.

Acceptance has been fundamental to this success. It is rooted in the ethnic diversity of the Omani population—around 46 percent of which comprises expatriates from Southeast Asia, Jordan, and Morocco—and the Ibadi branch of Islam that predominates in Oman, one that emphasizes tolerance and acceptance and denounces violence. Sunni and Shia Muslims can worship alongside Ibadis at Muscat's mosques, while religious protection enshrined in Omani law means those houses of prayer sit alongside Christian churches and Hindu temples. As Islam across the Middle East becomes increasingly sectarian, Oman—the only majority-Ibadi country in the world—has been widely praised as a beacon of religious acceptance.

Once a long-and-winding empire, which stretched from what is now Pakistan down the East Africa coast as far as modern-day Mozambique, Oman is no longer the trading power it once was, but retains some of its old influence and brokering ability: the legacy of a culture and national identity based on commerce and establishing good relations. Today it is relied upon as a diplomatic mediator in an unstable region, often acting as the host for summits and talks. Surrounded by factions, Oman's ability to accept different religions, different ethnic groups, and different needs has made it the ideal facilitator. It means that between nations which often have very little common ground, it can maintain strong ties on both sides, and act as a conduit.

The ethos of acceptance also governs the relationship between Omanis and their ruler, Sultan Qaboos. Despite his power being overwhelming—he is monarch, finance minister, defense minister, foreign minister, chairman of the central bank, and head of the armed forces—there is a broad agreement from people that his rule has been a good thing. Protests in Oman as part of the 2011 revolutions were limited, and quelled by promises of increased job creation. Generally speaking, for the best part of fifty years, Qaboos's absolute rule has been tolerated, while he has accepted the changing needs of the country, implementing greater democracy within local government and strengthening consumer protections.

As a rare example of stability and neutrality in a fractious region, Oman demonstrates the many virtues of being welcoming about other people, cultures, religions, and ideas. In the end, if we do not accept each other, we will fall into conflict whether great or small. The absence of this will always lead to suffering of some sort. Whether at an individual or international level, acceptance is what underpins good relations, creates greater harmony, and keeps the forces of ignorance and hatred at bay. It is also the cornerstone of progress. Change can only come when we accept ourselves, each other, and the circumstances we face together. To be accepting is to take a big step toward overcoming the divisions and hatred that undermine a peaceful society.

Family

El Nido, Palawan, Philippines.

'm on a rickety boat that's seen better days, on a three-hour crossing from Manila to the island city of El Nido. My six-month-old son, Naryan, is in my arms. On the surface, it's one of the more challenging journeys I have taken: an unstable vessel and an even less stable co-passenger.

In most parts of the world, it would have been as bad as it sounds. But in the Philippines, it was exactly the opposite. On that boat people looked after us, lifting our spirits, giving us shade from the sun, and making a game of how the boat rocked from side to side. It was the opposite of cultures where children are to be seen and not heard.

We had been traveling widely, through three continents including stops across Europe and the Middle East. But it was only in the Philippines that I felt the people around us really had an ease about the presence of a young child, and an understanding of how to respond.

It was my first experience of the Filipino emphasis on family, and the fact that they will treat everyone else's children like their own. In such a family-centric culture, I had nothing to fear about what a difficult journey would bring.

On dry land, it was no different. It's impossible not to notice how families stick together. And in the Philippines, that means not just parents and children, but also the entire extended family. As I know from having lived in an apartment above a Filipino family in London, a two-bedroom that often felt like it had about fifteen people living there, Filipinos like to keep their relatives close. But it's always a happy environment, and not one where tensions rise because of the lack of personal space. It's the same on the road: on buses in Manila, people tend not to get on in ones and twos, but a whole family unit at a time: parents, children, nieces, nephews, and cousins all together.

The Filipino focus on family goes beyond blood relatives. Your neighbors, your guests are all treated as family too. Their chidren are yours, and yours are theirs to look after. You always get the sense that other people's needs come first. This is *pakikisama* (getting along with others), a form of camaraderie and togetherness often identified as one of the defining Filipino characteristics. In the evenings, in El Nido, there would always be people to look after the children, so I could sleep, rest, or go out.

For Filipinos, *pagpapahalaga sa pamilya* (putting importance on your family) is one of the fundamental pillars of life. Indeed, the central role of family is enshrined in the constitution of the Philippines. "The State recognizes the Filipino family as the foundation of the nation," it reads. "Accordingly, it shall strengthen its solidarity and actively promote its development."

In recent times, some have feared that the importance of family is being undermined by the fact that so many Filipinos go abroad to work. Over ten million are estimated to work overseas, leaving behind around nine million children to be looked after by other family members. According to government figures, between 2010 and 2013 an average of five thousand Filipinos left the country to seek work abroad every day. The impact of this significant migration on families has been criticized, among others, by figures within the Filipino Catholic Church.

But, of course, the reason for parents seeking work abroad in the first place is to provide for their families. The remittances they send home make up an estimated 10 percent of the Philippines' national GDP. And those journeys, and that wealth creation, is only possible because of the incredible support provided back at home by other family members, enabling them to go abroad and earn. Whether the economic benefit of migrant work outweighs the cost on families back home is a debate that continues. But without doubt it shows the extent to which Filipinos prize their families and will do anything to look after and provide for them.

Many countries and governments talk about the family unit as the foundation of society, but Filipinos—in the way they look after not just their own, but also others around them—show what it really means: family as our peace and security, the source of joy, and the basis of longevity; the lasting legacy that we will leave on the world. Family brings together so much of what really matters in life, and the Philippines shows the world how to really make it count.

Cleanliness

Sacola dancing, Prefecture de Ruhengeri, Rwanda.

Arriving in Kigali, it is impossible to miss the emphasis on keeping Rwanda's capital clean. Posters declare that message, and you will not see a piece of litter anywhere, even though this is one of the most densely populated places in Africa. Cleanliness is maintained, as my guide Steven told me, not by bribing or punishing people, but through a sense of common purpose—what Rwandans call *umuganda*.

Since the genocide in 1994, there has also been a mental cleanup. The government does not tolerate mind pollution in the form of ethnic division. "Tutsi and Hutu are words that are not said, for here we are all one. We are one people, belonging to one nation—Rwanda," Steven explains. "We are the same. We are all good and bad. What is in our control is what we choose to focus on, and I choose to focus on forgiveness." It works because Rwandans are obedient, disciplined, and community-minded.

You will see this on the last Saturday of every month, as traffic stops for three hours to allow *umunsi w'umuganda*, a collective tidying-up of towns and villages across the country. All able-bodied adults are required by law to participate. Can you think of any other place in the world that drops everything to clean up?

Rwandan cleanliness reaches beyond the environment. Personal cleanliness is important too. If a child comes to school in the morning with a dirty face, he is sent home to wash. In 2018, Rwanda banned the import of secondhand clothing, a policy partly designed to prop up the domestic textile industry. Nearly every form of work requires a uniform. Needless to say, they are invariably crisply ironed. Steven even irons his T-shirt for Casual Friday.

All understanding of modern Rwanda must begin with the horrors of the 1994 genocide. No Rwandan will ever forget that out of a population of seven million, up to one million, the great majority of them Tutsis, were hacked or shot to death by Hutus, their fellow Rwandans. But if the horrors of the past cannot be wiped away, there is still an overwhelming desire for a clean slate and fresh start, one that the obsessive focus on cleanliness seems to embody.

I was approached by a woman as I was waiting at the airport for my bag on the conveyor belt. "Do you have any plastic in your luggage? In Rwanda it's forbidden. If you have any plastic bags, we confiscate them. But don't worry," she reassured me. "We replace them with cloth bags. Welcome to Kigali!" I was given a sweet smile that also managed to intimate that in Rwanda there are no exceptions to the rule: the national ban on nonbiodegradable plastic bags was instituted in 2008. I had heard that Rwanda was one of the least corrupt countries in Africa, which, by implication, means one of the most law-abiding.

I had been keen to visit because I wanted to know how Rwandans were getting on with their lives since the genocide. I was particularly interested because Sikhs experienced genocide in 1984 in north India. What could we learn from Rwanda about moving forward?

President Paul Kagame, an exiled Tutsi, had led the guerrilla force that halted the genocide by chasing the *genocidaires* across the border into the Democratic Republic of the Congo, Tanzania, and elsewhere. This feat has invested him with the moral authority to transform the country's darkest hour into an opportunity to reunite a fractured nation and start anew.

When the government decided to no longer be francophone and to join the Commonwealth instead, the country switched to English overnight. Literally. One afternoon lessons were being held in French. The following morning the teachers were using English to teach from an English curriculum.

There is a price to be paid for such totalitarian management. There is no freedom of speech. Journalists and political opponents have been jailed. Beggars, sex workers, and the homeless are rounded up and detained. Rapid progress, it seems, comes at a cost.

The application of any value can become distorted when it is extreme. Even so I took away with me a sense that with cleanliness comes order and transformation—"a fresh start." It is a simple, practical act that anyone can undertake. For those who are doing it, it can be as beneficial as a religion, education system, or cultural tradition. Cleanliness is celebrated in Rwanda, as it is by Sikhs and others, as being next to godliness. There's a lesson in that. We need cleanliness in our homes, our places of work, and in our minds to succeed. It clears away both the mental and physical clutter that can impede us in pursuing our goals. Mess is a distraction, an inhibitor, and something that weighs us down. By contrast, when you are surrounded by a clean environment, the way ahead starts to seem clearer. You're more focused: ready for anything.

Let It Go

Art embraced lightly, Dakar, Senegal.

Throughout my time in Senegal, I heard people talking about *musla*: taking life lightly, not being too serious about things that don't warrant it.

But I only appreciated the full significance of this right at the end of my stay, when I was getting ready to leave. Dakar, the capital, had just opened a new airport, a shining beacon of modernity, but one that was notably far from the city center. Having spent over an hour getting there, down one new toll road after another, I arrived with a little over ninety minutes until my flight. And then I realized. My passport was missing. Panic flooded through me. There definitely wasn't time to go back and retrieve it. Already, I could see the nightmare of delays, logistics, and extra costs ahead of me. Frantically, I told one of the airport staff what had happened.

Don't worry, he said. In a second, I had been given his phone and was calling my hotel. Don't worry. The passport was found, put in a car, and rushed to the airport. Don't worry. Regular updates were phoned in. Don't worry. Calmly, everyone who needed to know was informed: security, passport control, check-in staff. As my stress receded, the small crowd of people who had come to my aid started to tease and joke with me. And the precious cargo duly arrived, just twenty minutes before takeoff. I was escorted through security, rushed to the front of the queue, and swiftly boarded as the last passenger. By contrast, I've missed flights at Heathrow or O'Hare with much more time to spare, and much less to worry about.

That was my personal experience of a value that is distinctly Senegalese. The very relaxed shrug of the shoulder: things happen, don't worry about it. Just let it go. Stress only makes things worse. In so many different ways it is an easygoing country: people intervene not to escalate potential arguments but to defuse them. If there is a car crash, people don't rubberneck in the secret hope that something will kick off. They get out of their cars and try to calm people down. In a country that has, in its southern region, seen one of the world's longest-running civil wars, between people there appears to be a real aversion to unnecessary conflict. Rather than holding grudges or starting arguments, people prefer to tease each other; to defuse tensions with humor. Don't let situations or conversations get too heavy; instead keep things light and informal. Why make things difficult if they don't need to be?

The same attitude extends into personal relationships and even marriages. Polygamy is common, but doesn't create the dynamics you might expect, with second and third wives resenting their predecessors. Instead, being the second wife is seen as something to be prized: you have less responsibility, greater freedom, and more time to yourself. Don't worry about what you don't have; look at the advantages of your own situation. Don't create an argument where there doesn't need to be one. Let it go!

There are all sorts of indirect benefits from such a relaxed, calm, and easygoing culture. One is a thriving art, music, and comedy scene. In Senegal, you find the opposite of bureaucracy. If you need to go somewhere, find something out, or track someone down to interview for a story, people try to help you. The ethos is about making things happen, not putting barriers in their way. And if an individual can't help, they will usually try and find a friend who can. It's a permissive environment and creativity thrives as a result. I met artists who had come to Senegal specifically because they found it an ideal place to work.

Of course there are the less convenient sides of such a relaxed culture. The easygoing ethos extends to time. People won't mind if you are late for things, and they certainly won't expect you to mind if they are. In the same way, zebra crossings and traffic lights are treated more as decorations than instructions. Things get done, rules are observed in spirit, but the ticking clock and the letter of the law are not what people worry about. The attitude to religion is similar: in a country where 95 percent of the population is Muslim, belief is worn lightly, and people are given the freedom to practice as they see fit.

The easygoing culture of Senegal might not be for everyone. But we could all benefit from thinking, as many Senegalese do, about when is the right time to take something seriously, and when we should just let it go. In our personal and professional lives, there are so many things that can be magnified into seeming like much greater disasters than they really are. And by engaging in disputes, holding grudges, and worrying about things or situations that don't warrant it, we waste so much energy that could find more useful outlets. Senegal shows that we can go a long way on letting things go: it helps us to forge better relationships, relax in ourselves, and focus on the things that really matter in life.

Enjoyment

La Feria de Abril, Seville, Spain.

We tend to think of memories as grand, momentous things, but often what sticks in the mind is a small detail. The smell and taste of freshly baked bread, the smile on the face of a friend, the sun on your face and the coolness of the water on an early morning swim. These are the flavors and feelings of life well enjoyed, and nowhere are they more readily savored than in Spain.

I had never been abroad until I visited Spain at the age of eleven, driven from England through France to stay with my pen friend, Luis. Come the weekend, a family lunch was planned. The first thing that surprised me was the number of people who came round to enjoy the meal. And then there was the length of the occasion, like nothing I had encountered at home. I remember helping to set the table, with the midday sunlight flooding through the windows. By the time the guests departed, the sun had set. I sat there, soaking up the conversation, watching the colors of the day change around us.

It was my first introduction to the distinctive Spanish tradition of *sobremesa*. The literal meaning (over the table) does little to capture the essence of the ritual, which reflects a national culture where to enjoy is to fully savor the good things in life. *Sobremesa* is not the meal itself but what happens afterward. The lingering time spent together with family and friends to chat, share the moment, and let everyone say their piece and be heard. The meal is about so much more than the food: making sure no story is left untold, no opinion unexpressed, and no matter of importance undiscussed. The real savoring is not over full plates, but long conversations that unfold free form and without restriction of time or topic.

Sobremesa helps explain Spanish working hours that can seem odd to the outsider: with a two-hour siesta between 2 and 4 p.m., and the working day not concluding until around 8 p.m. Anyone looking to eat their evening meal around seven would be considered strange. At eight you leave work and step out for a drink, and you sit down for your evening meal often around 10 p.m.

The tradition reflects a belief that you don't necessarily need much to be happy. A meal can be a simple thing: you bring the ham, I'll bring the cheese. Most important, we both bring ourselves.

This enjoyment of simple things explains how the humble tomato has become the basis for one of the country's most famous festivals, La Tomatina. Each year, tens of thousands of people come together in the town of Buñol, near Valencia, to throw approximately 160 tons of tomatoes at each other. Something as simple as a food fight has become a national, cultural event that brings people from around the world to this one small town. In the wine-producing Rioja region, there is La Ballata del Vino (the Wine Fight), another annual festival where the weapon of choice is red wine. Events such as these are not unique; in the U.K. county of Gloucestershire, where I come from, giant wheels of locally made cheese are raced down a hill in an annual event that similarly attracts visitors from around the world. But where that is a competition, the Tomatina and other similar events are done for pure pleasure, joy, and enjoyment. A food fight!

The Spanish capacity for enjoyment, and making the most out of what you have, in part arises from the economic realities of a country with one of the worst poverty rates in Europe. According to Unicef, around 40 percent of Spanish children were living below the poverty line in 2014. Over a quarter of the entire Spanish population is at risk of poverty or social exclusion. In a country with high unemployment and growing income inequality, the enjoyment of things that don't cost money—good relationships, and time spent together—becomes even more important. This ability to enjoy life is also part of Spain's global reputation. We went there on our first family holiday, when I was fifteen, because my father, Resham, had heard about its relaxed and contented culture, one that mirrored his own personality.

The Spanish approach to enjoying life strips away much of the ephemera of modern life and focuses on the things that really matter: the people in our lives, the time we spend with them, and the relationships we nurture. In Spain, enjoyment points the way not just to having a good time but how to live an enriched and fulfilling life. And a long life too: Spain is forecast to have the highest life expectancy in the world by 2040, overtaking Japan. And if we're not following the Spanish example and taking the time to really enjoy life, then what is the point?

Unity

Reducing the distance between Zanzibar and mainland Tanzania.

"When you get to Dar-es-Salaam, just say my name, they will know who I am." That was the breezy promise offered to me while I was traveling through Tanzania, a nation whose unity can make what is a large country feel like a small place: one big village where everyone knows everyone, and people stick together. This unity is no accident, rather something that has been stressed and encouraged by the nation's politicians since the foundation of the country.

Indeed, the entire existence of modern Tanzania is an act of unity: the combination of what were Tanganyika and Zanzibar into a new "United Republic" in 1964, one that expressed its unity by taking a name combining both parts into a new whole. It was also the defining theme of Julius Nyerere, the founding president of the new Tanzania. Writing in 1964, he spoke of the "fundamental unity of the people of Africa," defined against the still present colonial rulers, but also warned that "the feeling of unity which now exists could . . . be whittled away if each country gets its independence separately and becomes open to the temptations of nationhood."

Over three decades later, speaking near the end of his life, Nyerere reflected that his original vision, of a wider unity of African states (one advanced with other African independence leaders such as Ghana's Kwame Nkrumah), had not yet come to pass. "I reject the glorification of the nation-state we inherited from colonialism, and the artificial nations we are trying to forge from that inheritance," he said in 1997. To the next generation he implored: "work for unity with the firm convictions that, without unity, there is no future for Africa." The pan-African dream advanced by Nyerere may have failed, but the unity ideal he preached has lived on in Tanzania itself. It is a country that is notable for how its people stick together, across tribal, cultural, and religious boundaries, the most notable being in the national language.

At independence, Swahili was adopted to provide a common language for the many different ethnic groups (over 130) and dialects that the new nation was bringing together. It was about one language, for one people and one country. And even though more than one hundred different languages are still spoken in Tanzania today, Swahili has become the unifying tongue just as Nyerere intended. Indeed, in 2015 it was announced that Swahili was to become the sole language of Tanzania's education system, which had previously been bilingual (Swahili and English).

Beyond language, the Tanzanian attitude to religious differences helps show how deeply embedded unity is in the national culture. In many other parts of the world, you will see that for events like religious festivals different groups split off and observe separately. In Tanzania, religious events and customs are much more of a shared experience. Christians will fast in solidarity during Ramadan, and Christian women will wear the hijab; Muslims will equally play a part in Christmas and Easter celebrations. Religion, so often a cause of division and separation, is used in Tanzania as a source of unity.

Religious leaders are also prominent in preaching the gospel of unity. The archbishop of Dar-es-Salaam said on his ordination that "we are obliged to put emphasis on the need to maintain the country's unity. Blood[shed] shouldn't be allowed to disrupt the country's unity."

But the real power of Tanzania's unity culture has been to make it one of the region's most peaceful nations, fulfilling the name of its largest city, Dar-es-Salaam (the Home of Peace). The Global Peace Index ranked it as East Africa's most peaceful country, and in the top ten most peaceful African countries.

Tanzania, then, shows what can be achieved when unity is made into a national mission, as it was by Nyerere. And in a disunited world, where it often feels like people focus more on divisions than on common ground, Tanzania offers a model to the world of how unity can be fought for and achieved. What company, country, or community could not benefit from being more united in its approach? Anyone saying that divisions are unbridgeable and differences irreconcilable might look to Tanzania for an example of why that doesn't have to be the case, if the will is there to focus on what unites people, nations, and cultures.

Devotion

Barkhor Street, Lhasa, Tibet.

was lost in a monastery that was itself a labyrinth of many monasteries, paths snaking out in every direction. I felt like I might be condemned to climbing stairs forever. What rescued me was the music. Drifting toward me, from a place I could hear but not see, was a melody of voices: chanting first at one pitch, then echoed in another, growing in volume and pace, voices rising up and up. Lost in the paths, I followed the music until I finally found where I was meant to be, and an extraordinary sight greeted me. The whole roof of the main building was being fixed, in a collective motion that was like a dance: one group would brush, while the other cemented, and a third laid more tiles, all chanting and singing in rhythm as they worked. This was devotion in action: a mundane task turned into something spiritual and filled with awe.

This devotion is everywhere in Tibet, a country I had long dreamed of seeing, but which many well-informed people told me not to visit.

Even Rinpoches (Precious Ones) that I know well within the Buddhist community in Dharamshala advised me against it. The Tibet I had in my mind, everyone told me, was not the country I would find with the Chinese army stationed everywhere and watching everything.

There is certainly no escaping the constant presence of the Chinese occupation, from the moment you cross the border, having first disposed of any material (guidebooks, maps, anything related to the Dalai Lama) that might suggest to the guard searching your luggage that you even acknowledge Tibet as a country. Yet as I spent more time in Tibet, though prevented from seeing and exploring the country in the way I normally would, there was one thing that shone through even this restrictive view. That is the extraordinary spirituality and devotion of the Tibetan people, one that has survived even the violent repression of Mao's Cultural Revolution and the straitjacket of the ongoing occupation.

During that time, over 95 percent of Tibet's monasteries were destroyed while in those that remain, the monastic communities have shrunk to almost nothing. Today, China permits only a small handful of young Tibetan men to enter holy orders, reducing a once all-pervasive monastic tradition to a token presence. Monasteries are increasingly placed under the supervision of Communist Party committees; mandatory "patriotic reeducation" programs force monks and nuns to accept a Chinese version of Tibetan history, law, and religious policy, and work to identify those the Chinese perceive as dissidents. Famously, in 1995, a six-year-old boy who had just been declared the Panchen Lama—the second most important spiritual leader in Tibetan Buddhism, after the Dalai Lama—was abducted by China and remains a political prisoner over two decades later.

Yet what Tibet shows is that you can destroy people's shrines, deny them their full religious freedom, and force them to sign up to ideas that they do not believe. You can do all of that, but you cannot fundamentally undermine such deeply held devotion. When you see pilgrims to the Jokhang Temple, one that has stood for over 1,300 years, you realize that this is something that can never be destroyed or taken away.

You can find this devotion everywhere. I followed incense- and music-fueled funeral processions, where according to Bon and Zoroastrian tradition, the body is laid at the peak of a mountain for vultures to consume and recycle back into the universe. And, most memorably of all, I joined people making the pilgrimage to Lhasa, the highest city in the world, and home to Tibetan Buddhism's holiest sites: the Jokhang Temple and the Potala Palace, the ruling seat and burial site of Dalai Lamas since the fourteenth century. Every few steps, pilgrims will fall to their knees, prostrating themselves toward their sacred destination. Knees padded and foreheads blackened, they walk sometimes hundreds of miles in pursuit of their pilgrimage.

All of this would be extraordinary in its own right, but is even more so because of the repression that surrounds it. Our tour guide's husband had been imprisoned for over seventeen years, as an academic who was seen as a dissident. Their son, Jinpa, reflected the impossible choice facing Tibetans, for whom it can be as hard to leave their homeland as it is to stay. "I constantly worry about my family. Conditions are so precarious that it is important I am here. Although I wouldn't call it 'home,' it is the best place to live our faith, because it is the most testing place on earth for us right now."

A group of male monks, in a similar vein, told me that their sole daily prayer is that they may one day have the opportunity to meet with His Holiness the Dalai Lama. They cannot leave to join him in exile; they can only pray that one day he will return to them.

That, perhaps, is the truest and most profound expression of Tibetan devotion: the idea that, even as repression and denial of religious freedom surrounds them, a different and better future may lie in wait. The Chinese occupation will soon enter its eighth decade, but that is a mere speck of dust for a religion whose heritage is well into its second millennium. As the Dalai Lama himself has said, as humans we have a choice in how to respond to every situation, with destructive emotions such as anger or hatred or with calm and mental clarity, seeking to rescue the positive out of even the most difficult circumstances. When I interviewed him, he told me that although the pain of Tibet's current situation is difficult to bear, in its own way it provides a service to the world: demonstrating the enduring power of devotion and spirituality even in the harshest circumstances.

This sense of perspective has been essential to sustaining Tibetan devotion, even in the face of horrendous oppression. In the world's highest region, Tibetans also take the moral high road. And they show that, by devotion to a certain idea, a particular cause, you can overcome any opposition. Those who believe differently from you may be more powerful and influential, but one thing they cannot buy or take from you is your own devotion. Tibet shows the enduring power of being devoted to a cause, however difficult it may be.

Performance

Evan Davis onstage at the Hay Festival, Hay-on-Wye, Wales.

Think of Wales and you think first of the voices. The voice of a choir in full swing, or a Cardiff rugby crowd reaching full pitch. The voice of Shirley Bassey or Tom Jones belting out a ballad. Of Katherine Jenkins or Bryn Terfel in full operatic flight. Of Richard Burton or Anthony Hopkins declaiming from the stage. Of Aneurin Bevan or Neil Kinnock hitting the heights of political rhetoric. Of Dylan Thomas cresting the airwaves with his poetry.

Welsh culture and identity are rooted in performers and performance. Whether it is a global superstar on the theatrical stage or the rugby field, or a male-voice choir or community rugby club, the act of coming together to perform in music, theater, sports, or politics is a cornerstone of identity. The Welsh national anthem reflects this participative, vocalist culture, variously describing a "land of poets and singers," the "paradise of the poets," and "the sweet harp of my land."

It is through its performers that Wales has gained global renown and influence. Some of the most influential British politicians of the twentieth century were Welsh nationals who harnessed the Welsh spirit of performance to attract loyal supporters and advance the causes they held dear. Although it is Winston Churchill who has since gained precedence as the great wartime orator, in his time it was David Lloyd George, U.K. prime minister during the second half of the First World War, who enjoyed this esteem. Before becoming prime minister, his speeches played an important role in making the case for war to the people. He blended the humorous with the grandiloquent, rooting his rousing calls to duty and service ("the great pinnacle of sacrifice, pointing like a rugged finger towards heaven") in the experience of his Welsh childhood, always holding the audience in the palm of his hand. "Lloyd George could send an audience rolling with laughter by just raising his eyebrows," a friend later reflected.

The "Welsh Wizard's" spiritual heir was the Labour minister Aneurin Bevan, a trade union leader who led the creation of the U.K.'s National Health Service and won renown as the greatest public speaker of his generation. Bevan too had the ability to make his audience laugh, cry, and cheer at will. Later came Neil Kinnock, who led the Labour Party for a decade, and though never winning power established his reputation as another memorable platform speaker in the great Welsh tradition. As with Lloyd George and Bevan, a Kinnock speech was an exercise in performance and personal history. "Why am I the first Kinnock in a thousand generations to be able to get to university?" he famously asked in a speech linking the British Labour movement to the cause of social mobility.

The political arena is just one in which the Welsh fire of performance burns brightly. A small nation has produced a surfeit of world-famous actors, singers, and performing artists: not distant figures, but global stars who had emerged from the same mine-working backgrounds as their homegrown fans.

Perhaps the most significant arena of all remains the rugby field, a proud area of Welsh tradition that has produced some of the most lasting national heroes and defining moments. Decades later, matches such as Llanelli's defeat of the mighty All Blacks in 1972 are still commemorated and form a foundation of local identity and pride. There are few more significant dates in the Welsh calendar than the annual rugby match against England and the opportunity to earn cross-border bragging rights for the year. When these big games come around, the performance on the field is guaranteed to be backed up by the one off it, as tens of thousands of supporters combine to try and sing their team to victory. All rugby fans sing, but none perform and contribute to the match itself quite like the Welsh.

The Welsh performance culture is enshrined in an annual event that is Europe's largest festival of competitive music and poetry. The National Eisteddfod, held every August, attracts thousands of competitors and around 150,000 spectators to a weeklong event of performances and awards, all in Welsh. The event has its roots in the twelfth century, and is the centerpiece for a tradition which is also enacted locally across the country.

Whatever the chosen arena, the Welsh understand perhaps better than any other the nature and significance of performance: the passion that drives it, the togetherness that delivers it, and the joy that derives from it.

This matters because performance is essential to success in almost every field, even if you are someone who will never pick up a musical instrument or sing in public. We all find ourselves in situations where we have to perform, seeking to persuade, to win support, or to inspire others around us. The great Welsh performers show how minds can be changed, causes rallied, and arguments won. Their art is universally important, one that we all can and should learn from.

Part V: Core Values

There are certain values that are about something more fundamental and overarching than how we seek to achieve change, relate to others, or play our part in our communities. They speak directly to our core being—the kind of people we are and the lives we want to lead. Our control center.

In every country there is something of a prevailing personality: a unifying trait or behavior that makes a national culture distinctive. In some this is stronger and more apparent than others. And in the countries I will look at next, the shared value is so clear, so immutable a part of the national fabric, that it has become all-encompassing: something recognized, caricatured, and in many cases endlessly debated as to its benefits and drawbacks.

Passion

The mighty falls of Iguazú, Argentina.

In Argentina it is never quiet. Walking through Buenos Aires your senses quickly switch to high alert, and are constantly being engaged: the sound of street singing and shouting that might be an argument or just a friendly conversation; the smell of meat cooking from the innumerable *parrillas*, where the world's most avid meat-eaters congregate; the sight of murals and street art on every corner, and buildings painted in a rainbow of bright colors. Argentina's capital is officially the loudest city in South America: a place of constant protest marches, impromptu tango dancing, and exclamation in every corner.

Home to a third of the Argentinian population, Buenos Aires is where the nation's many and various passions find their outlet—a passion for football (soccer), for dancing, for red meat, and Malbec, for political action, for your friends, for love, for life. This is not a place for half measures. If you have a belief, you pursue and defend it to death.

Something is either the best or the worst. You win or you lose. You love or you hate. But above all, you are deeply, loudly, passionate!

Football is the purest expression of Argentinian passion, the one thing that can make the country stop and be still. Banks close, schools shut, and tools are put aside when La Albiceleste step onto the field. It is not for nothing Argentina has been called the most football-obsessed nation on earth.

Argentina's most famous footballing son, Diego Maradona, epitomizes the umbilical relationship between the people and their *futbolistas*. Revered for his extraordinary talent, and adored for his unpredictable outbursts, Maradona is not just one of the greatest ever players, he is also the ultimate representation of Argentina's footballing culture. When, as national team manager, he celebrated qualification for the World Cup by belly-sliding onto a soaking-wet pitch, or as a supporter he gave the finger to opposing fans from his corporate box, he captured the unwavering passion that rules Argentina's raucous relationship with its national sport.

Political protest is another regular pastime, one capable of massing people both in huge numbers and around a significant range of issues. When a referendum was held on abortion in 2018, which ultimately blocked liberalizing legislation, both sides arranged protests that brought together over a million supporters across the country. As my colleague Patricio described to me, you might be walking to work or eating breakfast, but when you see a protest in the main square you go along to join, if necessary finding out its purpose when you get there.

Argentinian passion arises from a heady cocktail of pride and instability. There is pride in national distinctiveness, its European heritage that sets it apart from the rest of South America, and in its exports, from footballers to beef, red wine, dance, and music. But Argentina has also been a place of profound political and economic unrest, from the Dirty War of the 1970s and 1980s, when the ruling military junta "disappeared" thirty thousand Argentinians as political dissidents, to the savage financial crisis of the early 2000s, when the country defaulted on its debt, the economy shrank by over a quarter, and tens of thousands were left destitute.

Some cultures embrace passion more easily than others, but Argentina reminds us that its importance is universal. Wouldn't life be better if we had the courage to follow our passions, pursuing the path we really want rather than the one we think is expected of us? And wouldn't organizations be stronger if people really stood up for what they believed, rather than constantly toeing the party line? Passion is energizing for the individual and galvanizing for the collective. It is the truest expression of ourselves and what we believe. It is an expression of our humanity and our fallibility. Any life, business, or community that lacks passion will be so much poorer for it, in so many ways.

Modesty

Nun returning to her cloisters, Bruges, Belgium.

If a Belgian invites you over to their place for lunch, or the weekend, then prepare (and dress) for all eventualities. Twice, when working in Brussels for the EU, I accepted invitations and arrived at the given address to find that my new friend lived in nothing less than a castle. This is something they would never have dreamed of mentioning. The defining national characteristic, Belgian modesty, would prohibit anything that might be considered ostentation, and I never picked it up from my friends' words or behavior.

Whereas in some countries it is the norm to flaunt your wealth and possessions, Belgians take the opposite approach. Their overwhelming tendency is to be modest about themselves and their lives: to downplay, self-deprecate, and avoid standing out from the crowd wherever possible.

Self-promotion and exaggeration, the everyday currency of some cultures, are anathema to Belgians. They might be a world-leading expert in their field, but would rather die than make a point of telling you this. As a case in point, you probably know that Tim Berners-Lee is the founder of the World Wide Web, precursor to the internet. But can you honestly claim to have heard the name of his partner in developing it, the Belgian Robert Cailliau? Did you know that French fries are actually a Belgian creation? Or that America's best-selling beer, Bud Light, is owned by a Belgian company, AB Inbev?

Belgium, used to being disparaged by outsiders as not even a proper country—and which Donald Trump described as a "beautiful city"— finds comfort in shrinking from the limelight. Sandwiched between major European powers, it has assumed the unassuming role. Surrounded by forthright cultures, like the Netherlands, Germany, and France, Belgium opts for a softly spoken style, one that tends to mask both collective and individual achievements. Belgian modesty also helps to bridge divides and encourage amity between its two distinctive halves, Dutch-oriented Flanders and French-speaking Wallonia.

The Belgian economy might not be lauded as a model for others to follow as its Nordic near-neighbors often are, but the OECD ranks it as one of the most productive in the world. Its business culture doesn't get headlines, but modesty has proven a considerable corporate asset, with recent CEOs of Volvo, Heineken, and Nestlé all coming from Belgium. And while other countries brag about their technological developments, Belgium just quietly delivers, as it has in pioneering one of the most effective prototypes of a solar-powered car.

Nor has modesty held Belgium back from taking a key role in European politics. As Belgium's deputy prime minister Alexander De Croo told me, it is no accident that Belgium serves as the primary headquarters of the European Union, thanks to its ability to act as a political, economic, and geographical crossroads.

Belgium is also the source of what has been judged the world's best beer, brewed by Trappist monks at Westvleteren. But is this made on an industrial scale to capitalize on the demand and maximize profits? Not a bit of it. The monastery brews for just seventy days each year, just enough to meet their own needs and those of customers who must travel to the abbey to collect their limited supply.

The prevailing culture of modesty means that status symbols are shunned and gratuitous presentation frowned on. Instead, most Belgians focus on the straightforward goal of a comfortable, grounded life. The phrase "every Belgian is born with a brick in the stomach" reflects the national desire to own their own home and small piece of land. A modest ambition, but an essential one nonetheless.

Belgian modesty is so entrenched that some worry it can become a liability in the wrong circumstances. The Fulbright Commission, which organizes scholarships at American universities, has told prospective Belgian applicants that they need to cast off their modesty and do a better job of selling themselves in the highly competitive U.S. higher education marketplace.

But while there may be circumstances in which modesty can prove a barrier, for the most part Belgium proves that we could all benefit from its virtues. Being more modest means putting less emphasis on material wealth and possessions, and more on the essence of human relationships. It demands that compromise is sought ahead of argument, and that people focus on working together rather than proving themselves to somehow be superior. Modesty may be a small, hard-to-notice thing, but Belgium shows us how valuable it can be when embedded within a culture. It turns out that those who brag less often achieve more.

Health

Tomato, Tatarevo Village, Plovdiv, Bulgaria.

"How are you?" In many countries this is an innocuous inquiry, a conversation starter that you expect to have batted back at you with "I'm fine." But in Bulgaria, it's an invitation for people to steer the conversation toward the nation's favorite subject: health. Their hips will be sore, their posture wrong, or they might just have found a natural alternative to iron supplements.

Bulgarians will talk about health care much as the British do the weather. It's the discussion topic of first preference and last resort; universal among both young and old, between friends and around family kitchen tables.

When you are in Bulgaria, the conversation about health is all around you. People swap recipes not for cakes, but homemade remedies and treatments. Shopping channels are dominated by health-related products. Visiting for the first time, it felt to me like a large proportion of TV and radio was about health too.

Staying with my friend Dan, I would watch his grandmother bring out a bag of pills with every meal: one for arthritis in the knee, one for back pain, some drops for dry eyes, a nasal spray, something else they'd seen on the TV the other day and wanted to try. His friends would do exactly the same. Most over-fifties in Bulgaria are walking, talking pharmacies: popping pills and swapping treatment plans as their daily pastime.

Bulgarians take as much interest in other people's health as their own. If you so much as sneeze, expect advice to start coming your way immediately. People will fuss over you, telling you to close the window and keep the cold air out, to keep your socks on, to try this new remedy they've just brewed up. It's not that Bulgarians are nosy or nannying by default, but the national obsession with each other's health means people don't hold back from looking after you. The only motivation is that everyone should live as healthy a life as they possibly can. In the post-Soviet era, where everything else has to be paid for, your health is one thing that you can maintain and protect without being required to pay.

That said, not everything about the Bulgarian lifestyle is entirely healthy, especially when it comes to the national diet, unlikely to win a doctor's or dietitian's full approval. A typical day might begin with a savory pastry at breakfast time, a *banitsa* (baked, with an egg and cheese filling) or a deep-fried *mekitsa*, followed by a lunchtime salad, and a generous portion of meat and potatoes in the evening. On New Year's Eve, special flatbreads are made containing fortunes for the year ahead, which will often be a wish for health. This is all washed down with copious quantities of alcohol, always including *rakia*, the Bulgarian national drink that can be made from plums, grapes, or apricots. This is often produced at home, and I can well remember the smell of it, brewed up by Danny's hypochondriac parents in their basement. It is enjoyed either hot or cold, depending on the season, but rarely in moderation.

Other elements of the Bulgarian diet would be more familiar to the health-conscious, in particular yogurt, a ubiquitous part of the Bulgarian diet today, and which some claim was actually a creation of

Bulgaria in the first place. It's certainly the case that a Bulgarian scientist, Dr. Stamen Grigorov, discovered the bacterium that could turn milk into yogurt, naming it *Lactobacillus bulgaricus.* A yogurt-based diet has been linked to Bulgaria's unusually large population of centenarians. Today, yogurt remains a staple of Bulgarian dishes, from their version of moussaka, often served with fresh yogurt on the side, to the traditional Snezhanka (Snow White) salad of chopped cucumbers in a yogurt and dill sauce.

But it is not so much that the Bulgarian lifestyle is especially healthy, although the outdoors culture and some of the food definitely is; it's the collective obsession with health that is important. You might not live the perfect, health-conscious life in Bulgaria (which is no great performer in global health, obesity, or life awareness statistics), but you do definitely talk and think a lot about being healthy. It's also part of how the country sells itself: bucolic advertising images of red, ruddy-cheeked families out on the farm—all reinforcing the connection between health and happiness.

Think about the last time you went to the doctor for a checkup unless there was a serious problem that made it unavoidable; think about the last time you did something because it was in the best interests of your health and well-being. The reality is that many of us ignore these things; we let busy lives dictate our habits and we only think about our health after something has already gone wrong. Despite the obvious truth that our health is the most important thing to any of us, without which nothing else is possible, most of us are nowhere near giving it the priority it deserves. In Bulgaria that would never happen: a parent or grandparent would be badgering you, remedies would be pushed at you, and the first signs of an ailment would be seized upon. Many of us pay much less attention to our health than we should; so even if you don't have an actual Bulgarian grandmother, try and think occasionally what she might be telling you to do. Health is wealth, and we forget that at our peril.

Perspective

Atacama Desert, Chile.

have flown on planes all over the world, but never felt closer to the sky than on the floor of the Atacama Desert. The stillness, the dryness, and the lack of pollution make it probably the best place in the world to stargaze (and explain why it's becoming home to the world's largest telescope). It's hard not to gain a new perspective on your everyday grumbles when you are faced with something so awe-inspiring, sharp, and endless as this.

The Atacama's flawless night skies are just one part of the country's dramatic geography and climate that help Chileans to keep life in perspective. Bordered by the world's longest continental mountain range, featuring its second longest chain of volcanoes, and more earthquake prone than almost any other country, Chile is shaped in every sense by its geography. A country of extremes and extreme contrasts—from the world's driest desert to the lush plains of Patagonia—has created a culture that is by necessity philosophical. With natural disasters accepted as a normal part of life, Chileans have more perspective than most on what does and doesn't matter.

Such perspective has also been enshrined by Chile's history of political upheaval, from the military coup that overthrew Salvador Allende, the first democratically elected Marxist, in 1973, to the repressive seventeen-year dictatorship of Augusto Pinochet. The same period saw the Chilean economy swing from Allende's socialist program to the monetarist approach of Pinochet's advisors, borrowed from Milton Friedman and the Chicago School. Both left damage, from the sky-high inflation of the 1970s to the unemployment that grew to a third of the working population in the mid-1980s.

All of this strife has given Chileans their perspective. Pinochet was ousted not violently, but through a 1988 referendum in which his opponents won a majority for a return to democratic elections. The victorious campaign did not seek to visit on Pinochet and his supporters the kind of repressive violence that had characterized his regime, in which over three thousand Chileans are estimated to have been disappeared or murdered. Instead, as the director of the campaign against him, Genaro Arriagada, recalled years later: "Our conviction was that if we . . . put in jail or in exile the people of Pinochet, that will be the end of the country. It was necessary to have room for everybody." As he told *The Atlantic*: "This was a matter of creating tolerance between former enemies. About building a country in which [everyone has] a place."

Some say it was this perspective that allowed Chile to move on from the Pinochet years and create the democracy and mostly thriving economy that exists today. Between 2000 and 2015, the share of the population living in poverty fell from over a quarter to 7.9 percent, having been over 40 percent at the end of the Pinochet years.

Perspective also means that Chile has a strong track record in organizing around its problems. A combination of advanced warning systems, stringent building regulations, and rigorous disaster planning means the impact of major earthquakes is less than in other countries where earthquakes are devastating to human life and infrastructure. Also, economically, it has taken measures to lessen its reliance on copper exports, including through diverting some commodity-related income into sovereign wealth funds.

Chile shows that an environment of extremes does not have to generate extremism as a result. Through keeping perspective on its challenges, Chile has navigated a path through political instability, climate stress, and economic uncertainty—if not unscathed, then without the extremes that have affected neighboring countries, including Argentina.

In our own small way, we will all face situations in our lives and careers that seem to be impossible. The decisive question is what happens next. Do we get overwhelmed and panic, or succeed in keeping the perspective that allows us to make clear decisions? Crowned by the world's clearest sky, Chile has time and again demonstrated a degree of clarity in the face of chaos. Perspective has been the key to national progress, as it should be in all our lives.

Diversity

Stilts offer a different view of the streets of Bogotá, Colombia.

Succulent, stimulating, and sometimes slightly strange fruits are my overriding sensory memory of Colombia. The fruits are wildly diverse and unlike anything else on this planet. Then there are the musical beats. And did I mention magical realism?

Colombia is the birthplace of this literary genre, which inserts the surreal and the fantastical into normal circumstances. Its most famous author, Gabriel García Márquez, is considered the pioneer and the preeminent master of the art. His classic work, *One Hundred Years of Solitude*, was described by one reviewer as "the first piece of literature since the Book of Genesis that should be required reading for the entire human race."

It is no accident that an author such as García Márquez should have emerged from a nation like Colombia, which can feel like an adjacent, elevated reality of its own: one defined by the vibrancy and diversity of the colors, flavors, climate, and nature. Spending time here is an immersive, almost overwhelming experience; as if the entire world of geography, living organisms, and food and drink has been compressed into this one country. It is a place that delivers constant sensory overload, and it does so through its extraordinary diversity.

To understand Colombia you also need to understand its unique location and geography, with coasts on both the Caribbean Sea and the Pacific Ocean, a nation of marshlands and mountain ranges, coastlines and rainforests, huge cities and vast, uninhabited open plains. Caribbean beaches, the Amazon rainforest, the Andes mountains: all these sit within the endless diversity that is Colombia's geography: one country that contains many different lands. In fact there is no single Colombia, but six regions all with their own very distinct geographies, culture, and traditions. This makes it one of the most biodiverse nations on Earth, ranking second behind Brazil though it is only a fraction of the size. It is home to 56,343 registered species, of which over 9,000 are found nowhere else. A tenth of all the plant and animal species in the world can be found in Colombia. "If Earth's biodiversity were a country, it could be called Colombia," *National Geographic* has written.

The biodiversity may be almost unmatched, but it is also under threat. Colombia is home to extensive mining activity, while approximately 2,700 of its species are threatened, and deforestation is occurring at speed, with more than 2,300 square kilometers of forest destroyed each year.

Because Colombia values its biodiversity so much, it is taking radical measures to ward off these threats. Juan Manuel Santos, president from 2010 to 2018 and winner of the Nobel Peace Prize, has said that "it's so evident that we are destroying Mother Earth." His measures to counteract climate destruction included adding thousands of square kilometers to the nation's protected nature reserves, which took Colombia's total number of national parks to sixty. Santos also canceled plans for a major new highway that had been planned to connect Venezuela with Ecuador through Colombia, because of the impact on protected areas in the Amazon, and dozens of species threatened with extinction.

The preservation of Colombia's diversity has also gone hand in hand with attempts to heal a divided nation, where a half-century civil war came to a temporary end in 2016. Members of the main antigovernment group FARC have since been drafted into the battle against deforestation, with over one thousand trained in sustainable farming and methods to track and combat illegal logging.

Colombian diversity extends far beyond the natural environment in which it is rooted. You also see it in the food, the music, and the culture. Eating your way across Colombia is a banquet of culinary traditions—from the spicy fish and rice of the Caribbean coast to the Brazilian and Peruvian flavors found in the Amazonas region and a diverse set of influences inland that range from the European to the Incan. Music is the same story, with the sounds of Colombia's six regions reflecting traditions that range from African dance to European big band and South American salsa.

It is impossible to spend time in Colombia and not feel both enriched and uplifted by the experience. The diversity of people, of flora and fauna, of sounds and flavors creates an experience that is as immersive as it is joyful. No surprise that Colombia has frequently been ranked as one of the world's happiest and most optimistic countries. Because that is what diversity achieves: it opens up the mind and the heart to new influences and experiences, it sparks creativity and aids common understanding. Without diversity we are limited and restricted, holding the world at bay rather than inviting it in. With it we discover, explore, and develop. And most importantly, we have fun, we relish the unknown, and we learn how to truly live.

Craftsmanship

Red soils of Nová Paka, Czech Republic.

Visit a Czech home and you will be struck by the small details: the carefully carved roof tiles, the neatness of the garden fence, hand-made furnishings and decorations. Everything from the door you walk through to the chair or couch you sit on and the small decorations will have been carefully considered and crafted. The same is true across the country as a whole: of the bridges you walk over, the glasses you drink from, and the food you drink. Craftmanship abounds.

Czech craftsmanship spans the biggest monuments and the smallest parts of everyday life: from the towering architecture that has helped make Prague one of Europe's most important tourist destinations, to the tiny details of how people design and decorate their homes. People take a deep pride and satisfaction in the process of putting things to-gether: how a room is furnished or a sausage seasoned.

It's obvious that there is craftsmanship in something so grand as a cathedral, and Prague, the "city of a hundred spires," has no shortage of magnificent architecture. Yet it is the small details that show you how deeply the culture of craft is embedded. In the capital, you might easily dismiss the ubiquitous sausage stands as ten-a-penny, no different from hot dog vendors in New York or *kestane* (chestnut) sellers in Istanbul.

But Czech butchers elevate the sausage from a humble staple into an art form. To ask generically for a sausage in Prague is like going into a Florentine gelateria and asking for some ice cream, or a Viennese *Kaffeehaus* and ordering an americano. The craft of Czech sausage making means you have a huge amount of choice, with subtle variations from the choice of meat to how long it has been aged, and how it is flavored. You could opt for the paprika and marjoram-spiced klobasa; an *utopenci* (literally, "drowning man") bratwurst, pickled and served cold; the sometimes foot-long *parek*, which puts the American hot dog in the shade; or the ring-shaped, offal-based *jaternice*.

If variety really is the spice of life, then Czech culture comes well seasoned. The mass-produced and generic is shunned in favor of the craft, original and distinctive. Less IKEA and more your local DIY store. Even Prague's lampposts, including one in the Cubist style, said to be the only one of its kind in the world, are eye-catching and distinctive.

There are deep roots to Czech craftsmanship, with traditional Bohemian industries such as glass production that are still going strong today, and which are a global byword for handmade quality. The culture is also said by some to have been strengthened by the shortages experienced during the communist years: often there was no alternative but to make what you needed yourself, with whatever materials were available. The shortages may have become a thing of the past, but the desire to make do and mend hasn't gone away.

If there is a deep tradition to the craft culture in the Czech Republic, it has become no less strong for the passage of time. When you visit, it is not uncommon to be woken up early in the morning by the sound of drilling, as people work on their homes—to make improvements as well as repairs. There is an element of frugality here, in not wanting to waste money or materials (which may also have its roots in the shortages that were faced under communism), but the fundamental driver is about the pride and satisfaction that comes in creating something with your hands. You may hear the phrase *zlaté ručičky* (golden hands), reflecting the national pride in their ability as craftsmen and engineers.

Above all, what becomes clear when spending time in the Czech Republic is the value of caring about the small details of how things look and sweating the process of how they are put together. This is a value that is not just seen in objects and buildings, but that also lives in people; it is celebrating small but important differences, and respecting the craft of the production as much as you judge the quality of the product.

There is a deep satisfaction to be had in making something yourself—whether it is cooking a meal, creating something with your hands or doing some painting. There is something satisfying and personal about having achieved something like this for yourself, especially in a world where many of us have become distant from these skills and traditions. To see Czech craftsmanship up close is to have your eyes opened to the beauty that can exist in even small, everyday things; a new perspective that shows the importance of taking time to do things properly.

Enlivenment

Vice President Margarita Cedeño de Fernández and
(former) President Leonel Fernández, Santo Domingo,
Dominican Republic.

You have heard about body language, but you've never really seen it unless you visit the Dominican Republic. Here, people talk, work, and live with their whole body and being. A conversation is never just a quiet chat or a mumbled aside. Dominicans speak by moving: hands waving, pacing forward, eyes getting larger and larger. An everyday interaction between friends might look like a raging argument, as the volume gets louder, the pitch higher, and the parties closer and closer to each other. Not so fun when it happens between balconies at 6 a.m., but better than no communication at all.

Here there is no being quiet, laid-back, or understated. There is none of the chilled-out vibe that is often associated with the Caribbean. Instead people live in a state of enlivenment, with a constant sense of pace, noise, and action. All around there is music, dancing, fashion:

a dizzying cocktail of the Latin, African, Caribbean, and indigenous cultures that today's Dominican Republic has blended.

Enlivenment is, as the name suggests, alive: firecracking, sparkling, spritzing. It's everywhere, no more so than in the country's proud dance tradition, which has spread across the world. From the quick-stepping merengue, which has its own national day and annual festival, to the hip-thrusting bachata, which was once illegal on the island, dance is in the blood. From the moment they can stand up and walk, boys are being introduced to the dancers in their family to learn the tradition, while no party or family gathering is complete that does not feature copious dancing. Not that Dominicans need a good reason to dance: it is going on everywhere, almost all of the time. The ubiquitous music is not seen as something to be passively listened to, but to throw yourself into: embodying it, swinging with it, acting out the rhythm.

The dances, and their accompanying music, reflect the republic's complex history. You dance to the beat of African drums, a Spanish accordion, and a Taíno (native) *güira* (metal scraper). Dance traditions that are themselves a fusion of cultures have continued to evolve over time. Pop, jazz, and the guitar have found their way into the traditional mix and been adopted. Tradition is not fixed but constantly evolving, as it has done since Christopher Columbus landed on the island in 1492 and imposed Spanish rule, beginning centuries of outside influence.

What goes for music and dance is equally true for the republic's thriving fashion industry, one that has been brought to the world by legendary Dominican designer Oscar de la Renta, who won global fame in the 1960s as Jackie Kennedy's couturier of choice, and whose legacy is continued today by Leonel Lirio. The Dominican Republic's annual fashion week is the central event in the calendar of Caribbean couture. Flavors too are another part of Dominican enlivenment, especially in the republic's world-famous chocolate. It is one of the largest exporters of organic cocoa, an industry that provides employment to forty thousand farmers on the island.

Spend time in the Dominican Republic and you cannot avoid being swept into the unique pace and richness of its lifestyle: the sounds, the sights, the flavors. Conformity, passivity, and caution all go out the window. This is a place and a people who really know how to live—at high speed and in full Technicolor. Surrounded by so much enlivenment, it is impossible not to be uplifted and inspired. And it begs a question. If we all tried to live a little more with this much life, energy, and commitment, how much more could we be? And how much more fun would we have!

Humor

Smiling pharaoh on the Nile, Egypt.

"Please leave now, Mr. President, my wife is pregnant and our baby does not want to see you."

"Please leave now, Mr. President, my team has said they won't win until you do."

"Please leave now, Mr. President, my arm hurts."

These were some of the protest banners that were pictured around the world as the 2011 revolution that ousted Hosni Mubarak took hold in Tahrir Square. Egyptians were massing in huge numbers at a moment of critical national importance. And, as only Egyptians can, they were doing it with wit and humor.

When state television accused the protesters of being foreign interlopers, bribed with money and American fast food, people filmed themselves brandishing KFC. Others wore pots and pans on their heads as mocking protection against assaults by the military. While

Tunisia had the Jasmine Revolution, Egypt had the Laughing Revolution. Not for nothing are Egyptians known as Ibn Nukta, the sons of jokes.

Khafiift id-damm, "light of blood," is a phrase you will often hear Egyptians use about themselves: a people who are militant about refusing to take life too seriously, and will always make a joke out of even the most serious circumstances.

It doesn't matter where you go in Egypt or what you are doing—from being with someone's family to getting on a bus to work or joining a protest march, there will be someone, probably most of the people there, making a joke of some sort or other.

In a country that threw off one dictator in the 2011 revolution, only to end up with another in the form of current president, Abdel Fattah el-Sisi, humor plays an essential role in allowing people to express their political opposition in what is a one-party state.

Political satire has long been a part of Egyptian culture, flourishing despite often harsh censorship. It is said that President Gamal Abdel Nasser used to send his secret police out to report back the jokes that were being made about him; while his successor-bar-one, Hosni Mubarak, was the subject of a biting refrain about his supposed lack of intelligence.

As the journalist Megan Detrie reported in 2012: "Three decades ago, when Mr. Mubarak was new to the presidency, one popular joke ran like this: 'They asked the presidents of Egypt to name the most difficult year in their lives. Gamal Abdel Nasser thought and said, "the year of the Naksa [setback] in 1967." Anwar Sadat thought and said, "the year of the Ramadan War, 1973." But Mubarak immediately said, "my second year of high school."' "

Egyptian humor is not just informal but has its roots in organized performance from theater and puppetry to film and television, and today social media. The Egyptian National Theater, which began in 1869, helped spark the nation's organized comedy scene, and remains one of Egypt's most important cultural landmarks. Comedy in Egyptian cinema has its roots in the black-and-white films of Ali Al-Kassar to the films of Nagib el-Rihani. While today there is the *Joe Show*, which mocks all leaders and positions of authority, and until recently there was a spin-off version of the American satirical show *Saturday Night Live*. Comedians such as Adel Imam are hugely popular national figures. All these modern iterations have a much deeper root: the first ever court jester on record attended the court of the Egyptian Pharaoh Pepi I, in the twenty-fourth century BC.

Living under a dictatorship, in an often repressive environment, Egyptians find comfort in laughing at themselves and the circumstances they live in. With frequently rising electricity prices, it was not uncommon to hear people joking that they would rather walk the streets naked than get ripped off for air-conditioning. The misery of frequently rising prices, the lack of political fairness and freedom, and the iron grip of the older generation on political power, provide both the foundation and ample material to fuel this satire. It is how people cope and express themselves. "It is our means of opposition," I was told.

But there is more to Egyptian humor than political expression. It is also what greases the wheels of everyday interactions between strangers and binds together family gatherings. My Arabic was never good enough to know exactly what joke had been made around a dinner table, but there could be no mistaking the contagious atmosphere of humor and people relishing each other's company and banter. You quickly find yourself laughing along with everyone else, including the bus driver as you mount an overcrowded vehicle.

Egyptian humor shows that, even in difficult circumstances, there is often a chink of light to be found. Their approach is to take life lightly even when it seems incredibly serious: allowing your body to shake with laughter and fill with the dopamine hit of a joke well told, and laughter shared between people. Your health, your mood, and your friends will thank you for it. In Egypt you learn that mockery can truly be the best medicine.

Steadfastness

Commuters crossing the Thames via the Millennium Bridge,
St. Paul's Cathedral, London, England.

"England expects that every man will do his duty."

"We shall fight on the beaches, we shall fight on the landing grounds, we shall fight in the fields and in the streets, we shall fight in the hills; we shall never surrender."

"I know I have the body but of a weak and feeble woman; but I have the heart and stomach of a king, and of a king of England too."

The words, respectively, of Admiral Nelson, Winston Churchill, and Queen Elizabeth I, these are some of the most famous and resonant phrases in English history. Spoken (or in the case of Nelson, signaled) on the eve of pivotal military confrontations—the Battle of Trafalgar, the Dunkirk evacuation, the Spanish Armada—they capture the essence of one of the most powerful forces that has shaped

English culture for millennia: steadfast resolve in the face of a dire external threat.

England, an island in identity as much as geography, has been defined throughout its history by its response to the threat of would-be and successful invaders: from the Romans to the Vikings, Normans, and Nazis. From Boudicca to Churchill, leaders who have rallied their people in the face of existential threats have gone down in history. On the flip side, the English have been more often invaders than invaded: countries that were occupied under the British Empire might have reflected on a different side of English steadfastness, manifested in the long-standing refusal to allow people around the world their independence.

Steadfastness has been a historic English characteristic, and it continues to inform contemporary identity and culture. Much of this is rooted in the experience and memory of the Second World War: the "Blitz spirit" that remains a shorthand for steadfastness and the role of "The Few," the Royal Air Force pilots who defied the German raids during the Battle of Britain. Whatever the real truth, the notion of an essential refusal to give up or be intimidated ("we shall never surrender") has become a powerful national myth, one that continues to echo in the debate and negotiations around Brexit.

But steadfastness is not just about stirring statements made on the eve of battle. It is also about the quirks of English culture for which it is world-famous: standing patiently in line to queue, carrying on with the barbecue even when the rain is pouring down, never complaining even when you are served the wrong meal in a restaurant, insisting that a cup of tea is the cure to all ills. The steadfastness that defines English culture relates as much to the everyday as it does to the exceptional. The stiff upper lip manifests itself in all sorts of ways.

Steadfastness is also something that the English are drawn to, and willing to throw their support behind. Politicians as ideologically diverse as Margaret Thatcher and Jeremy Corbyn have been successful because they have steadfastly held to their views in the face of fierce criticism and pressure to change, especially within their own political parties. The fact that they were or are, in their very different ways, unwilling to change or bend with fashionable winds has become one of their core selling points.

Whether in deadly serious or wholly frivolous circumstances, steadfastness has defined the English ideals of nation and character for millennia. In times of trouble, it is the national story—mythical or otherwise—to which leaders return and around which they seek to unify people.

It is relevant because, in all our lives, there will be moments where we want to give up. Whether you are building a business, raising a family, or creating art, there will come a moment where it all seems too much and your mind and body are screaming at you to quit. This is exactly how I felt running my first marathon in London, before I was saved, as many runners say they are, by the support of the crowd. The people massed around the course were not going to let me or anyone else give up; they cheered every last tired step to the finish line. The ability to remain steadfast in these moments, to separate the short-term pain from the long-term goal, is immensely valuable. Every now and then, as the tea-towels say, we all need to just keep calm and carry on.

Silence

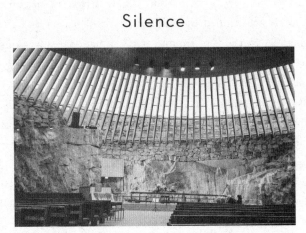

Temppeliaukio Rock Church, Helsinki, Finland.

A sign of intelligence is to listen with attentive ears and think, before forming an opinion and speaking. Otherwise, when only looking with open eyes, often subconsciously, one has already decided what the story is and what the picture looks like.

It is commonly understood that 70 to 90 percent of all communication is nonverbal. According to "The Art of Communication," a study from the University of Pennsylvania, it is actually 93 percent, with 70 percent of communication coming from our body language, and 23 percent expressed in our tone and inflection. So what is unspoken, matters—and Finland is perhaps the best example of the power of silence, allowing both parties to think, listen, and absorb what is being said.

Finland is a magically serene country. It's the most sparsely populated in the European Union. This, the eighth largest country in Europe, hosts only 5.5 million people, and while a quarter live in Helsinki, the rest are very spread out over those 130,000 square miles. There aren't many people but it's how they live that is interesting. In the countryside houses are isolated, people preferring expanse rather than being clustered together. What was even more surprising to me was the students continue to model this preference in the way they live. At a time of life when the rest of us in the world tend to huddle into dorms together, the Finns would rather rent a single studio twenty meters square, and spend some time alone.

Silence, solitude, and space are prized here, and this is something that struck me as a first impression before I even met or got to know anyone. Walking through the streets of Helsinki, I could hear a pin drop, day or night, and the same was true in more rural parts. There is hardly any traffic (people prefer to walk or bike in the center), and people do not move around in groups, but would rather walk by themselves. Finns are curiously silent in the metro, the bus, or the tram. Strangely, it was hard to find a café, restaurant, or bar that played music while people ate and drank together. Listening to one another was, for them, more important than "drowning out the noise in one's head," said one bartender. This is a country that embraces quality communication with one another and with themselves.

A Finn does not grow nervous if there are breaks in the conversation; silence is regarded as a part of communication, and although many Finns are competent in several foreign languages, they usually speak unhurriedly. As a result, Finns have a special attitude to words and speech: words are taken seriously, and so people are held to what they say. "Take a man by his words and a bull by its horns," says a Finnish proverb. So slow down for three minutes, allow yourself to settle, and pay attention.

Reflection in silence continues into their recreation, as people like to take long runs by themselves, or walk alone. People are quiet and so is the design they create and use—which is minimalist and uncluttered. Their most common way of relaxing is the sauna, a nation of 5.5 million has 1.5 million saunas, where "you stop—to hear nothing but your own heartbeat." And what is one of the most visited tourist spots? A high rooftop with a spiral staircase, which only allows just one person to climb at a time, giving them (they say) the freedom to just be.

I loved the harmony they had with themselves and with nature— over a quarter of the country consists of lakes, and the rest is largely forested. This link with nature is also reflected in their sense of patience and calm. People are obedient and respect others, as for instance in quietly waiting for the green man at the lights. The down-to-earth Finns are sober, modest, and rational, not attaching themselves to status, and they are incredibly self-reliant. Society has been set up so that they can manage via daytime child care and work on making life manageable. Even Finland's president (Tarja Halonen) does her own shopping, cleaning, and chores.

Perhaps it is this introspection, awareness of others, and attention to detail that leads to its regular innovation in technology and design. Patent applications to the U.S. Patent Office from Finland place the country consistently in the top twenty in the world (and remember by population they're 117th). Both Nokia and Neste are Finnish. At its peak, Nokia, from this tiny nation, managed to take 41 percent of the mobile phone market worldwide. According to Alexander Stubb, the Finnish minister of European affairs and foreign trade, the success of Finland has been mostly defined by Nokia: "We used to be a top thirty country in the world out of two hundred, now when you look at international standards and measures of education, competitiveness, GDP per capita, we're top three. We became a very affluent nation with the rise of Nokia."

In its wake, Nokia has sparked a wave of fellow innovators, including Angry Birds, which has become one of the most internationally recognizable video game icons of the twenty-first century.

It is interesting how technological communication was led by such a nation, similar to its contemporary Japan, where there is respect for silence with no obligation to talk without a reason. Perhaps this is why mobile phone use was embraced here—mobile phone discussions in Finland are typically short and informative. In Finland the use of mobile phones is governed by a loosely defined etiquette that objects to their use if disruptive or dangerous, making them forbidden on airplanes and in hospitals, inappropriate during meetings, concerts, and church, and irritating in restaurants, etc. As the sociologist Sherry Turkle highlights, even the presence of a mobile phone on a table during conversation can alter the speed and depth to which people share, increasing superficiality.

Although Finland was relatively late to industrialization and largely agrarian until the 1950s, it developed an advanced economy rapidly. It overperforms economically and intellectually, having four 10-billion-euro companies and four Nobel Prize winners since 1939. It's a top ten global performer in education and is fourteenth in the world in terms of GDP per capita. Not bad for a place so small.

But isn't it all a bit dour and depressing? asked a skeptical American I know. Not for me it isn't and it certainly isn't for the Finns. Yes, the rate of suicide has traditionally been higher in the Nordic countries (yet at thirty-third in the world it's close to the United States at fiftieth, behind Russia by a dozen places, and alongside placid Belgium, Finland isn't that suicidal at all), but it is more of a feature of places that lack natural sunlight for over half the year than being connected to silence.

Finland is consistently in the top ten happiest countries in the world based on a report published by the U.N.'s Sustainable Development Solutions Network (SDSN). This year it was sixth, way ahead of the U.S. or U.K. It was also one of the first countries to allow every citizen to vote (1906); in 2010 *Newsweek* chose it as the best country in the world; and in May 2015, it was ranked as first in the World Human Capital Index, by the World Economic Forum, meaning it has the world's most productive population.

But you didn't know about any of this because Finland is modest and keeps quiet about its achievements. In an age that's eagerly espousing mindfulness and meditation Finland may prove to be a role model and show us that silence really is golden.

Goodness

Temple of Apollo, Delphi, Greece.

The value that defines Greece is so long-standing, so all-encompassing, that it has been talked about by luminaries of both the ancient and modern worlds: from Pindar to Plato, Saint Paul the Apostle, and Barack Obama.

This is *philotimo*, an idea with deep roots in one of the world's oldest civilizations, which everyone knows but no one can entirely agree on an apt translation for.

With *philotimo* you are literally a "friend of honor," but the etymology of the word only goes so far in explaining its meaning and significance. Often quoted is the explanation of the ascetic monk Paisios, who wrote, "*Philotimo* is the reverent distillation of goodness, the love shown by humble people, from which every trace of self has been filtered out. Their hearts are full of gratitude toward God and to their fellow men, and out of spiritual sensitivity, they try to repay the slightest good which others do them."

I am choosing to follow him and define *philotimo* for this purpose as goodness. Because *philotimo* is about seeing the good in people, it is about doing good and helpful things for their own sake, and trying to be a good person who contributes positively to the lives of your friends, family, and community. It is about what is good for the world around you, not for you as an individual; and about what's good not just for now, but the long term.

Under *philotimo*, you always seek to do the right thing, looking at the big picture. And by aspiring to goodness as the Greeks do, we can also demonstrate many other values: respect, selflessness, humility, empathy, generosity, and gratitude. All these are things that *philotimo* represents and supports.

At the core of *philotimo* is to help others in need, something that has been brought into sharp relief in Greece by the refugee crisis sparked by the Syrian civil war. At its peak, over a million refugees arrived on Greek shores in 2015 and 2016. This came in the context of the soaring unemployment and poverty that have afflicted Greece since the economy collapsed under piles of debt in the aftermath of the financial crisis, and stringent austerity measures imposed by the EU as part of its bailout.

Yet just at the moment when Greeks were dealing with so much economic pain domestically, many showed *philotimo* to refugees arriving in precarious vessels and in desperate need. Stories abounded of Greek islanders who waded into the water to help people ashore, families who offered accommodation, and shops that donated scarce supplies. As a nation, Greece has struggled in some ways to cope with the demands of the mass migration, with shocking conditions reported in several refugee camps. But as a people, Greeks proved the statement of one of their nation's earliest philosophers, Thales of Miletus, who said that "*Philotimo* to a Greek is like breathing. A Greek is not a Greek without it." They showed that *philotimo* is a timeless value and one that will be demonstrated regardless of context or circumstance. You do the right thing without thinking about what the consequences might be—in the mold of ancient Greek figures such as Pheidippides, the original marathon runner who died after running the 26.2 miles to Athens from the scene of the Battle of Marathon, to deliver news of the Greek victory.

Greece is a place where you cannot help but reflect on yourself and your values. This is especially true if, as I did, you visit the Temple of Apollo at Delphi and its famous inscription: "Know thyself." This is the saying that prompted an equally famous Socratic aphorism—"the unexamined life is not worth living"—and a Shakespearean echo in *Hamlet*: "To thine own self be true." This is something that matters hugely to me: unless you are honest to yourself—and live by your values—you can never give of yourself in the way that *philotimo* demands.

Observing the power of Greek goodness and *philotimo* in action is a powerful spur for self-reflection and introspection. When we decide to err on the side of goodness, and to do the right thing regardless of our self-interest, it can change everything about us and how we see the world. We become more generous, more considerate, more open to other people and conscious of their needs. We see the bigger picture—one beyond our own interest and the short-term imperative, and gain important perspective on what matters. *Philotimo* is not just an important value in its own right, but one that acts as a gateway to many of those I have written about in this book.

Faith

Harmandir Sahib (Golden Temple), Amritsar, Punjab, India.

Until you have worn one, it can be hard to understand why a piece of cloth worn around your head is so meaningful. It wasn't until I lived in India for the first time and donned the *dastaar*, a traditional Sikh cloth turban, that its power became clear to me. The simple act of wrapping up my hair transformed me from a girl, vulnerable and objectified, into a "don't mess with me" spiritual warrior. What's more, by signifying myself as a person of faith, I became a beacon of safety, reliability, and trust for others. Old women would come and sit by me at railway stations and ask if I could ensure that they got onto the right train. Men would treat me as an equal, or even better, with respect. I had become desexualized and the *kara* (iron bangle around my wrist) added to my own feelings of strength, defiance, and resilience. I stood taller, with my head held higher, as if my *dastaar* was a crown—an effect magnified when the cloth is white, as bold as a beacon of light, symbolizing service, discipline, and committment. It was in these moments that I recognized the power of faith for the first time.

On that visit, I spent a month living at Harmandir Sahib, more commonly known as the Golden Temple, in Amritsar, a rite of passage that helped me—as a Sikh who grew up in Church of England schools—both understand more about my own faith, and more broadly the power of faith in people's lives. Sitting by the *sarovar* (sacred pool) that surrounds the temple, you would see people who had traveled huge distances to share their greatest problem or fear, believing that the waters would heal them. It was an education in how people can derive strength, comfort, and purpose from their faith.

Faith doesn't have to be manifested through the rigors of regular prayer or specific rituals. It can exist in so many different actions and interactions, some of them seemingly unremarkable. Even a greeting as simple as *namaste*—meaning: the divinity in me recognizes the divinity in you—is a profound signifier of shared faith.

Anyone who has ever gotten behind the wheel of a car or rickshaw in India will understand the importance of faith to life in the world's second most populous country. If you didn't believe, you wouldn't be able to travel on the roads at all. There's a reason that every God, messiah, or messenger that has ever been invoked in prayer festoons the windshield of any Indian vehicle.

But faith is not just a necessity for navigating India's famously chaotic and danger-filled roads. It is also the defining characteristic of a country that has been birthplace to some of the world's most prevalent religions (Hinduism, Sikhism, Buddhism, and Jainism), is home to over a billion Hindus, the biggest population of Sikhs, and also the world's third largest Muslim population.

Across contemporary India's multi-religious society—also containing substantial Christian and Jewish communities—there are almost endless variations in religious belief and practice, but one unifying factor. Faith matters.

That is no surprise when you consider the role that faith plays in Indian life. From the way your name is chosen to the person you will marry, many of the most meaningful decisions are taken according to the faith that you have chosen or been born into. Faith is something that accompanies almost any significant moment in your life, whether you are wishing for it or celebrating its arrival: from starting a new job to moving into a new home or having children. People will trust in faith: praying, following customs (such as making a tiny paper cradle when wishing for a child), or making offerings of water, food, flowers, or incense to the deity.

Faith is also seen as essential to work: during Ayudha Puja (the worship of instruments, part of the annual Navratri festival), craftsmen's tools, rickshaws, and other machines will be specially cleaned, garlanded, and worshipped (while being left untouched) for the day. This is important because the things you work with are not simply tools of the trade; they connect you to something deeper: the soul and spirit of people, and of the work we do. My mentor Raghu Rai, a renowned photographer, uses his camera not just to observe and capture, but also to reveal the spirit of the people, places, and moments he records.

The festival's existence shows the extent to which faith permeates all aspects of everyday life; there is little in Indian life not touched by faith or surrounded by religious worship. All around, you will see signs of religious observance and devotion. Almost every Indian home will have a shrine for daily prayer, whether that is a room, an altar, or just a dedicated corner. At acknowledged spiritual sites, you will see trees covered with pieces of colorful cloth, tied by people for a specific desire or promise.

The Beatles, Julia Roberts, Steve Jobs, Mark Zuckerberg—everyone goes to India when they decide they need a little or lots of spirituality or faith. Individual worship is supplemented by moments of collective observance, whether you are gathering at the feet of the many Gurus,

Saadhus, or Rishis, or preparing for pilgrimage. There are so many mountains and sites for pilgrimage, and then there's the Kumbh Mela, which rotates around four sacred rivers every three years (visiting each every twelve years) and is the world's largest religious gathering. On its busiest days, it has been known to bring between 30 and 40 million people together in one place. Concepts that are grounded in Eastern faiths play a defining role in how many people live and understand their lives: from the well-understood notion of karma, whereby good deeds are rewarded and bad ones punished (thereby giving people faith that they control their own destiny), and dharma, divine law governing human conduct (literally duty), which informs key traits of respect and worship for the environment.

Thus in many ways, faith was and remains the birthmark of India. It is faith that allows us to discover the true depths of our resolve as people, discovering the inner belief that we need to get through the tough times, support each other, and ultimately be our greatest selves. Faith cannot be proven or disproven—but if you have it then you are empowered to find solace even in the darkest of times, and trust when something is beyond your comprehension. Faith fills gaps that nothing else can. It is what allows us to reach beyond ourselves—from the known to the unknown, from the possible to the impossible. It changes our perception of the world—allowing us to see wonder in the place of indifference, and to embrace belief in place of skepticism. It represents one of the most important things in any life, secular or religious, which is the power of belief to overcome the force of accumulated logic, reason, and expectation.

Commitment

Sufi mystic, near the Kurdistan Region, Iran.

Our journey was a long one, into the heart of the mountains of Kurdistan, which span Syria, Iran, Iraq, and Turkey. There, hidden in a sacred valley, a house sat in a clearing that seemed to be pulsating with an otherworldly energy. Having removed my shoes I entered and immersed myself in the rhythmic, overpowering, almost transcendental music and poetry that was coming from within.

We weaved through corridor after corridor, past a thousand bodies rapt in worship. Finally, hidden at the center of the labyrinth, an inner courtyard emerged. Here the incense was thick, the light dim, the beat much faster, and the eyes of those singing were closed. Arms were locked together, feet rotating and heads spinning. Eyes were pulsating and voices were being raised in a frenzied pitch that almost seemed beyond human. It was more rapid, more energetic and sustained in a way I hardly thought possible.

These were the Sufis in worship, and they strive for *ihsan*, which means "perfect worship," and to the witness it appears to be the practice of Islam with intensity. It was a spiritual, emotional, and above all a high-energy experience—one symptomatic of Iranian culture as a whole, where everything is done at full throttle—and with total commitment.

Iranians are a dramatic, passionate, and above all committed people. They throw their whole selves behind the things they say, believe, and desire. This is what has helped the nation produce so many outstanding poets, architects, and musicians. As Anglo-Iranian comedian Omid Djalili has joked, the Iranian way of writing love letters is to cut your arm off and write it in your own blood.

Iranian language is the language of commitment. In many cultures, the words "I love you" are some of the most meaningful and precious. But for Iranians they do not go nearly far enough. An Iranian wanting to express their love or commitment would say *Ghorboonet beram* (I will sacrifice myself for you). To a loved one or family member you might joke *Jigareto bokhoram* (I'm dying to eat your liver). An expression of surprise or frustration would be *khodah margam bedeh*, literally "God give me death."

I witnessed what Iranian commitment looks like when attending any of the many events and ceremonies, religious and otherwise, that populate the calendar. Here, worship and ceremony is taken to a whole new level. On Chaharshanbe Suri (Red Wednesday), an outdoor festival held as a precursor to the Iranian New Year, people will make bonfires and jump over them, chanting a Zoroastrian refrain that translates roughly as "take away my sallow yellow and give me your fiery red": in other words, be rid of the old, tired, yellow year and bring in the vibrant, fresh, new red one. The heat and purity of the fire, sacred to the Zoroastrian faith that was born in Iran, symbolically cleanses the problems of the year past. This continues even though it is now formally prohibited by the Iranian government.

During Ashura, the month-long commemoration of Husayn ibn Ali, martyred grandson of Muhammad and the founding father of Shia Islam, self-flagellation is common. I saw people whip themselves; some (although I am told this is a tiny minority) will beat themselves with chains, others will even use sharp blades to draw blood, a practice now officially forbidden; all to share in some of the pain suffered by Husayn, who was killed and beheaded at the Battle of Karbala in October 680. Watching quite elderly women slashing themselves was a stark and quite frightening demonstration of how committed Iranians are to their traditions and beliefs.

Yet it would be wrong to characterize Iranians as religious in the traditional, narrow sense. What I frequently encountered was something closer to spiritualism than traditional religion: people praising, worshipping, and connecting with Allah through music, song, and dance. Although Iran is filled with formal places of worship, much of this happens informally within the home, away from the prying eyes of the regime. It is about the nature of the commitment rather than the specific religious practice.

We all need things to which we can commit—beliefs, people, responsibilities. Commitment is what grounds us as people, providing anchors in our lives, and reminding us what is important. No one ever became an accomplished poet, architect, musician, or athlete without an absolute commitment to their craft—a total involvement in becoming the best they could be. The beauty, depth, and richness of Iranian culture reflects exactly this commitment. The Iranian willingness to commit to things without a shred of doubt or self-consciousness should inspire us all. Half-baked promises and vague notions do not help us. To be fulfilled we need to pick the things that matter, and commit our bodies, minds, and souls to them.

Chutzpah

Wailing Wall, Jerusalem, Israel.

If you want to understand why chutzpah is so intrinsic a part of Israel, start with the name itself. Its meaning—"he that fights with God"—tells you everything you need to know. What greater chutzpah could there be than picking a fight with a divine power? (The fact that many Israelis thumb their nose at organized religion only reinforces the impression.)

Chutzpah is a value that captures both admirable and less attractive characteristics. It is about the determination and inner strength to do things even when people tell you it can't be done. And it's just as much about stubbornness, bloody-mindedness, and even rudeness. They are two sides of the same coin.

In its original Yiddish meaning chutzpah is more about bad manners and arrogance than audacity we should admire. Today, where mold- and rule-breakers are generally more celebrated than shunned, chutzpah has taken on a more positive meaning. It is about the relentless pursuit of things that shouldn't be achievable, but which can be made so by sheer force of will. It's about the unshakable belief in your ideas and ability to fulfill them. Start-ups seeking to overturn much bigger, more established rivals have chutzpah; political outsiders railing against the establishment have chutzpah. In a world increasingly defined against the status quo and in favor of disrupters, chutzpah has moved from being a character trait to chide to a behavior that is celebrated and imitated.

And if you are looking for the best example of chutzpah in action, look no further than Israel. Chutzpah is in every pore of Israel, in its history, present, and the behavior of its people. It took chutzpah to create the modern state of Israel in the first place, and for it to survive for over seventy years in the teeth of violent opposition both near and far. It takes chutzpah for a country that is 60 percent desert to be home to such thriving agriculture. It takes chutzpah to be a country as small as Israel to be one of the most innovative, entrepreneurial economies in the world.

I had met plenty of Israelis before ever setting foot in the country, and had known the vast majority as highly motivated and extremely successful people. But it is only when you actually experience Israel, see at first hand how such a small country can achieve so much, that you understand the real scale of its success and the true meaning of chutzpah. At first I thought the word just meant that you really go for it. But it was sitting around Shabbat and seder tables in Israel that helped me understand there is a deeper meaning and motivation. The stories that are told and the history that is recited—of suffering, struggle against the odds, and survival—are the real cornerstone of chutzpah. It is through the regular, ritual remembrance of what has gone before that the greatest strength is derived. If we can survive this, we can survive anything. And not just survive, but thrive. This connection to the past is what grounds the chutzpah that defines Israel today in the millennia of experiences that have brought its people to this point. The chutzpah that is helping Israeli companies invent the future is rooted in the chutzpah that allowed their country to be created and survive in the first place. It is about beating the odds and finding the inner strength to triumph, whatever the circumstances. Israel is a nation whose very existence is an act of chutzpah.

Whether the problems we as individuals face are large or small, they all become more manageable, more conquerable, if we adopt—with due moderation and sensitivity—the art of of chutzpah.

Work

Lavender Village, Vilnius County, Lithunia.

Wherever you go in Lithuania—across its awesome and unexpected natural environment, from the lakes and forests to the lavender farms, and the sand dunes of the Curonian Spit that connects it to Poland—something follows you around. A buzzing noise. It's the sound of an important Lithuanian symbol, the honeybee, constantly working away in the background.

With roots in the nation's long-standing pagan culture, the bee has a unique place in Lithuanian tradition. Austėja, the ancient Lithuanian Goddess of Bees, remains a popular girl's name; honey is both an important Lithuanian export and an essential part of the national cuisine; while the word for the death of a bee is the same as that for a human (different from that used for all other animals). In most places there are colonies of bees; Lithuanians speak about families of bees, as they would families of people.

The bee is not just a revered part of Lithuanian culture, but also a symbol of its defining value: work. This is not a country where people slack off or opt to take a personal day, much to my son Saiyan's dismay on our visit. Hard work is something that is practiced and preached in equal measure. There could be no more appropriate representation of Lithuania's defining value than the worker bee.

For the older generation especially, the imprint of the Soviet era means that work is widely seen as one of the most important facets of life. What matters is having a job, and what wins praise is how quickly, effectively, and efficiently someone can get their work done.

Whereas in some countries having multiple jobs is seen as a negative—suggesting the inability to support yourself from a single source of employment—in Lithuania it is something to be proud of. Someone with two or three jobs is seen to have the commitment and work ethic that Lithuanians respect. People tend not to specialize in one thing but to have a portfolio of different jobs: driving, cooking, caring for the elderly. What's more, there is no real hierarchy among jobs: a doctor or teacher will live a similar life to a trash collector or gardener.

The greatest compliment you can pay to a Lithuanian is not that they are charming, good-looking, or a good parent, but that they work hard. The value also comes through strongly in Lithuanian proverbs, with some of the most popular translating to sentiments such as "Don't get happy before the work is completed" and "He that doesn't work, doesn't eat." A Lithuanian friend who had moved to London was taken aback when she encountered colleagues taking days off sick. This, she said, would never have been dreamt of back home. It had simply never occurred to her before.

Work ethic is something instilled in Lithuanians from a young age, where they start supporting their parents in whatever job they are doing. Perhaps that is why some of the most prominent Lithuanians have started early in their field of expertise. The award-winning actress Ingeborga Dapkūnaitė made her first onstage appearance at the age of four, in a performance of *Madam Butterfly*. Swimmer Rūta Meilutytė won a gold medal at the London Olympics in 2012 at the age of just fifteen, having moved with her father to the U.K. a few years earlier to access better training facilities. The world-renowned accordion player Martynas Levickis first picked up the instrument at the age of three.

Lithuania is a proud nation, which in the fifteenth century was one of Europe's largest and most influential states, and also played an important role in bringing down the Soviet Union through its elections and subsequent protests in 1990–91. Yet it has often had outside rule imposed upon it, and faced harsh economic conditions, making hard work a necessity for survival. Since the end of the eighteenth century it has only been an independent nation between the world wars and after 1991.

Today, when so many countries are divided on the issue of large-scale immigration, Lithuania faces the opposite problem. Its population fell by almost 15 percent between 2005 and 2017, an emigration trend especially prevalent among the young seeking economic opportunity elsewhere (and, one person told me, to escape the often-nepotistic hiring system). The political focus on the diminishing workforce and the problem of low wages helped spark the election of the previously unheralded Lithuanian Peasant and Greens Union to government in 2016. In a country where work matters above all else, the question of how to ensure the workforce isn't hollowed out by a brain drain has become one of the most pressing.

Lithuania's commitment to work reminds us of its importance in all our lives: how fundamental it is to physical and mental well-being, and creating a sense of purpose and self-worth. We live at a time when the nature of work is fast changing, but its essential value remains: it anchors our lives and offers the opportunity to achieve, improve, and provide for those we love.

Autonomy

Former president Tsakhiagiin Elbegdorj, Ulaanbaatar, Mongolia.

'm six months pregnant, I've been riding on horseback across Mongolia for days, and it feels like an age since I last felt my baby kick. I've asked to see a doctor and been told one won't be accessible for days. This is the consequence of autonomy: I've done exactly what I wanted, ignored all the warnings, and now all I can imagine is what I would do with myself if something were to happen to my baby.

But as we accustomed ourselves to the Mongol lifestyle—living in a *ger* (yurt), surrounded by animals, moving from place to place—I soon felt my son kicking more strongly than ever. In this land of the outdoors and setting your own path, something seemed to come alive in him, as it had in me.

This is a way of life that stretches back to the era of Genghis Khan and his descendants, at which time the Mongol Empire was the largest the world had ever seen. A nomadic people stretched itself across over 16 percent of the world's landmass, greater even than the Russian Empire at its height.

Modern Mongolia may be a small fraction of its former self, but much of the same culture that powered its empire building remains. It is still a nation where the autonomous, self-determining lifestyle of the nomad prevails like nowhere else, stretching across Mongolia's vast open spaces and grasslands.

Perhaps this mind-set is summed up best by a single word, *temul*, the basis for the birth name of Genghis, Temujin. According to the historian Jack Weatherford, *temul* "[occurs] in several Mongolian words meaning to rush headlong, to be inspired, to have a creative thought, and even to take a flight of fancy."

He continues: "As one Mongolian student explained to me, the word was best exemplified by, 'the look in the eye of a horse that is racing where it wants to go, no matter what the rider wants.'"

The horse is an appropriate symbol for Mongolian autonomy. Although, after Genghis, the wolf is often held as the national symbol, horses are the defining animals of the Mongolian culture and way of life. As the proverb goes: "A Mongol without his horse is like a bird without its wings." Mongolia built its vast empire on horseback, and horses remain central to nomad culture for hunting, riding for leisure and in competition, and as status symbols. The Mongolian national drink, *airag*, is fermented mare's milk, while for a Mongolian child, learning to ride is as much a rite of passage as learning to walk. In Mongolian folk culture, horses are also thought to have spiritual significance; Mongolian warriors were traditionally buried with their horses, and mare's milk was sprinkled on the ground before a battle. Today, horses are routinely given as diplomatic gifts to politicians and world leaders who visit Mongolia.

Like their horses, Mongolians go where they want, not where others lead. While lots of people might say they have personal freedom, Mongolian nomads truly have the autonomy to choose where to pitch their tent and graze their animals from one day or week to the next.

Many still live in the same *gers* that have been used for centuries, including in the rapidly expanding capital of Ulaanbaatar. The *ger*, as an open and mobile space both inside and out, symbolizes something about the autonomy of the Mongolian mind-set: no restrictions on where they take themselves, the freedom to move around, and the free will to determine the course of one's own life. Indeed, much of Mongolia's steppe is given to its people for free by the government, with every Mongolian citizen entitled to claim a plot of land as their own without charge. There is something about experiencing the Mongolian environment that fires up the autonomous spirit—the ability to see the whole horizon, be surrounded by openness on all sides, with no check on which way you can go or how far.

The same spirit suffuses Mongolian government. When I met then–Prime Minister Sükhbaataryn Batbold, he told me about how Mongolia was determined to build its rapidly growing "Wolf Economy" on its own terms, and in its own model. This is in contrast to the Asian "Tiger" economies: an economy that, like the wolf, will be strong, clever, and able to survive even the harshest conditions.

Spend any time in the country and you will soon realize that Mongolians are not a people who can be hemmed in, whether by expectations, deadlines, or conventions. The Mongol culture is to explore, to test the unknown, and do the unexpected. To pursue a life defined by autonomy and the opportunity to go where the will takes you. If freedom is often about the battle for shared rights, autonomy is a more personal thing: the ability to set the course of your own life, and to follow your own unique path.

With many of us living lives and pursuing careers that are cased in structure and routines, real and imagined, there can be few among us who would not benefit in some way by embracing a little *temul,* and the Mongolian urge to be free.

Obedience

New Year's prayers at Shwedagon Pagoda, Yangon, Myanmar.

"Would you like a cup of tea?" In Myanmar, the answer is always yes. Whether or not you actually want a hot drink, when someone offers, you accept.

This is *anade*, a deep empathy for the feeling of others and overwhelming desire to avoid causing embarrassment. Even to refuse a drink or second helping of food would be seen as a potential loss of face for the person offering it. So you say yes, even if only to avoid social embarrassment. You show restraint, subverting your individual preferences to the greater good of social harmony, one maintained by the national culture of obedience.

Anade informs how people think about every aspect of their everyday lives. It is a prism for every small decision you make: how can I avoid awkward situations for other people, or putting them to any trouble? One time this goes completely out of the window is during the water festival before the New Year: where everyone sprays each other with water for four days, to cleanse the sins of the past year. Obedience to this tradition overrides any sense of embarrassment.

Myanmar's culture is underpinned by *gadaw*, the hierarchical principle that respects age and social class, with elders and those of higher social standing automatically given respect regardless of the circumstances. A Burmese friend's father is a professor, and I would see the way his students doted on him, hanging on his every word and never questioning his arguments. It is the same in the workplace. No 360-degree-feedback here: what the boss says goes, even if they are only marginally older or more senior to you in the organization. You put obedience to the hierarchy and wisdom of your elders before expressing your own opinions and criticisms.

Obedience is deeply engrained in Burmese culture, arising at least in part from the *sila* (morality) that is the cornerstone of the Buddhist path to enlightenment, in a country where 90 percent of the population practice the religion. The national religion also dictates a collective focus on the importance of karma: maximizing your good deeds while mitigating the bad. As Buddhists, most Burmese are heavily concerned with the attainment of *punna* (merit), which may help explain why Myanmar has frequently ranked at the top of the World Giving Index, which measures a combination of charitable donations, volunteering, and the willingness to help strangers and those in need. What's more, no one will ever accept a tip in return for services, on the basis that it isn't their money to take. Obedience is seen as part of what it means to be a good person, and to maintain good karma. People try to live in the path of the Buddha—good words, good deeds, good thoughts—as obediently as they can.

A long history of oppression, from the British colonial regime to the military junta that ruled from 1962 to 2011, and the atrocities that have subsequently been committed against the Rohingya Muslim minority, are another root of the obedience culture, with dissent and protest routinely suppressed in the most violent way. Where obedience is not found in Myanmar it is imposed, often brutally so.

During the pro-democracy protests of 1988, thousands were killed by the military and security forces. Hundreds of monks were beaten and arrested in protests as part of the Saffron Revolution against the junta in 2007.

Obedience, as something both demonstrated and demanded, has been fundamental to Myanmar throughout its recent history. And while its implications have been far-reaching, its foundation and lesson is simple. It is really about thinking of others before you think of yourself. It means you honor hierarchy, custom, and tradition because to subvert them would be to risk others losing face. You do not have to be a respecter of hierarchy to appreciate the benefit of this principle. By thinking through the consequences of our actions, and putting ourselves in the shoes of those around us, we can all become better friends, better employees or employers, and better family members. Whether or not you consider obedience to be a good thing in its own right, the basic principle that others should come first is applicable to us all.

Positivity

On Lares Trek, Cusco, Peru.

Peru's appearance at the 2018 Football World Cup was the nation's first in thirty-six years. But the long history of disappointment did nothing to dim the expectations of Peru's fan base, who quickly established themselves as the tournament's most passionate and positive supporters. It might have been half a lifetime since Peru had qualified for the World Cup, let alone challenged for it, but Peruvians still believed they could win it.

YouTube was flooded with positive motivational videos; and over fifteen thousand Peruvians flooded into Russia, many of them making significant sacrifices and undertaking extraordinary long-haul journeys to experience the special moment. Stories were shared of people who had given up their jobs, taken five separate plane journeys, and sold possessions to be there. Whole families traveled together, including those who had been at Peru's previous appearance in 1982 and could now attend with their grandchildren. That outpouring of support for the national team reflects the positivity that is Peru's defining characteristic.

If a friend or family member is about to do something important, like taking an exam or going for a job interview, you don't wish them good luck. Instead you send *buenas vibras* (good vibes) or *energía positiva* (positive energy) and wish them *éxitos*. The implication is that you shouldn't have to rely on luck, and that the result is in your hands. You can will the outcome you want into being, if only you are positive enough in your mind-set. On TV news bulletins, you will similarly hear editorializing about how things might have turned out differently if people—athletes, politicians—had tried harder.

The same impulse drives Peru's budding self-help industry. In Peru, a chef is not just a chef, and an athlete is not just an athlete. They also double up as high-profile motivational figures, championing both Peruvian culture and the national spirit of positivity. Gastón Acurio, Peru's highest-profile chef, is credited with rebuilding the national food culture and putting Peruvian dishes such as ceviche on the map globally. Well beyond running restaurants, he has become a global ambassador for Peruvian cuisine. "Calling Acurio a celebrity chef today is like saying Oprah is a talk show host," *Washington Post* reporter Nick Miroff has written. "He is more of a modern food shaman: artist, interpreter, healer, impresario and national pitchman." As the man himself has said: "We can use our cuisine as a weapon of change." Perhaps it is no surprise that Peru does not just export any old foods, but superfoods like quinoa and lucuma, which are being widely adopted for their positive benefits to health and well-being.

Where does this innate positivity come from? In part it is the strong indigenous culture and inheritance in Peru, with over a quarter of the population still comprising indigenous peoples. These strong roots—represented in everything from cuisine to World Heritage Sites such as Machu Picchu—show us there is both pride and belief in what it means to be distinctively Peruvian, and what that culture can offer to the world.

It is also perhaps born out of the necessity to leave behind the legacy of the wars Peru has fought with its South American neighbors, and the brutal civil war that cost seventy thousand lives between 1980 and 2000.

Now Peruvians look to the future with confidence, with an economy that is frequently the fastest-growing in Latin America, and a culture that is increasingly recognized as important and influential on a global level.

On the Inca Trail around and across Lake Titicaca, I was moved to write in my journal about the "lake of a million diamonds." Objectively these were just ripples in the water and the crystals in the salt flats. But surrounded by Peruvian positivity, I was seeing things in a new light. Positivity can have the same effect in all aspects of our life. Whether you are starting a new job or major undertaking, dealing with a problem or seeking self-improvement, a positive mind-set is the basis of success. Peru shows us the importance of willing what we want to be, into being.

Fortitude

Kremlin, Red Square, Moscow, Russia.

"Delete the picture right now."

I am standing in the middle of St. Petersburg and a pimp is shouting at me. I have stumbled across an unlikely, eye-catching scene: a line of scantily clad girls being paraded through the city. Out of instinct, I photographed it. Now the camera is being grabbed out of my hands. Any thought of protest is quelled when another bulky man steps into view. I am shaking and not because of the cold. These people are not messing around. The picture is gone but I have learned, in my own small way, the big lesson about Russia: it is a harsh, unforgiving place, and the only way to survive is with fortitude.

Most Russians will have their own personal and family story of fortitude, the experience of living through struggle. In Russia, fortitude is not merely a value, it is a way of life: strength is power, but also a necessary component of survival. And, whatever your view on Russian politics and foreign policy, when you are in the country it is hard not to admire the iron resolve of its people. In Russia, hard times mean not that you consider giving in, but that you dig even deeper into the reservoir of fortitude and self-preservation.

People wear their fortitude as a badge of honor, almost a sign of nationhood. My host Olga told me how her mother, a university professor, for nine months after the collapse of the Soviet Union, when the system broke down and nobody in academia was paid, would do a day's work and then go over the border to sell Russian goods for money (while also picking up products she could make a profit on back home). For her troubles, she would be tailed by the mafia.

Such harshness has bred its own culture, one in which fortitude is both held close and brandished aloft. Displays of military strength accordingly have a central place in Russian culture. The annual May 9 Victory Day commemorations, celebrating the end of World War II and victory over Nazi Germany, have become one of the most important annual holidays in Russia, with military parades held nationwide. The seventieth anniversary event in 2015 saw over sixteen thousand soldiers marching through Moscow.

Tales of past victories, especially those that symbolize great fortitude, also have a prominent place in the collective memory. Dom Pavlova, an apartment block that held out for sixty days in the face of the German onslaught, symbolizes the defiance of the Battle of Stalingrad. The Soviet commander at Stalingrad, Vasily Chuikov, is said to have boasted that the Germans lost more men trying to take this one building than they had taking the entire city of Paris. This is the meat and drink of Russian folklore: strength and struggle in the face of the outsider and the invader.

The same spirit is still celebrated today; in early 2018, a Russian pilot shot down in Syria blew himself up with a grenade to avoid capture, with the reported last words, "This is for our guys." The story was lapped up by the Kremlin and Russian media as a classic example of Russian fortitude in the face of peril.

Today, the hardship faced by many ordinary Russians is the product of economic sanctions rather than military action. The asset freezes and trade restrictions imposed by the EU and U.S. following Russia's 2014 invasion and annexation of Crimea have sent the economy into deep recession, and the numbers living in poverty close to 20 million (a significant spike, though still half of what it was in 2000).

Yet talk to Russians about their current plight, and you will get a mostly defiant response. "We don't need to eat," one told me. "It feeds us to know that we are being feared." As a foreigner, you are constantly being asked about the view from outside: what are they saying about us? There is always something of the siege mentality.

We may not experience extreme hardship in our lives, but that does not mean we cannot find inspiration from Russian fortitude. On a relative scale, we will also experience difficulties and setbacks. We will all have to find a way to battle the odds. At this point, so much depends on your inner core of fortitude: something that gives you the will, the confidence, and the determination to keep going and ultimately achieve your goals. Without that fortitude, even the best ideas, the best-positioned careers, and the most capable people will ultimately falter. We all need a little Russian fortitude in us to pull through the hard times and succeed.

Joy

Children of Colombo, Sri Lanka.

I was woken early, with a hot cup of tea and a smile that was every bit as warm. We were headed to Sri Pada, the Sacred Footprint, one of the highest and holiest sites in Sri Lanka. At the summit of this 7,300-foot mountain is a footprint in the rock that—depending on your religion—is variously believed to be that of Buddha, Shiva, or Adam. The trek takes around four hours, so it's an early start if you want to reach the top in time for sunrise.

Not everyone can summon a smile when they've been woken up in the middle of the night, or wants to do much in the way of talking. But throughout that predawn ascent, I was surrounded by joy: people chatting away, uplifting and inspiring each other. I almost felt like I was being carried up the mountain by the energy and goodwill of the people around me.

Visitors often comment on the friendliness of Sri Lankans, and how people are always smiling. One travel writer dubbed it "the isle of smiles," while Indian journalist Jug Suraiya has written of the contrast between the two nations: "You don't see too many smiles in public in India . . . but in [Sri] Lanka there were smiles and to spare." Muttiah Muralitharan, the cricketer who is Sri Lanka's most famous and successful sportsman, was for years known by the nickname of "Smiling Assassin."

It is true that wherever you go in Sri Lanka smiles will follow and surround you. What I witnessed, however, was more than just cheerfulness. There was something more pervasive and profound: a joy and an elation that informs how Sri Lankans approach so many aspects of their life, whether that is sharing a political opinion, playing a game on one of the country's ubiquitous cricket fields, celebrating religious traditions such as monthly *poya* (full moon) days, or just glorying in the nation's extraordinary outdoors.

There is a joy in the fundamental approach to life, one that springs in large part from Sri Lanka's extraordinary natural environment, where you are surrounded by mountains, forests, and oceans; elephants, cheetahs, dolphins, and whales. It's impossible not to have your spirits lifted, and to feel some of your worries slip away when surrounded by such awesome, overwhelming beauty on all sides. You find yourself constantly living in the moment, as Buddhist teaching instructs. You feel powerfully the sense of being part of something greater: socially, environmentally, and spiritually.

Joy helps us make the best of difficult circumstances, and is centered on the idea that everyone has a role to play. As Jug Suraiya aptly summarized: "the Lankan smile affirms an underlying social contract, an acknowledgement that my well-being is inextricably linked with your well-being, that the one necessarily must ensure the other in order to exist itself."

Among people who have experienced devastating environmental disasters, and been through a long and bloody civil war (exceeding one hundred thousand deaths), there seems to be a conscious will to move beyond the suffering. A war that some thought would never end has finally been brought to a close, and the country can now look forward to the once impossible prospect of demilitarization; after the tsunami in 2004, which killed over thirty thousand people and displaced 1.5 million from their homes, much of Sri Lanka has been rebuilt. In 2019, Anders Holch Povlsen, the retail entrepreneur and CEO, lost three of his four children in the ISIS bombings in Sri Lanka. His fourth child was so moved by the typically Sri Lankan reaction of positivity and action that he has taken a gap year to give back with the same joy, and Povlsen has done the same in his contributions via healthcare hubs and more.

In a country where both problems and progress are long-term in nature, there is little focus on instant gratification. Joy arises from deeper sources: people coming together, being part of something, giving their all to a task. Being present in the moment and being there for others.

From Sri Lanka I learned the true value of what people sometimes describe as a positive attitude, but which really is about more than just your personal outlook on life. It is about taking joy in the things you do, however mundane, and finding meaning and fulfillment in countless small acts of kindness and generosity toward others. And, in doing so, by looking for joy and spreading it to others, we might just succeed in finding it for ourselves.

Dignity

Courtyard of the Umayyad Mosque, Damascus, Syria.

"We do not want your bread. We want dignity." Words shouted in the southern city of Daraa, at a funeral for protesters killed by Syria's secret police; funerals that would spark huge attendance, more protests, and then more funerals.

As revolution spread across Syria in the spring of 2011, one defining theme was a call for dignity: the dignity of work in a country where employment was hard to find and often precarious; the dignity of political freedom and democracy, in a nation that had been ruled by one family for thirty years; the dignity of living in a fair society, where wealth was not siphoned off by a corrupt system; and the dignity of living in a free society, without looking over your shoulder for the secret police at every turn.

In March, during the early weeks of the revolution, a "Friday of Dignity," with widespread protests against the Assad regime, was one of the early flashpoints in the uprising. An estimated thirty-eight people were killed when the military opened fire on multiple groups of protesters. That November, a nationwide Dignity Strike was organized, a coordinated campaign of civil disobedience, prompting further crackdowns.

In the face of a murderous regime, knowing the deadly consequences of protest, Syrians still stood up to fight for their dignity. In the words of nonviolence activist Yahya Shurbaji, who became famous as the "man with the roses" who approached security forces with gifts of peace: "I would rather be killed than be a killer."

The story of Shurbaji shows the shocking way in which the dignity of ordinary citizens was violated with impunity by the regime. He was arrested in September 2011, and his family campaigned for years for his release, only to be informed in 2018 that he had been killed in prison some five years earlier. One of the many bitter tragedies of the bloody civil war that emerged from the revolution is that those who protested in the name of dignity in 2011 had so much of theirs stripped away in the years that followed.

That tragedy is compounded still further when you pause to consider the country Syria had been before the civil war, and the way it was defined as a nation by dignity—the dignity of religious freedom and tolerance, of one of the world's oldest and most important civilizations, and of the extraordinary constellation of cultures that could be seen and experienced on the streets of Syria's cities. Anyone who thinks that New York or London represents a melting pot should have seen Damascus before the revolution, as I did on my honeymoon: a place where you could feel the living history of one of the world's oldest cities through the courtyards and streets, smell the jasmine that it is named for, and taste the food that has been flavored by millennia of immigration, invasion, and traders passing through. In Damascus, the history of empires, of religions, and of trade intersect. It has the dignity of the oldest inhabited city in the world, one that has seen almost all the world's major cultures and religions leave their mark.

Syria was a country of historic, cultural, and religious dignity—so much of which has been attacked and torn down by the horrors of its civil war. Hundreds of thousands have been killed, millions displaced from their homes and forced to flee the country, and cities turned into rubble.

Not a shred of dignity has been shown to the people of Syria by a dictatorship that has tortured, murdered, and used chemical weapons against them with impunity. But dignity is still what oppressed and displaced Syrians long for. In 2018, as the seven-year civil war appeared to be nearing its end, thoughts began to turn to whether, how, and when the millions who had been forced out could return. For many, the starting point to rebuilding their country, their culture, and their lives, is to regain some of the dignity that has been so brutally stolen. As one refugee interviewed by the BBC said: "We want a solution that will give us back our dignity—no more, no less." For Syria, whose past was so defined by dignity, there can be no future without it.

Humility

Taken from a "rusty garden chair" overlooking
the Rio de La Plata, Uruguay.

B e humble! Those were the words that Carolina, the daughter of my Uruguayan host family, said would be ringing in her ears every time she stepped onto the court to play handball. It was her mother's first and most important commandment, one she had internalized. A talented player, you would never hear her boasting about her own skills, celebrating her achievements, or excluding those less capable from her team. It reminded me a little of my own mother, who used to say "never be proud."

This is a small example of the Uruguayan humility that is a national characteristic stretching from its people to its political leaders. José Mujica, president from 2010 to 2015, was nationally revered and globally recognized as one of the most humble premiers in the world, with an approach completely at odds with most people's idea of a political leader.

His political philosophy—"It's a mistake to think that power comes from above. It comes from within the hearts of people"—is about as humble a belief as you will find among politicians, reflecting the priority of serving those who have elected you over advancing your own position.

And Mujica lived as humbly as he spoke. A guerrilla revolutionary, who spent fourteen years in prison under the Uruguayan military dictatorship, he had a lifestyle as president that could not be further from the norm of luxurious residences and lavish state occasions. Instead, the septuagenarian continued to live (and work) on his wife's farm. He gave away over 90 percent of his salary to charitable causes, bringing his income in line with that of the average citizen (approximately $775 a month). His official form of transportation was not a tinted-window limousine, but a 1987 Volkswagen Beetle, in a battered faded blue that symbolized his lack of interest in outward displays of wealth or prestige. All his international travel was done in economy class. Visitors to the three-room farmhouse would be greeted by Mujica's most prominent bodyguard, his three-legged dog, Manuela.

Both geography and demographics help to explain the humility inherent in Uruguayan culture. Sandwiched between giant Brazil and Argentina, the "little country" (*paisito*) is a nation of just three million people, and the second smallest in South America after Suriname. By landmass, Uruguay could fit itself over forty-seven times into neighboring Brazil. Its small population is largely made up of people who came with little or nothing, and who have stayed close together, from the Spanish and Italian migrants of the nineteenth century onward.

As a visitor, you see empathy and humility all around you, in small, everyday gestures. People will wait for you to board the bus ahead of them, and offer you a seat. Humility means you never push yourself forward, literally or metaphorically. Ostentation and self-aggrandizement are anathema. You do not show off your talents, wealth, or success; restraint is both expected and widely practiced.

Humility is a value that we often overlook or discard, in our rush to pursue this ambition or achieve that status symbol. In a loud, competitive world, some feel that to be humble is to shortchange yourself, and to lose the opportunity of getting noticed. Yet such an attitude ignores how humility helps you see differently: improving your appreciation of how your successes have really been achieved, and the variety of factors and people that have contributed toward them. Humility is really about a social contract, one that celebrates balance, empathy, and community.

Being humble does not have to mean that you lose out. José Mujica was often given the tag of "world's poorest president," which he rejected. As he told *The Guardian* at the end of his tenure, sitting on a "rusty garden chair" outside his now famous farmhouse: "Living light is no sacrifice for me—it's an affirmation of freedom, of having the greatest amount of time available for what motivates me. It's the price of my individual freedom. I'm richer this way."

Happiness

Dragon King of Bhutan—King Jigme Khesar Namgyel Wangchuck, Dechencholing Palace, Thimphu, Bhutan.

I promised 101 values, but there is one more I couldn't possibly leave out: the Bhutanese example of how to achieve happiness. The idea of happiness perhaps feels less like a value and more of a fundamental right, but it's something that comes up time and again in the workshops I hold. So have it as a bonus chapter here, and decide for yourself if happiness is going to be one of your defining values.

Happiness and positive psychology have only recently become a focus of study, and the one nation we have to thank for that, who brought it to the U.N. and to scholars as a pursuit, is the Kingdom of Bhutan.

Happiness is what most people say they value above all else because it just feels good, and research shows that when we are happy we are also healthier, more productive, creative, and have fewer conflicts. Yet happiness is difficult to attain because it requires so many of our needs to be met, balanced, and agreed upon by the wider system. In our meeting with His Majesty, Jigme Khesar Namgyel Wangchuck, locally known as

K5 (the Fifth King), he explained how he saw it as the responsibility of the government to create an environment where its population can pursue happiness, and it is only since Bhutan opened its gates to the world in 1974 that we can begin to examine how they go about it.

Bhutan is a tiny Asian country with a fledgling economy, and one might expect it to pursue economic development, but they have seen that a common price to pay is the loss of one's culture, environment, and social system. This is why Bhutan decided that gross domestic product (GDP) indicators are inadequate to address human needs and that it needed a more comprehensive indicator: Gross National Happiness. "We believe that the source of happiness lies within the self, and that there is no external source for contentment," the King told me. "The faster car, bigger house, more fashionable clothes might bring you fleeting pleasure but not contentment." As part of this approach, the Kingdom has been actively encouraging ruralization—creating amenities in countryside areas that encourage people to stay rather than make the default move into cities. You can see the impact of this reduced urbanization in that Thimphu is the only capital city in the world without a single traffic light. And you can see the importance of Gross National Happiness in decisions like the refusal to fully exploit Bhutan's hydroelectric capacity—which could be commercially lucrative, but only at the cost of flooding valleys and forcing people to leave their homes.

Bhutan also shows the importance of having a higher purpose, whether that is religion, spirituality, or a philosophy of life. Bhutan remains a deeply Buddhist land and thus they have everyone's well-being as their interest, not just their own. For this reason there are approximately seven thousand monks in the mountains of Bhutan, spending their lives meditating not only for personal development but also societal well-being. Often the eldest son of a family will be offered to the monastery at age five, bringing great prestige to his household.

Bhutan, the last Shangri-la, nestled in the Himalayas between the giants of China and India, is not intimidated, but rather lives according to its own terms, hence it is one of the few Asian countries that has never been colonized. The Druk or "Thunder Dragon" is the national symbol and appears on the flag of the country, and the jewels it is holding represent a different kind of "value." Bhutan is aware that there are many human needs that have to be met for human happiness, not just the material ones. Similarly, positive psychologists encourage finding fulfillment through having goals that are interesting and enjoyable to work on, and that use our strengths and abilities.

Good governance is important to the Bhutanese. This is why His Majesty Jigme Wangchuck, the world's youngest head of state, was given the throne in 2006, at age twenty-six, by his father, who wanted to groom him as a leader on the job. As king and head of the government he must take a long-term view that ruling parties can lack. He says, "I pray that while I am but king of a small Himalayan nation, I may in my time be able to do much to promote the greater well-being and happiness of all people in this world."

The greatest lesson is that the pursuit of happiness does not work if pursued at an individual level. It's about our relationships and how we help each other. It's about us, all of us, together. It's about having a cause greater than ourselves and improving the world in which we live.

Conclusion: Living Your Values

I want to offer some advice about what happens next: how you can take the values that have resonated with you over the course of reading this book, and make best use of them. Recognizing your values is one thing, and an important step that many people never take. But you should try to go one step further and focus on how to actually implement them. Used in this way, they can help you make the decisions, build the relationships, and set the ambitions that will shape your purpose, life, and strength as a leader.

This is the kind of process that some of the world's most influential companies have been through to define who they are and what they stand for. Bob Moritz, the global chairman of PwC, explained to me how it undertook a survey of 234,000 employees to understand what mattered to them most, before whittling it down to a few core values that relate to their entire workforce. David Craig of Refinitiv described how their values of being bold, open, and focused can have a healthy creative tension resulting in a productive environment of debate and progress. McKinsey puts aside one day a year to reflect as a group on what their values mean to their work and lives, updating them in small ways to reflect changing times. As such, the process I outline here is one that can be done either as an individual or collectively—as a family, business, or institution.

To put this into action, the first step is to go from the initial list of values you have highlighted while reading to a core group of five. It's too simplistic to try and boil down everything you believe to a single value, but equally there is no point having so many values that you forget what some of them are. Your fundamental values are ideas you need to carry with you, in your head and heart; if there are too many to immediately remember, then they can't matter enough to you. Remember, a compass only has four fundamental directions.

This process is a valuable one in itself. What we are looking to end with is not values that merely strike you as interesting, worthwhile, or relevant. There needs to be a stronger bond than that. These should be principles that are intrinsic to you, and beliefs that you cannot live without. Sorting the essential from the important is how we discover what truly matters to us, those values that define us and that cause us pain when they are trampled on.

Start by writing down your top fifteen or twenty on small cards. These might provide a cross section of change, continuity, community, connection, and core values, or they might be weighted in one or two key areas. Group them, seeing what connects various ideas, and where there might be crossover. You will find that there are a number of obvious overlaps: some values will be horizontally connected, creating a cluster around a central theme, while others will be vertically connected, pointing to an ultimate word that you value most. From these clusters you need to start making choices and establishing priorities.

To do that we need to start with ourselves: the values that resonate most powerfully with us and speak directly to our experiences. Then these need to be put in context, with an understanding of how the world in which we live and work has shaped our values. Then finally, we need to find an accommodation between the two: understanding how our values help us to navigate our lives, personal, and professional, and how they can help us to be our best authentic self and achieve our mission in life.

In doing this, I encourage you to ask yourself four questions, and then follow four steps:

The questions

1. Think about a time in your life or career when you have been truly happy. What was present at that moment? What needs were being met, and how? What made you feel fulfilled?
2. Think of a particularly disappointing time in your life. What was missing? What went wrong? Which needs were not being met?
3. Think of the time in your life you were most upset. Why was that, and what values had been violated?
4. What is your ultimate aim in life, your biggest accomplishment, and your greatest regret? Does anything connect them?

The steps

- First, go back through your list and whittle away the ones you know to be slightly less important.
- Think about how you feel as you read the words and ponder their significance to you and in your life. Your entire shortlist will comprise values that matter to you; your job now is to feel your way toward the difference between those that are important and those that are fundamental. Are you more concerned about order or vision, precision or relaxation, etiquette or informality? This should help you get your initial fifteen or twenty down to a final eight or ten.
- Then, take guidance from three people who know you well: a close friend, a family member, and a colleague or professional peer. Share your shortlist with them.
- Ask them for their views on your values (and of course, offer to do the same for them in return).
- This helps us to understand ourselves as others see us, and to get an objective perspective on how reality—through external eyes—matches up to our own perceptions. Getting a variety of perspectives—from loved ones through to those who know you professionally—will provide a reality check if one is needed, and help iron out any anomalies. There is a difference between who

you think you are, how you actually spend your time, and what you wish for—your aspirational values. Be honest with yourself. And listen to your core team, whether personal or professional.

- Finally, it's back to you. Take the shortlist you have compiled and scrutinize the values again. Think not just about why each value matters to you, but also how you would feel if it was taken away from you. Ultimately you should be looking for those five values that you would fight the hardest to maintain, whatever the circumstances. Because loss aversion is so important a psychological impulse to us as humans, it can be easier to decide between things based on what we least want to have taken away from us. This helps us to choose what is really most important—the five values we simply cannot countenance losing in any circumstance.

You may find this final stage challenging, and that is a good thing. Examining ourselves in this way can be hard, but it is also beneficial. Having stress-tested your values, through your own eyes and those of people around you, you can feel confident that these truly are the values that matter to you above all else.

What happens next?

Once you have the five core values, I encourage you to rank them in order of priority: this brings power and focus. Right now, which of these values is doing the most to drive the decisions you take and the priorities you set? What has the most everyday relevance in the circumstances of your life as they currently are?

I know from experience how important it is not just to think about your values in isolation at one point, but to continually return to them as the circumstances of your life change. I have used the technique I outlined here at a number of crossroads in my own life. When my children were born, family came to the forefront of my priorities and stayed there for the first five years of their lives. This was the value that mattered most at the point in time I felt I could give the most to my children, in the formative stage of their development. But there were other parts of my life that family had started to overwhelm: my health and work among them. I've also come to recognize that, over time, your values shift as they relate to other people. At eighteen, my mother's values of family and tradition above all else were suffocating to me; and my appetite for exploration anathema to her. In the end, the two converged: ten years later I married Gavin, who had been to Oxford but was nothing like my mother's *Brideshead Revisited* caricature. In fact, to her delight, he met all of the criteria—hers and mine. As the children have grown, my priorities have balanced out and my hierarchy of values has evolved in turn. It's by looking at these questions—which many parents face—through the lens of values that I have been able to make decisions consciously rather than simply being dragged along by circumstances.

Bear in mind that, while these five values are unlikely to change over time, the priority of them almost certainly will. Values are not fixed but dynamic: different ones mean different things to us at different stages in our life. Just as we might read a favorite book through new eyes as we age, learning or recognizing something new every time, our appreciation of values will evolve over time. This means that after a goal has been met, you might wish to check in with your list with your new context in mind, asking yourself if the prioritization still holds true, or if not, what has changed and why.

With the values now clear in your mind, and neatly prioritized, it's time for the really good bit: making use of them in everyday life. Over time this will become instinctive: your values become an essential lens on the decisions you are making, a way of cross-checking your gut instinct and satisfying yourself that you are being true to yourself. Start by asking yourself these questions about each of the five values on your final list:

1. Why does this value matter to me?
2. In what areas of my life is this value most relevant?
3. How well do I currently live by this value?

This exercise should reveal both where your values are making a difference, and areas of your life where they could have a greater role to play. Now it's time to get specific. What can these values do for you?

In an immediate sense, they can help you to reassess three areas of your life: your work and career; your relationships with family and friends; and your life goals. In all cases, think about the decisions you are currently facing and the priorities you are choosing. What if anything have you been struggling over?

Where you might previously have used a list of pros and cons, now turn to your newly codified list of values. Go down in order of priority: What would this particular value have you do? Is the decision you are inclined to take in line with your most important values? Or if you don't know which way to jump, which way are the values pointing to?

Right now, this might help you to adjust in some areas of your life, recognizing where you have either drifted away from your values, or where they can help resolve something you have been pondering for some time. And in the long term, these values will become your companions as you go forward in life—together they will form an expression of your deepest beliefs, and a mechanism for helping you feel your way toward the right decisions and priorities.

Instinctively, we all know what we stand for in life. And we are making decisions based on our values all the time, even without necessarily recognizing we are doing so. Yet there is a huge difference when you start to actively acknowledge those values, and use them to arbitrate how you pursue your objectives, manage your relationships, plan your time, and align your priorities. When you have your values clearly defined, the hard thinking has already been done, simplifying your choices and eliminating angst. There is no excuse to say you don't know what you want in life, what to do next, or how to make a difficult decision. Now you have a compass, one that might stay in your back pocket most of the time, but is always there ready to point the way forward.

A life lived with values in mind is one that allows you to be more conscious, more confident, and more committed about the things you choose to do. Recognizing your values doesn't change who you are so much as clarify it—helping you to understand yourself better. This is vital, because we can only have the things we want by being comfortable with our personalities, our priorities, and our potential. Having our values clearly in mind allows us to appreciate ourselves for who we are and why—everything in our life that has brought us to this point. As a leader, it allows us to stand tall with the decisions we make, and to provide comfort and consistency to our teams. With our values, we can live in the moment, be more dynamic in how we make decisions, and feel empowered about our sense of self.

Values are how we obtain the level of self-knowledge that is a platform to achieving success and fulfillment. They provide the foundation for so many happy, successful, and fulfilled lives. I wish you all the joy in the world embracing and exploring yours.

Acknowledgments

Firstly, this is for my parents, Gurpal Kaur and Resham Singh, and my siblings Rajdeep and Manreshpal who personify Nishkam—selfless service and support. My partner in everything, Gavin Dhillon, for he listened to my dreams and kept me going. To our parents, Surinder and Sucha Dhillon, and our absolutely stellar family on both sides, we are nothing without you. My grandparents, Narajan and Amar Rai, Mohinder and Harbajan Atwal, Swaran and Gurmail Dhillon, Piara and Naranjan Sher-Gill. Foreparents, Udam and Piara Mann (Nanke), Maha and Bhago Rai (Dadke), and ancestors upon whose shoulders we stand. My children, Naryan and Saiyan, whose preeminent birth created the sense of urgency, and who illuminate every breath I take through their very existence. Most importantly, I am grateful for spiritual guidance from our Gurus, Sri Guru Granth Sahib Ji, and mentor Bhai Sahib Mohinder Singh Ahluwalia. This is for each and every person I have met along my journeys both near and far—some have been mentioned in these pages but countless have not. You have created my belief in humanity, contributed to me endlessly, and it is my aim to pay it forward, always. Forever in your gratitude.

I want to acknowledge all of you who have shared yourself with me. You know who you are, and believed in me when I didn't even know how to believe in myself. To the schools that I attended including Denmark Road High School, Gloucester, and the fabulous teachers I have met throughout life. To those I have worked for since my first job at age seven, including my first mentor, Roger Poolman from Aeros, who rewarded my work with flying lessons that led to a private pilot's license. My professors at the University of Manchester and Melbourne including Prof. Ralph Young, and everlasting friends like Kiran Singh and Co. To Jo Ryan, who spotted me for JP Morgan during the milk-round, and has never stopped believing in me and supporting my potential.

To my Fairy Godmother, Kathy Eldon, who trusted completely from the moment we met, always sees the best in me, and has gone on to inspire so much of my life since, AND our entire Creative Visions extended family. The London School of Economics and Destin, for transforming me into a master, and continuing to inform and engage us still today. Keith Bowers, who ignited my training and journey with the BBC and World Service, and brilliant producers who have encouraged me again and again, from Jasper Bouverie to Richard Collings and Lamine Konkobo, and compassionate colleagues who have been so generous with me at every turn. My wonderful peers at the European Union, United Nations, and then Reuters, including Chad Ruble, and Nathan King of FSN. To Tony Orsten, who saw my light and employed me as his second employee for twofour54 in Abu Dhabi to create the first media venture capital fund in the Middle East, and then for inspiring characters from Noura Al Kaabi to Khaldoon Al Mubarak in the UAE. I am indebted to the lifelong relationship with London Business School, MIT (Boston), and Harvard Business School. Particularly, Madeleine Tjon Pian Gi and Natalia Donde, and the life-changing guidance of Dean Nitin Nohria, who helped seed this concept of values within me through our work on the MBA and Global Business Oath.

Most importantly, to Deepak Chopra who fully saw my potential and turned this (infinite) potential into a reality, which led to Trident, Robert Gottlieb, and Amanda Annis, who saw this as a career-making book. For seeing all this before even I could—I can never thank Deepak enough. Thank you to Michele Martin of North Star Way for seeing the vision so clearly and powerfully. To Richard Hall for seeing the beauty and leading me to Josh Davis, who believed from day one and checked through every little thing with me—deserving a gold medal. To Simon Trewin, who put a rocket under *The Values Compass* by championing me through his invaluable mentorship. And to my incredible editor at Simon and Schuster, Julianna Haubner, who has been there with full encouragement at each and every deadline.

Thank you to Raghu Rai for his gem of a photograph depicting my India, and for Angela Fisher and Carol Beckwith for their Zuwadi of African Ceremonies and the photograph of Congo. To Dr. Kapoor for my long study in values, which slowly created my PhD, to Dav Panesar for keeping it real and Malini Vishwakaram keeping it alive. To my daily supporters and to my global tribe, my gratitude for you is in every step I take.

None of this would have been possible without people from all countries, backgrounds, and walks of life sharing their insights, opening themselves up with authenticity, and allowing me to interview them. I am beyond grateful for the values people have operated from, the heartfelt kindness they have shared, and the beauty I have seen in humanity the world over. To Andy Taylor, who first suggested the idea for this book as "Letters to my Unborn Child." Most of all to most beloved friends who believe in me and keep me moving forward. I am a reflection of you.

So very grateful for the family and children's values classes that we hold, the organizational and corporate workshops we deliver, and the individuals we are fortunate enough to work with. Most of all I am indebted to you, dear reader, for as you evolve further into your very best self, this entire world becomes a better place for it. Please keep in touch, for we are stronger together—always. Thank YOU.